D1447328

POLITICAL RELIGION

Political Religion

How Christianity and Islam Shape the World

THEOLOGY AT THE FRONTIERS

Felix Körner, SJ

Paulist Press
New York / Mahwah, NJ

BR
115
.P7
K645
2020

Unless otherwise noted, the Scripture quotations contained herein are from the New Revised Standard Version: Catholic Edition, Copyright © 1989 and 1993, by the Division of Christian Education of the National Council of the Churches of Christ in the United States of America. Used by permission. All rights reserved.

Cover image DavidZydd/iStock.com
Cover design by by Dawn Massa, Lightly Salted Graphics
Book design by Lynn Else

Copyright © 2020 by Felix Körner

All rights reserved. No part of this publication may be reproduced, stored in a retrieval system, or transmitted in any form or by any means, electronic, mechanical, photocopying, recording, scanning, or otherwise, without either the prior written permission of the Publisher, or authorization through payment of the appropriate per-copy fee to the Copyright Clearance Center, Inc., www.copyright.com. Requests to the Publisher for permission should be addressed to the Permissions Department, Paulist Press, permissions@paulistpress.com.

Library of Congress Cataloging-in-Publication Data
Names: Körner, Felix, author.
Title: Political religion : how Christianity and Islam shape the world / Felix Körner.
Description: New York : Paulist Press, [2020]. | Series: Theology at the frontiers | Includes bibliographical references and index. | Summary: "Few would deny these religions have played, and still play, a major role in world affairs. But what exactly does the interaction between religion and society consist of? Körner, a Catholic theologian and student of Islam, looks at seven models of how Christianity and Islam have influenced society. He concludes that religion is most authentic when it uses its power to shape the world not through violence, but in a positive manner: in "acknowledgement of the other.""— Provided by publisher.
Identifiers: LCCN 2019029372 (print) | LCCN 2019029373 (ebook) | ISBN 9780809154968 (paperback) | ISBN 9781587688942 (ebook)
Subjects: LCSH: Christianity and politics. | Christianity—Influence. | Islam and politics. | Islam—Influence. | Political theology. | Religion and sociology.
Classification: LCC BR115.P7 K645 2020 (print) | LCC BR115.P7 (ebook) | DDC 322/.109—dc23
LC record available at https://lccn.loc.gov/2019029372
LC ebook record available at https://lccn.loc.gov/2019029373

ISBN 978-0-8091-5496-8 (paperback)
ISBN 978-1-58768-894-2 (e-book)

Published by Paulist Press
997 Macarthur Boulevard
Mahwah, New Jersey 07430
www.paulistpress.com

Printed and bound in the
United States of America

Contents

Contents

Acknowledgments and Dedication

When I had just arrived in Rome, Johannes Schidelko, a fine Catholic journalist, asked me the question that triggered many of the thoughts I develop here: Why can religions be used to justify violence? Thank you for asking.

When Pope Francis published his apostolic exhortation *Evangelii Gaudium* in November 2013, Mark-David Janus, CSP, of Paulist Press, made a decisive move in the direction of this book, too. He saw that this era was becoming the second phase in the reception history of Vatican II. That is why Mark-David, together with my fellow Jesuit Gerard K. Whelan (Gerry), launched this book series. Francis himself seemed to define its paradigm when he challenged us scholars in March 2015: "Do not settle for a desktop theology. Your place for reflection is the frontier." Gerry, the fundamental theologian from Ireland, was able to set up an editorial board for such a theology at the frontiers from an international team of Jesuit professors, each of them with a link to the Gregorian University, Rome: René Micallef from Malta, myself, and (at Ateneo de Manila University, Philippines) José Mario Francisco, who bravely accepted to coordinate the group. Well done, *Eppur si muove*, things are actually moving!

Apart from the board members, it was Kathrin Misera-Lang, a German lawyer, diplomat, and friend, who (in spite of all her professional and family business) read the first draft and suggested many meaningful modifications. Very helpful.

Then Patrick McNamara, senior editor at Paulist Press, took over. I think that the text now really sounds English, things look solid, and the book has become wholly readable. Great job, Pat!

And then, there are my brother and my sister and their families, who keep encouraging me (pulling my leg, deflating my ideas…); there are two interlocutors who on nightly walks were part of the book's production process: Ulrich Rhode, SJ, and João Vila-Châ, SJ; and there are two men here in Rome who help me survive: H. Miguel Yáñez, SJ, and Xavier Jeong Yeon Hwang, SJ.

I dedicate this book to Mrs. Hilke Pannenberg. She was her husband's healthy-minded support when he was doing theology and when he was no longer able to. It was to her that Wolfhart Pannenberg dedicated *Was ist der Mensch?* of 1962, the 1967 *Grundfragen* collection, his *Anthropology* of 1983 and, in 1997, the *Problemgeschichte*. Now she is ninety-one, still a healthy-minded support to theologians and therefore this book's obvious dedicatee.

Introduction

Religion is the realization of the sacred: that is, perceiving the sacred, and allowing it to become real. Politics, conversely, consists of the attempt to shape the world through the exercise of public power. If these two definitions are used, it becomes clear why politics and religion are two of humanity's great claims at shaping the world. That is often why religion and politics tend to view one another as competitors, occasionally disrupting one another and using one another as instruments of power. But religion's goals are different from politics. They transcend politics. If, then, a religion seeks to shape the world, is it committing a political abuse in the name of God?

The Prussian statesman Otto von Bismarck once declared the impossibility of running a state based on the principles of the Sermon on the Mount. Yet why should this be impossible, or even illegitimate? The Qur'an, for that matter, seems to have a straightforward approach when it comes to political issues. In the light of new intellectual and political developments, then, is a new political theology needed?

The very term "political theology" arouses controversy. In late antiquity, it marked the path that a theologian ought to avoid. Theology was "political" if it simply tried to do justice to the *polis* (the state) rather than to the divine. If political theology originally implied a servile submission to state power, should the concept be abandoned altogether? Perhaps not. The term "political *philosophy*" does not, after all, raise controversy. So why avoid employing a useful term because of past controversies? Political theology, rather, is a scholarly discipline that studies the interrelations between theological understanding and political world shaping. Its fundamental questions are twofold. First,

ix

how can a religion influence human relations, such as an association or domination? Second, how do human relations affect religion? What is being developed in the following pages, then, is indeed a political theology.

If the interaction between religion and politics are to be studied here, what makes this study specifically theological? While it does utilize history and philosophy, sociology and political science, it will go further. Rather than simply submitting to the claims of the humanities and social sciences, it tries to check whether those claims are justified. To nonreligious readers, this study offers alternative ways of understanding and shaping society: theological concepts, explanations, and methods. Theology has an original contribution to make in the dialogue between the different schools of knowledge. It employs largely unused approaches, paths of understanding that arise from fundamental theological questions. It studies a specific religious confession and asks in what sense it is true.

Organization

In the political theology being developed here, specifically Christian contributions will be featured: the references to Israel's scriptures and to Jesus, the recognition of human life as inscrutability, the message of the kingdom of God and its particular representation, and the Church. What is new here is that, along with Christian themes, another voice will regularly appear: that of Islam. The political theology of Islam has played a key role in many societies and poses difficult questions. It will be asked which form of state power the Qur'an favors: theocracy, autocracy, or democracy. Does Islam allow for different patterns of political order? Also addressed will be the call for violence in sources claimed to be revelation. With the addition of the Qur'anic voice, the Church finds an important interlocutor. Looking at specifically Christian and Islamic profiles, they can thus be chiseled out more clearly and enrich one another.

So how do religions become world-shaping entities? Seven politico-religious models will be discussed here. Each will first be formulated in nontheological terms, thereby allowing for greater dialogue and enrichment.

Introduction

It needs to be noted at the start that most people do not select their own religion. For many, religion seems to have always "been there." So chapter 1 looks at *religion as culture*. Its counterpoint is the promise that human beings will acquire authenticity by means of a faith decision; hence chapter 2 examines *religion as the foundation of a new identity*. Throughout history, religions have served as the basis for political order and justice, but also for the rule of injustice. Chapter 3 discusses *religion as legitimation of rule and violence*. Against this, however, many religions have a prophetic element, critical of the powers that be, questioning also religion's political abuse: *religion as the relativization and critique of worldly power* (chapter 4). Another key theme for religion in the public sphere, right next to the power question, is that of powerlessness. Religion can give space to the human incapacity to understand failure, as well as highlight the voices of the forgotten, the suppressed, and the unfulfilled. It thus becomes the voice of the deprived. *Religion as the presentation of weakness* is the subject of chapter 5. If, however, a religion becomes aware of its own weakness, whether through interreligious or antireligious competition, it will no longer claim a complete following. It will expect objections, emphasize personal credibility, and will try to be meaningful also to nonmembers. Therefore, *religion as inspiration in a plural society* is the subject of chapter 6. This survey will eventually lead to a new concept that can shed new light on all six of these forms of religious presence: *religion as acknowledgment of the other*, the focus of chapter 7.

Each of these models will be elucidated with the aid of biblical themes. The dynamics thus designated are those that have motivated and oriented Christianity's political involvement throughout the centuries. This applies to both individual and institutional involvement. In addition, it will be determined which biblical images were most influential. Programmatic concepts from both the Old and New Testaments can provide key images to be explored, modes of understanding to be fathomed, and also offer new ways of living. In each chapter, one such concept will account for the development of the model under discussion. Each time the original concept will be paired with a concept of development. This will be from the New Testament, too (along with a nonbiblical Greek background), making it philosophically compatible. The book is then organized along the following scheme:

Politico-religious model	Dynamic	Development
1 Culture	World	Spirit
2 New identity	Vocation	Community
3 Legitimizing rule	Authority	Justice
4 Relativizing power	Kingdom of God	Congregation
5 Presence of weakness	The poor	Faith
6 Inspiring a society	Conscience	Witness
7 Acknowledging the other	Coming to know	Love

Some Particularities

In the book's subtitle, Christianity and Islam are listed on an equal footing. But one should not expect they will be treated with the same amount of attention. The choice of quotations indicates, for example, that I am not a Muslim theologian, but rather a Catholic theologian who is a scholar of Islam. Although I have a great interest in Islam, I am nevertheless an outsider. Furthermore, this book is not a comparative study, but a Catholic ecclesiology seeking to benefit from Islamic testimonies.

This book was initially the result of a lecture delivered together with the Qur'an exegete Ömer Özsoy, for Protestant, Islamic, and Catholic theology students. Afterward, I also used this material at the Gregorian University in Rome, for my ecclesiology class in the dogmatic licentiate program. The students' questions, objections, and suggestions were gratefully received.

Three particularities need to be explained. In the following pages, the history of concepts will be explored, occasionally with the aid of excerpts from an original text. Stories of personal experience will also be related. The significance of these will vary for each reader. No single definable agenda motivated the choice of these. Readers can allow themselves to be moved by the words of the text, by scriptural passages, and by stories of personal experience. The question of why the author put this precisely in that part of the book will then no longer be important.

One last thing on this subject: what I mark as my own experience is neither invented nor generously rewritten. It is really what I remember to have happened.

Books I Found Inspiring

What can I recommend for further reading? What should one read? In Lebanon a young Jesuit once asked me how he could find his own philosophical or theological "hero," and how he could tell that he had found him. I replied, "The one you want to read even on a Sunday afternoon is the one." I have to find out for myself what kind of questions I actually have, at which kind of thoughts everything seems to fall into place, and which styles of answering upset me rather than lead me forward. And that's something you only find out by reading.

That was also how Wolfhart Pannenberg became my preceptor. I have read everything by him. And even rereading him is full of discoveries! For the questions around "political religion," his 1983 *Anthropology in Theological Perspective* is altogether worthwhile. A political theology, if Christian, also needs to explain why we need a Church. Pannenberg tackles the ecclesiological theme especially in the third volume of his *Systematic Theology* (1993). But also his lectures on human nature, election and history, given in the United States between 1975 and '76, opened up new worlds to me, as can be felt in the following, I hope.

Via Pannenberg I came to know another exciting author, Eric Voegelin—a giant of which I only know one foot, so to speak. But the category through which he considers human power is a key: What is "represented" in this or that political order? I have tried here to continue Voegelin by combining his optics of representation with Jesus's presentation of God's kingdom. Behind this, of course, are Pannenbergian insights, too.

The fact that Weber and Troeltsch can only be read with amazement and profit hardly needs to be emphasized. Likewise that Jürgen Habermas is always worthwhile and that one should have Johann Baptist Metz in one's working memory for a political theology is obvious. But I would like to mention two other contemporary voices. Hans Joas often proposes impressive new perspectives on our theme. Here, for example, I will bring to bear his concept of reflected sacrality. And Charles Taylor's *Secular Age* really changed my mind. If I will claim in the next pages that religion should be understood as something like culture (with its wild, even embarrassing, but not conceptually reducible elements), I owe that to my reading of Taylor. By the way, I read the book during a Jesuit vacation in Sardinia. It turned out that one of the others had the same book in his baggage. In the evenings we were fighting for an understanding of that wildly written work, and for answers to the quest what follows from it.

Basic Bibliography

Casanova, José. *Public Religions in the Modern World*. Chicago: University of Chicago Press, 1994.

Crone, Patricia. *Medieval Islamic Political Thought*. Edinburgh: T & T Clark, 2004.

Pannenberg, Wolfhart. *Anthropology in Theological Perspective*. Translated by Matthew J. O'Connell. Edinburgh: T & T Clark, 1985.

————. *Human Nature, Election, and History*. Louisville, KY: Westminster John Knox Press, 1977.

Taylor, Charles. *A Secular Age*. Cambridge, MA: Harvard University Press, 2007.

Voegelin, Eric. *The New Science of Politics* (1951). In *Modernity without Restraint*, vol. 5 of *The Collected Works of Eric Voegelin*, 75–241. Columbia: The University of Missouri Press, 1999.

————. *The Political Religions* (1938). In *Modernity without Restraint*, vol. 5 of *The Collected Works of Eric Voegelin*, 27–73. Columbia: The University of Missouri Press, 1999.

CULTURE

Previewing the First Chapter

Religion may just be there, like the air around us. We need not even think about our faith lives. It can be simply our culture. If, however, we want to study that environment, preferably with words offered by the religions themselves, we quickly realize that there is no mention of the word *culture* in the scriptures. They speak of the "world," rather. What do religions say about their own relation to the world?

Coming to our attention first are two Christian thinkers who actually drafted a theology of the world: Johann Baptist Metz (1928–2019) and Karl Rahner, SJ (1904–1984). Following this, I examine the voice of scripture. We experience how the Bible sees the world as something in motion, and how the Qur'an explains the world as something symmetric, drawing from that the call to a new life.

The question of how much religion is like culture must be examined. The danger then becomes evident in a "puritan" form of religion, which rejects as "merely cultural" and "pagan" everything not originating through its own faith message. This is anything *but* world shaping. It may be the prelude before falling into radicalism and ultimately insignificance.

The right attitude is dialogue. But what is the goal of such dialogue between religion and culture? I will examine three models: that of conceptual compatibility; what Robert N. Bellah (1928–2013) termed "civil religion"; and, finally, what Georg Wilhelm Friedrich Hegel (1770–1831) called "spirit." There is a fourth model in store, but I will examine it at the end of the second chapter: religious community as sacrament of the world. Before that, however, it is necessary to look at religion as culture.

I

Religion as Culture

Not far from our church in Ankara, Turkey, is Adem, standing among the baby strollers. He is a salesman and a football fan. He is not very tall, but he is impressively muscular. And he is looking for a suitable wife. She definitely must wear the headscarf. But Adem does not like to talk to me about such questions, because he slightly fears the priest might take away his religion. When Adem and I talk, a few spectators usually gather: his boss and some of his friends. They know that always something funny happens in our short conversations. For example, he notes that it's the German, of all people, who does not know who Schweinsteiger is.

Today our conversation is about German soccer once again, a topic about which I know nothing. At that moment, the call to prayer arises behind us. Ḥayya ʿalā ṣ-ṣalāt, sings the loudspeaker from the minaret. "Do you know what the muezzin says?" I ask Adem. "Uhh," he hesitates, "that Muḥammad is the Messenger of God!" I answer, "That also, but ḥayya ʿalā ṣ-ṣalāt means 'Come on, to prayer!'" Bystanders confirm this, as if they could all have given the correct translation from Arabic to Turkish immediately. "So, are you going?" I ask them. "Later!" they answer defensively. That might mean, in half an hour, or once they have become fathers and made the pilgrimage.

CULTURE

What is religion? Even simpler than our introductory definition, "realization of the sacred," would be the following quote from political scientist Eric Voegelin: "By *religion* one understands such phenomena as Christianity."[1] If we define religions as phenomena just like Christianity, we admit right away that we are casting our own grid over reality. We look at what is foreign to us, with our familiar patterns. And for a start, that is fair enough.

If religions are indeed phenomena such as Christianity, how did Christianity first appear? As a society within society? Over a century ago, Ernst Troeltsch (1865–1923), a pioneer in the sociology of religion, gave a helpful answer. Troeltsch asked which "social forms" Christianity assumes. He found, in the style of his friend Max Weber (1864–1920), three "ideal types" under which Christianity could appear: institution, sect, or mysticism. Since Troeltsch, these three types have become standard vocabulary in the sociology of religion; in other words: institution of grace, community of contrast, and movement of enthusiasm. But there is another type of religious presence, altogether common, only less visible. Except for certain parts of Europe, a traditional and experiential reference to the sacred is self-evident to the majority of people in the world. For them, religion *is* culture. One only becomes aware of this when religion loses its self-evident character, when it becomes merely an option. Of all the ways in which religion has shaped the world, the most traditional is through culture. People are surrounded by religion. Studying one's own religion is like exploring your native language or the political constitution of your nation. Long before studying these, they have already shaped you. Thus, Troeltsch's three ideal forms of Christianity's social types require an additional model in culture. Once a religion can manifest itself as culture, the fundamental question arises of how religion relates to culture.

Of course, as noted earlier, the word *culture* is not featured in classic religious vocabulary. To found a theology of culture based on ancient texts, we must focus on another concept. In the language of many spiritual traditions, the word for the present time, for the "here and now," for our environment, is not *culture*, but *world*. Religion may then choose to explain, transfigure, or condemn the world. Faith and world seem to shape one another. In investigating a religious theory of culture, the first question is, How do religions understand what they call the "world"?

4

Theology of the World

THESIS

According to the New Testament, believers are the "light of the world." Religion's appropriate relationship to the world is not withdrawal, conformity, or takeover. Rather, for a faith seeking to understand, look beyond, and fashion the world, the phrase this world *indicates the place and time of commitment.*

JOHANN BAPTIST METZ: CRITICAL FREEDOM

There is in fact a theologian who has drawn out an explicit theology of the world: Johann Baptist Metz. In that tumultuous year of 1968, a collection of Metz's articles appeared under the title *Theology of the World.*[2] Several years previously, Metz started calling his thought "political theology," or rather, in order to avoid misunderstandings, "new political theology." Controversy arose as to the term. Since the early days of Christianity, the term denoted a piously disguised support of existing power structures: loyalty not to the divine reality, but to one's own *polis*. But Metz's point is that theology must look beyond the private, investigating and influencing society anew. In that sense, Metz's approach is "new political theology."

The Church's task in the world is to be that critical institution of freedom. Metz contrasts his own "political" theology with "dialectical" theology, which he feels avoids a decisive approach to the world, seeing it in ambiguous terms. It sees God's creation both as good, and as a stronghold of evil. For Metz, dialectical theology simply juxtaposes values into static paradoxical formulae such as "God and humanity," "eternity and time." It looks at the world in undecided contemplation. Metz sees this kind of theologizing as what he calls a nonhistorical "And." His counterproposal to this is the historic "Or." If we resign ourselves to the world, life merely happens. But if we acknowledge the world as history that we have an obligation to shape, then the world is what we can make of it, in the light of our future. The historic "Or" means that it is only through our lives that the world "happens."

With this impressive advance, Metz has also brought forth critics. Their main objection is that a Metzian theology of the political amounts to actionism, offering "hope without faith."[3] While God's promise does imply humanity's responsibility to shape the world, critics rightly argue, where is the serene confidence that the kingdom of God is already growing?

If one chooses to portray Metz as a theologian of hope lacking faith, one must however avoid falling into another trap. While Metz underplays a serving Church that is simply "there," unspectacularly patient, it would be a reductionist view of the Church's mission to interpret it just as an institution of criticism. Still, we have only hinted at Metz's main point, which is expressed in another formula he employs, "the worldliness of the world." Johann Baptist Metz's appeal to the Church is this: take the social reality seriously, in its intrinsic value, as Christians ready to learn and to act! Understanding this formula will allow us to see how the "worldliness of the world" provides for the decisive continuation of political theology.

KARL RAHNER: CHURCH AND WORLD

The trail leads first, to Metz's theological mentor Karl Rahner, who also discusses the relation of the Church to the world. His most important (albeit not his clearest) article on the topic is found in the second encyclopedia he edited, the postconciliar *Sacramentum Mundi*. In titling his entry "Church and World,"[4] he echoes *Gaudium et Spes* (1965), Vatican II's Pastoral Constitution on the Church in the Modern World. To clarify his own viewpoint, Rahner marks out what he rejects as heretical if not dangerous: integralism and esoterism. In doing so, he made a historically significant conceptual decision. While the Catholic magisterium had previously warned against integralism, it designated theological modernism as the opposite extreme. For Rahner, however, the opposite of integralist was esoteric. Although Rahner was never completely satisfied with the term *esoteric*, he used it to designate those who saw the world as altogether sinful. In that case, religion is seen as a flight from the world. As for integralism, Rahner takes the word from the French warning against *integrisme*, or fundamentalism. Integralism is the belief that everything should be "churchified," as Rahner calls it.

Rahner sees integralism as subordinating Christians under a ministerial Church where they are simply to execute what the clergy commands. (This provides a sense of Rahner's own experience with the institutional Church.) The dangers of these two extremes, though,

6

have their place not only in Church politics. At stake is a fundamental challenge, the theological problem of the world. The problem pops up today under a different guise. Think about the popular success of the radical, violent uses of religion. To many, they are fascinating because they offer simple answers in a confusing world with too many options. Salvation doctrines are marketed as the simple answer to everything. The reduction of complexity is an attractive proposition to many.

This comes at a cost, however. Religious integralism and esoterism share one basic conviction. Both reject what "true religion" has not yet transformed and approved. In one case, it must therefore be replaced by religion; that is the integralist option. In the other case, the religious group must keep away from it; that is the esoteric alternative. Each time, their fundamental error lies thus in their evaluation of the "world," its complete devaluation.

Religion that sees the world as all sinful can realize the Sacred only in

Esoterism   *or*   **Integralism**

Religion must escape the world.   *Religion must replace the world.*

Rahner devotes much space in his encyclopedia to the relation between "Church and world," but he never offers a formula to express how they should relate. Instead, what prevails has an activist sound, à la Metz. On three occasions, though, Rahner did actually propose elsewhere forms of thought to express a balanced relation between the religious and the secular.

Perhaps his earliest proposal, in 1937, was "the Ignatian mysticism of joy in the world." Although Rahner used the formula hesitatingly, it strikes a resounding note. Rahner's Jesuit spirituality is based on the experience of "consolation," which St. Ignatius Loyola (1491–1556) wanted to make accessible to all. Consolation is the gift of being able to "love everything in God and God in everything."[5] Within this context, nonreligious insights and activities are not distractions, let alone defections, from the spiritual realm. They are ways to God; indeed, they are God's ways.

Rahner proposed another way of speaking about the relationship between religion and the world. In the aftermath of the two world wars, European philosophers introduced, as the fundamental human activity, a word Rahner happily used elsewhere: "dialogue."[6] Its first expression in the magisterium occurs in Pope St. Paul VI's inaugural encyclical, *Ecclesiam Suam* (1964). This use of the word *dialogue* is about more than just talking. It employs the dynamics of conversation as a metaphor for a particular form of interpersonal relations. One might describe it in the light of four characteristics:

- Encounter (the novelty of the other)
- Dependence (each "I" owes itself to a "thou")
- Honesty (the risk of fully revealing oneself to the other)
- A reconciliatory approach (as opposed to combativeness)

The formula that Rahner preferred, however, was "the worldliness of the world," whereby he calls for the courage "to let the worldly world really be worldly."[7] For Rahner, "world" is the antonym to the ecclesiastical realm, the secular as opposed to the sacristy. Here he is referring to a fundamental theological insight for which he had, with others, successfully fought at Vatican II. It constituted a breakthrough in Church history. This insight was incorporated into *Gaudium et Spes* 36, which refers to "the autonomy of earthly affairs." This means theology must acknowledge that "created things and societies themselves enjoy their own laws and values." They must be "gradually deciphered, put to use, and regulated." By the "very circumstance of their having been created, all things are endowed with their own stability, truth, goodness." Why is that a consequence of being created?

When God creates, God allows realities to exist that are relatively independent from himself. Thus, the Creation account reads, Then God said, "Let the earth put forth vegetation: plants yielding seed, and fruit trees of every kind on earth that bear fruit with the seed in it" (Gen 1:11). So it is the earth itself, then, which is to bring forth plants, and these in turn themselves can then produce fruit—and seeds in it, so that history can continue. The Creator has manifestly handed over control. Once theology sees nature's relative independence, it can acknowledge that theologians are not in charge of defining and explaining natural processes. Accordingly, the council fathers affirmed the validity of scientific methods. Furthermore, they confirmed that science is not the enemy. Other sources of knowledge are not in need of theological correction, but are theology's partners in dialogue. To let the world be worldly means respectfully and positively encountering other forms of knowledge and other lifeforms; for example, quantum physics, or Mahāyāna Buddhism. That is not distressing, but good and even healing. If a faith tradition wants to contribute to the world's knowledge, and help shape it in a positive manner, it will be interested in all other approaches that seek to do the same.

Is the program then to simply let the world be? By no means. While acknowledging that autonomy is a remedy against integralism, religion has something to offer to the arts and sciences, as well as to other religions. It can synthesize and integrate these various forms of life and knowledge, while serving as a critical reminder of these spheres' respective limits. A continued exchange is needed. However, "the world" is not a clear-cut interlocutor standing in front of me. What is it, then?

The "worldliness of the world" formula must be traced back further to Rahner's philosophical mentor Martin Heidegger (1889–1976), who actually coined the phrase.[8] For Heidegger, the world is not a series of objects abstracted from the subject, but rather a network of cross-references grouped around me according to my intentions. It is worldly because it is a whole that encompasses and shapes me.

What Heidegger wants to point out is that we are caught up in our respective worlds, that our everyday experience is surrounded and shaped by a force not seen. Heidegger, however, did not sufficiently consider the fact that we can turn our attention to objects in a matter of fact manner, "objectively," in that sense. Can we not sometimes succeed in distancing ourselves from our own impulses? Do we not sometimes see things beyond how they function in our plans? We *can* actually see objects fairly objectively. Not everything is related to the mere element of our respective purposes. On the other hand, Heidegger emphasizes something that theologians often miss when they look at the world as a challenge to be turned into a "better place." True, we do exist in the midst of a network of cross-references we cannot simply remove. Religion, too, is not only in the world, but it is itself something *like a world*, an environment shaping us. Before studying this, though, it is necessary to look at how the scriptures see the world.

BIBLE AND QUR'AN: WORLD IN TIME

Why is it religion in particular that speaks of the "world"? Because it is precisely the religious view that transcends things to allow people to see all as one whole. In its theological context, the term *world* may sound like a place saints would shun. Or it could be the place a priest dreams of going to, when he starts to feel the air in the church getting musty. He may even believe that if he uses sociological terms and dresses fashionably, he'll finally be efficient and "professional." If one is interested in venturing beyond church doors, one should start by employing a nonreligious vocabulary. Look at what your favorite words and phrases are. Instead of saying "the world," theologians might utilize some alternative phrases such as the following:

- People
- The present
- Contemporary life
- The public sphere[9]
- Public reason
- Society
- Pluralistic society
- Postsecularism

Or, for that matter, culture. But we must be careful. Eliminating the word *world* would also mean sacrificing important insights. The concept and background of the term itself is worth exploring.

Bible: Temporality

Surprisingly, the Hebrew Bible has no word for the cosmos, for the order of all objects encountered. Occasionally, "world" can be expressed as "everything," "earth," or "land." Most common, however, are words denoting "duration."[10] The great Old Testament scholar Gerhard von Rad (1901–71) was wondering why "Israel was unable to conceptualize the world so philosophically, so objectively as if human beings were set in front of it." He found his answer in that people's particularly unsteady history; that is why for them "'world' was experienced as something that happened to human beings: in an ever new manner, in manifold ways." So rather than sensing a philosophical principle ordering the cosmos, "Israel saw, first, YHWH Himself much more immediately at work in these world affairs, and, second, Israel saw human beings as participating in it."[11]

If Metz claims in his "new political theology" that world is history, he gets support from von Rad and, indeed, from the Old Testament. As for the New Testament, it speaks of the "world" sometimes with a word that stresses unforeseeable change and at other times with a word that stresses stable order.

The biblical understanding of the world shapes other languages

The New Testament uses the Greek words kosmos *("beautiful order") and* aiōn *("temporal phase") interchangeably. Latin imitates this when Christians alternate* mundus *(literally "pure world order") and* saeculum *("aeon" or "era"). Such a concept of the world, pointing at its temporal rather than static character, also exists in English. "World" comes from the Old High German word* weralt, *meaning "age of the world" or "era." It seems to be a Christian coinage, translating* saeculum *literally. Thus it echoes the Hebrew temporal world concept (ʿôlām). In this way a sense of the world's temporality is silently transmitted from the Hebrew Bible to today's English language.*

The World of the Qur'an

In the following pages we will study key passages from the Qur'an. It is, to begin with, useful to know that the Qur'an today contains 114 texts known as "Suras." Though sometimes called "chapters," they are really more independent. The Qur'an is not a book arranged according to its contents. Rather, it is a lectionary in which texts are grouped according to length (like St. Paul's letters in the New Testament). It is historically possible to define quite precisely when Muḥammad's words were spoken, in four different stages. In 610, Muḥammad appeared in his hometown of Mecca, claiming that his proclamation was God's word. Twelve years later, he emigrated with followers to Medina. What he announced in Mecca, between 610 and 622, can be divided into three stages: early, middle, and late Meccan. What he said as Qur'an from 622 until his death in 632 is known as "Medinan." But what concepts of the world does the Qur'an offer now?

How the Qur'an Speaks about the World

In pre-Qur'anic Arab poetry, the hereafter is called *al-āḫira*, "what comes afterward," or "the later." The Qur'an adopts this word.

It is a temporal concept. It sounds like the New Testament expression *ta eskhata*, "the last things" (2 Pet 2:20), which can be understood as either "later" or "the hereafter." To say, "this world," as opposed to "the later," the Qur'an sometimes uses *al-ūlā*, literally "the first," in the early Meccan Suras. But the most common word used for "this world" is a spatial designation, *ad-dunyā*, "the lowest." In spite of this, temporal thinking pervades the Qur'an.

This corresponds to the rabbinic contrast between *ha-'ôlām ha-zê* ("this world") and *ha-'ôlām ha-bā'* ("the world to come"). The Qur'an also alludes to *'ôlām*, the Hebrew word for "world." It appears in a frequent Qur'anic expression for "God and human beings." God is *rabb al-ālamīn*, which seems to say, "Lord of the worlds." The surprising plural (as opposed to the expected *rabb al-'awālim*) is probably a contraction of *rabb al-ālamīyīn*, "Lord of the *'ôlām* inhabitants." This presents human life in a new light; humanity inhabits all that is called *'ôlām*, this world and the next. Hence the Qur'an sees human beings as having a dual citizenship.[12] Another word frequently used in the Qur'an is *arḍ*, which is related to the Hebrew *æræṣ*, meaning "land" or "earth" (Sura 55:10).

Sura 55 is perhaps the clearest representation of the Qur'anic worldview. Its recurring dual forms reflect the world's harmony. Here, we sense the symmetrical correspondence of creation, revelation, and action. And here the world is deciphered as God's sign. God is its merciful Creator, but God also warns of the coming judgment, thus calling humanity to exercise responsible citizenship in this world.

Studying Sura 55

This Sura, also known as *ar-Raḥmān* (from the first line), needs to be understood within the context of the ancient Arabic worldview, which is most fully expressed in the long pre-Islamic poems called *qaṣīdas*. These poems are polythematic, just like most Qur'anic Suras, but the *qaṣīda* always voices the same three themes. This type of poetry consisted less in finding new themes than in varying the language employed to express the ever-recurring topics.

The *qaṣīda* begins with a *nasīb*, or prelude, in which the Bedouin lover has left his dwelling place in search of his beloved. He reads footprints in the sand where his beloved's tribe had recently camped. They have moved on unexpectedly. The beloved is gone; the enchanted past is lost, leaving only an abandoned campsite (*al-aṭlāl*). The footprints signify loss. The ode's theme now shifts, as the Bedouin mounts his horse or camel. He sings out his animal's beauty, with no longer a thought to the beloved. What follows is a standard conclusion, a homage to the ruler.

Sura 55 offers no signs in the sand, no eyes cast to the ground, but a glance turned upward! Instead of a hostile environment, there is life in a cosmos created and maintained by a merciful Provider. People do not have to invent their own tasks anymore. Now, rather, human life discovers its task as a gift received from God. In view of this task, life in paradise, once understood, every element in the world speaks of meaning and purpose.

A chorus is repeated in this Sura (thirty-one times), a unique feature for the Qur'an, which makes the text sound almost like a psalm. This chorus never changes, but keeps asking, "Which of the favors of your Lord do you want to deny?" At first, this may simply sound like praise. Later, however, the chorus gets a very different context, and thus the favors (ālā᾽) have a different feel to them. The chorus now sounds almost threatening, but why? And why the dual address: "Which of the favors do you (the two of you) want to deny?" The Sura apparently raises many questions.

Sura 55 *ar-Raḥmān*—the Mercifier
In the name of God, the merciful Mercifier!
1 The Mercifier! (*ar-raḥmān*)
2 He has taught the reading (*al-qur᾽ān*)
3 and has created the human being (*al-insān*)
4 and has taught clarification. (*al-bayān*)
5 Sun and moon go according to calculation.
6 Stars and trees prostrate themselves.
7 He raised the sky and set firm the scales,
8 lest you be rebellious when weighing;
9 Set up the weights as is right!
Do not manipulate the scales!
10 He posited the earth for humanity;
11 on it, there are fruits and palms in clumps.
12 Grain on blades and fragrant herbs.
13 Which of the favors of your Lord do you want to deny?

14 The human being, He created from clay like the potter
15 and the *ǧinn* he has created from a blend of fire.

13

16 Which of the favors of your Lord do you want to deny?

17 The Lord of East and West!

18 Which of the favors of your Lord do you want to deny?

19 He let the two waters flow so that they meet;

20 between them is a barrier lest they commit any transgression.

21 Which of the favors of your Lord do you want to deny?

22 They bring forth pearls and corals.

23 Which of the favors of your Lord do you want to deny?

24 His are the drifting ships that tower on the sea like landmarks.

25 Which of the favors of your Lord do you want to deny?

26 Everyone who abides on earth must pass away,

27 but the face of your sublime and venerable Lord remains.

28 Which of the favors of your Lord do you want to deny?

29 It is Him whom those implore who are in the heavens and
    on earth; every day He is at work.

30 Which of the favors of your Lord do you want to deny?

31 We will take our time for you, you heavy ones and you
    light ones!

32 Which of the favors of your Lord do you want to deny?

33 O you multitudes of *ǧinn* and humans!
If you are able to penetrate the regions of the heavens and the
    earth, then penetrate! You will not penetrate unless by
    His power.

34 Which of the favors of your Lord do you want to deny?

35 Fire-flames and ore will be sent against you, so that you will
    be helpless.

36 Which of the favors of your Lord do you want to deny?

37 When heaven splits apart and shines in rose color like oil,

38 Which of the favors of your Lord do you want to deny?

39 That day, neither human nor *ǧinn* will be asked about their
    guilt [any more].

40 Which of the favors of your Lord do you want to deny?

41 The evildoers are recognized by their sign and then seized by
    their tuft and feet.

42 Which of the favors of your Lord do you want to deny?

43 "This is the hell the deniers have denied!"

44 They go back and forth between fire and boiling water.

45 Which of the favors of your Lord do you want to deny?

46 The one who has feared the power of his Lord will receive
two gardens—

47 Which of the favors of your Lord do you want to deny?

48 —with manifold species.

49 Which of the favors of your Lord do you want to deny?

50 In it, there are two flowing sources.

51 Which of the favors of your Lord do you want to deny?

52 In it, there is a pair of every fruit.

53 Which of the favors of your Lord do you want to deny?

54 One rests on beds covered in brocade; with the garden
fruits close.

55 Which of the favors of your Lord do you want to deny?

56 In it, there are women their glance cast down in chastity,
untouched before by either human or *ğinn*,—

57 Which of the favors of your Lord do you want to deny?

58 —they are like hyacinths or coral.

59 Which of the favors of your Lord do you want to deny?

60 Are good deeds repaid with anything other than
good deeds?

61 Which of the favors of your Lord do you want to deny?

62 Under it, there are two more gardens—

63 Which of the favors of your Lord do you want to deny?

64 —of deep green.

65 Which of the favors of your Lord do you want to deny?

66 In it, there are gushing springs.

67 Which of the favors of your Lord do you want to deny?

68 In it, there are fruits, palms and pomegranate trees.

69 Which of the favors of your Lord do you want to deny?

70 In it, there are good, beautiful women—

71 Which of the favors of your Lord do you want to deny?

72 —with black eyes, in separate tents,—

73 Which of the favors of your Lord do you want to deny?

74 —untouched before by either human or *ğinn*.

75 Which of the favors of your Lord do you want to deny?

76 They rest on green cushions and beautiful rugs.

77 Which of the favors of your Lord do you want to deny?

78 Blessed be the name of your Lord exalted and
venerable!

The text is from the first phase of the Qur'anic proclamation, when Muḥammad is gathering followers in his hometown. Hence this Sura is "late early Meccan." It introduces an innovation: the Jewish name of God, *ha-Raḥămān*, as God is called in postbiblical Hebrew. In Arabic, God is now called *ar-Raḥmān*, a term that becomes fundamental to listeners. The Arabic word for "merciful," *raḥīm*, sounds quite similar. Although *ar-Raḥmān* may sound foreign to the Arab ear, it is not incomprehensible. A sense of this is given in the English rendition of the Arabic name, "the Mercifier."

Sura 55's first verses strike an affirming note. The cosmos is under the control of the Mercifier, comprehensible and livable. The order of the stars, for example, calls humanity to the correct usage of measurements. Then, however, the world turns out to be only prelude to the final judgment, a testing ground for the all-decisive (and not far away) eschatological event, where judgment awaits (Sura 55:39, 41). The actions of evildoers decide their fate before the judgment.

This also clarifies the duality issue in the chorus ("both of you"). As soon as the question has been sounded for the first time (Sura 55:13), the Sura shows that it is not only the human being who is addressed, but also a *ğinnī*, which can be either an evil demon or a good spirit. Sura 55 makes strong use of doublets. This is a skillful way of depicting the earth as order, as instructive symmetry, as a prelude to judgment, as the place where decisions, good or bad, are made. The point of the Sura's duality is not to get lost in this world's distractions because the real thing is yet to come. God's beautiful order, therefore, is dangerously double-edged.

Double-edged

The biblical worldview is also double-edged. The classical expression of the Christian's earthly life situation is captured in the words "in the world but not of the world." This is an allusion to Jesus's prayer in John 17:11–14. The world is not the origin of the disciples' mission. It is the place to which they are missioned (John 17:18).

Why is the world seen as double-edged, both evil and good? God has created being that is *not* God himself.[13] God gives life. When creatures live out the dynamic of giving service, the world is the place of God's spirit. They both receive life and make life possible. To be created also means, however, exercising relative independence. Thus, with creation,

God allows creatures the opportunity to close in on themselves. But then autonomy becomes deadly. This is the world's primary problem. Although creation tends toward self-closure, this is nevertheless the world that Christ's Spirit must expose and transform, or "convict" (*elenkhein* in the original Greek, John 16:8).

World of Meaning

Something composed of several elements only becomes recognizable as one when contrasted with that which does not belong to it. All things, people, and events become recognizable together as one, as "the world," only when held in contrast to that which is nonworldly. Therefore to consider the "world" as such already means to transcend it; in other words, speaking of "world" has something religious to it.[14] But is that totality really ordered, is it beautiful and good? The entirety of everything can only be understood as good, if seen as leading to a good end. This brings us back to the first insight of the "new political theology," that the world is history.

Whoever experiences the historical change of events can only see the world as good if they understand the world as history, and that this history will end well. Such an insight lets us now respond to Rahner's question in his *Sacramentum Mundi* entry on the Church and the world. To restate it more sharply, What is the Church's mission, the task in the world that only it can fulfill? What is it that the Christian faith, and only the Christian faith, offers humanity? The answer is well expressed in the title of Pope Francis's first apostolic exhortation in 2013, *Evangelii Gaudium* (The Joy of the Gospel). Why is the answer to the question for Christianity's unique contribution the "gospel joy"?

Whenever prophets proclaim God's final judgment, a good end is at least presented as a just end. The gospel of the resurrection of Christ also proclaims the end of history, but in a distinctly different way from apocalyptic prophecy. First, in the risen Christ, his disciples see that there will be a *good* end: communion in the life of God and the individual's ultimate fulfillment. Second, even what seemed at first to thwart that good ending will from hindsight be understood as part of God's good history. Finally, because the end has already begun, people can be seized by joy. They can therefore live a life based not on anxious effort, but they can live as people grasped, moved, and liberated by that joy.

17

What is special about the witness of Christ? The joy people experience allows them to love beyond a normal human capacity. Perhaps the Christian relation with the world is best expressed in the Sermon on the Mount: "You are the light of the world" (Matt 5:14). Christ's disciples can see the world in the light of Easter. They recognize in the present moment a new pathway to completeness. The resulting confidence can be communicated to others, through words and deeds. It can also be communicated through a unique experience in which the verbal and nonverbal, history and community, play a role: in the celebration of the sacraments.

Those who claim, however, to have *defined* the Christian project by the "light of the world," may have fallen into the "integralist" or the "puritan" trap. If people can summarize their world purpose in a few words, they should be challenged with two questions: Do you think you have already understood the fundamental concerns of the people that make up "the world" for you? And do you think you have already fully grasped your own tradition (here, the Christian faith)? In reality, both "the world" and your own tradition have their hidden sides, lives of their own, that are not at the obedient disposal of a political theology. A religion cannot simply create world relevance through a slogan. We can never fully know the world or the faith! We therefore must learn to live with the provisional character of our knowledge and our words. Only then can being "light of the world" be more than a catchphrase. We need a different approach, one in which neither "faith" nor "world" are reduced to a mere definition. It can be expressed like this: religion can only be world shaping if it is being lived as culture, indeed, when it is alive as culture.

Having explored different religious ways of seeing the "world," we must return to the original question. If living with the sacred is the normal situation of many even today; if, in that sense, religion is often a culture, how does religion relate to culture, and vice versa? It is time, then, to look at what a theology of culture means.

Theology of Culture

What does "culture" really mean? Culture, simply put, is a group's style. To put it more precisely (perhaps too precisely), it can be understood as a community's form of life. In any case, culture is already at work before one begins to consider it. It cannot be understood, defined, or conserved completely. Nor can it be completely changed.

In Java today, no one adheres to the ancient Javanese religion any longer. For many Muslims, Christians, Buddhists, and others, however, treasuring Javanese culture—in language and clothing, art and architecture, particularly its unique shadow puppetry—is a safeguard against puritanism and radical extremism.

The Pakistani Christians, like their Muslim compatriots, are members of the Urdu culture now, but they do not fit in with the Islamic majority. The nation does not unite Pakistani Muslims and Christians into one "us." The nation is merely what political scientist Benedict Anderson (1936–2015) calls an "imagined community."

And in Latin Europe? From the Baroque era to the Second Vatican Council, the Catholic cultural project was fundamentally different from the Protestant one. Catholicism wanted to shape the whole culture, just as elsewhere; indeed Catholicism wanted to be the culture of its time. By contrast, liberal German Protestantism wants to be part of its homeland culture, both as its origin and as its future.

To answer the question of how religions relate to the culture they want to shape, which in turn shapes them, we must look at both the biblical cultural project and the Qur'anic cultural project.

THESIS

Religion can only be world shaping if it is alive as a culture. It cannot be understood completely, defined completely, conserved completely, nor be changed completely.

"CULTURE": AN APPROPRIATE DESCRIPTION OF RELIGION

Charles Taylor (1931–) offers a detailed interpretation of secularization, originally written for the 1999 Gifford Lectures. From this has grown his history of the modern *mentalité*, which he smartly titles

19

A Secular Age.[15] Smart, because in Latin, the title would be *saeculum saeculare* ("a secular century"). Does Taylor mean that if we do not see ourselves as the only possible world, but understand ourselves dynamically as an "age," if we relativize ourselves as one story among many, if we place it within the context of a grand narrative too vast to oversee, then we inevitably become secularized? Taylor does not argue this. He does not concoct a theory one could derive from one simple formula. He is a philosopher and a chronicler of the modern spirit. Taylor traces the interaction of ideas, interests, and institutions in society, especially with regard to religion and culture. In exploring what he calls the "social imaginary," Taylor wants to study three questions:

- How do societies *imagine* themselves? ("Imagination" is found in subconscious frameworks of perceiving and thinking. It is also alive in intuitions, images and symbols. The social imaginary, is, then, the alternative to theory.)
- How does a society see *itself*? (The "social" contrasts with elitism.)
- What *expectations* do people place on the polity, to enable political action? As the existing order's alternative, "imagination" then represents what we should be or could be.

Taylor's main question in *A Secular Age* is this: How do we find ourselves in a world where religion has become, not insignificant, but optional? A major factor he cites is found in puritanism. The "puritan" can be observed on many different fields of life. What is the puritan problem?

Reform and Reformation

Religious founders typically make a sharp distinction between salutary truth and human production; the latter is then often pejoratively labeled "tradition." The Prophet Isaiah, for instance, around 720 BC accuses the inhabitants of Jerusalem of having redefined the fear of God into a "human commandment learned by rote" (*miṣwat ănāšîm məlummādâ*, Isa 29:13), something artificial that is neither recognized by God nor resounds in the human heart. In the Synoptic Gospels, Jesus also criticizes his contemporary culture, particularly denouncing blatant injustice disguised as religion. Like Isaiah, he too applies the term *tradition* critically to his time.

One practice of his own time Jesus strongly critiqued was divorce. He sensed how it put women at a disadvantage. The same is true of the practice to piously exempt oneself from looking after one's parents. It is interesting to see how Jesus applied a critical approach to tradition in his own ministry. While he points out that the popular abuse of scripture cannot continue, he does not say that his arrival abolishes the Torah. Rather, he sees himself as bringing the law to "fulfillment," by observing God's intent from the beginning of the world (Matt 5:17; 19:8). What does God's intent consist of? In order to clarify this, Jesus does not only quote the Torah. He rather adduces a later voice, a prophet. Jesus retrieves Isaiah's reproach and carries it further. "Tradition" (*paradosis*) refers to what should be rejected. It is human work, sharply contrasted with the divine word (Mark 7:5–13).

But the question is this: What is God's central commandment? It requires us "to do something" for the needy (Mark 7:12), in the present case for father and mother—and to honor them (Mark 7:10). Jesus even offers a short formula for the social transformation caused by God's order: "I desire mercy and not sacrifice" (Matt 12:7). That formula is not from the Torah; rather, it is prophetic (Hosea 6:6); it is part of the tradition! Jesus is neither replacing the foundation (the word of the Torah) nor the tradition (interpretation of the Torah in light of the prophets, hope for the resurrection, the idea of angels, the experience of the spirit; see Acts 23:8). By this, nothing is being canceled. After all, Jesus has come to "fulfill." Jesus's coming is, then, not a fundamentalism but a reform. That is a renewal of all that has been transmitted, not through devaluation, destruction, or division, in view of a reconstructed original era; but in light of what becomes palpable now as God's original intention: mercy practiced.

Many religions are themselves reform movements that both transmit and transform their religion of origin. Hindus see Buddhism as *nāstika* (Sanskrit, "negative" or "atheist"), because it rejects the Vedas' cultic regulations. But Vedic ideas such as the circle of being, *saṃsāra* (Sanskrit, "wandering" or "world") survive in Buddhism. The Qur'an claims to be the "corrective confirmation" (Arabic, *taṣdīq*) of a Jewish and Christian "distortion" (Arabic, *taḥrīf*) of God's original revelation. The gospel of Jesus Christ understands itself, as we have seen, as the "fulfillment" (Greek, *plērōma*) of God's commandments and promises to Israel.

When a reform movement finds itself in mere opposition to the larger culture, hostility arises. It doesn't matter whether the reform aims to turn everything back to the past, or everything forward to the future. If a reform has no sense of tradition, it veers toward divisive reformation, thereby becoming an iconoclastic cultural revolution. Only where reform succeeds in shedding a positive light on its own starting point (the fruit of tradition), only where a reform succeeds in seeing its present culture's meaningfulness, can it become transformative rather than destructive.

Normative, and Puritan, Centering

In sixteenth-century Geneva, John Calvin (1509–64) ordered that the churches be locked during the working week. This was not because people only worshiped on Sunday, but because Calvin wanted to ensure that the they did not practice forms of worship running counter to his Reformation program. He worried, for example, lest they turn to images "just as to the ear of God."[16] Here, a fear seems to speak itself. Calvin's main work, the 1536 *Institutes of the Christian Religion* (*Institutio Christianae Religionis*), is a systematic catechism attempting to explain the Christian faith in all its ramifications. Religion established as *Institutio* prohibits popular religion, which must be transformed through enlightened religion, and converted into rational religion. Organized control of religion, however, tends to become religion as organized control. It is worthwhile to look at Calvin's programmatic title. *Institutio* actually means two things: rationalized information and public establishment. Such a rational religion wants to control the unregulated movements of lived tradition. In the longer term, however, regulation does not cleanse religion, but sterilizes it, making it unilinear and artificial. Such a legalistic construction loses its own energy. For Calvin, the criterion for allowing images was that they gave "instruction and encouragement."[17] In the ears of militant disciples, that came to mean that images must be destroyed. Although puritan reductionism may start as the attempt to intensify society's religious life, it often indirectly results in society's greater secularization.

Already in pre-Reformation Europe, one observes a specific type of religious reform, which proved a guiding pattern for the Reformation as well as Catholic reform circles. During the fifteenth century, what the Protestant church historian Berndt Hamm calls "normative centering" occurred in many places. Devotional piety, theological writings, even artwork, sought to concentrate faith's content and explicate it from that center. That core message should organize people's lives. A prime example is Jan van Eyck's Ghent Altarpiece (completed sometime prior to 1432). Its focal point is the blood of the Lamb of God. Sacrament, Church, life, the present moment—everything springs from it. Normative centerings provide an attractive clarity, but also contain dangers.

Such a brief formula runs the risk of becoming "puritan" when its followers aim to purge their environment of everything that is not corresponding exactly to that formula. Those other things are rejected as "pagan" or "disbelief." The relation of religion to culture becomes one of condemnation. The believer is required to reject everything in this world that is coming to life from other sources than faith. Dancing and carnivals, for example, were now prohibited. How is such a tendency to be designated? A term from the sociology of religion is useful here. It once had a very specific meaning but is now used beyond religious boundaries: *puritanism*. (Other examples of terms thus used include *gnosis*, *orthodoxy*, *reformation*, and *fundamentalism*.) Here the name, which was used for Calvinist Puritans in England and New England from the sixteenth century on, serves as a generic term. One can also label as "puritan" other movements wanting to purify themselves and the world in the name of a supposedly rediscovered "true faith," as opposed to a culture of unbelief.

An anticultural religion typically arises from a desire for clarity, since life can be confusing. Adherents of such a religion do not see themselves as the "light of the world." But the gospel can be a light whereby cultural expressions are "signs of the times."[18] This means recognizing one's surrounding culture as the place where God wants to start his kingdom, just as Jesus's public ministry was for those who saw him (Matt 16:13). Those who view their world in the light of the gospel can explore, scrutinize, and discern how far their world's movements are life giving or not, allowing themselves to be transformed by the gospel, in order to collaborate with it. Believers who take their faith as light of the world can perceive and develop other realities. By contrast, if people's conviction leads them to condemn their own culture, they face the puritan trap.

The dawn of a new historical era can cause confusion. It may even be perceived as a threat to one's roots, to an ideal that provided order

23

in one's life. Every reform will bear such traits and promise to bring people back to their original center. But where the choice of believing means a sharp rejection of all lying outside that ideal, what lurks behind is puritanism. For a religion, this is dangerous on six levels:

- Puritanism deprives a religion of its inner wealth.
- It can ghettoize people to the point where the positive aspects of their surrounding culture can neither purify nor enrich them.
- It quenches the positive tension between faith and reason. Thus rational claims of differing worldviews, of individuals, and even religions, are obscured.
- It creates a social atmosphere whereby religions appear as options or arbitrary decisions, largely irrelevant to others. Religion then becomes a private matter.
- Its focus on personal decision weakens one of religion's core values, the call to a responsibility that goes beyond any human judgment.
- It forces undecided people to leave their religion because it offers no variety in levels of identification, as cultures do, since belonging to a culture is not a choice.

Both the New Testament canon and the Hebrew scriptures challenge readers to study, to be intellectually flexible. They are stimulating, exciting, and at times disappointing, as well as contradictory, poetic, and inspiring. But they do not lead to an all-unifying formula. Scripture requires spiritual listening. It is not a catechism. When catechesis materializes into a manual for all of faith's and life's questions, the catechism becomes an ideological manifesto. In some circles, the Qur'an is seen as a handbook for unambiguity. Then, however, the book is being manipulated by fundamentalist propaganda, just as the Bible often is in analogous circles. A desire for clarity leads to normative centering. In desperate confusion, this can descend into militancy. But the image of an allegedly unambiguous Islam smacks of ignorance.

Challenge to Think: The Qur'an

The Qur'an is, in its own way, deliberately multilayered. It calls for new ways of understanding the world. It is full of "signs for those ready to think" (Sura 45:13). Thus, for example, it refers to God as both "the Manifest" and as "the Hidden" (*az-Ẓāhir*, *al-Bāṭin*, Sura 57:3). "Which of the two is correct?" one might ask. Sura 6 presents Muḥammad as being commissioned:

> Say: I am not telling you that I have the supplies which God has or that I know the invisible. Nor that I am an angel. I only follow what was inspired into me. Say: is the blind like the one who sees? Do you not think? (Sura 6:50)

This Sura expressly calls for critical thought. It is by no means a simple text, but challenges readers to engage in a new, different, and responsible way of thinking. The verse's argumentative structure needs to be seen in the context of the whole Sura. Muḥammad does not exercise judgement, so simply being his follower is no guarantee of salvation. The prophet is only a herald, a messenger of both joy and warning (Sura 6:48). He is not ominiscient. He simply faithfully delivers the message of God, the all-Seer, who knows what people do in secret. They will have to give an accounting to God in the future judgment. Listeners are called to reorient their lives immediately, to live responsibly, even if no one sees them.

Already in its Qur'anic beginnings, Islam wants to bring clarity to people. But if it is submitted today to people's desire for simplification, because they are unable to cope with modernity, the Qur'an loses its inherent dynamism. It is an explicit call to think. No wonder that an intra-Muslim intellectual debate emerged among Muḥammad's followers soon after the Qur'an's proclamation. Indeed, rather than being a stronghold of unambiguity, Islam has been called "the culture of ambiguity."[19]

Streaming Tradition

How can a religion free itself from the grip of both reductionism and instrumentalization? Like several past questions, this, too, contains a problem. It ascribes to religion its own dynamics. But isn't it rather religion's adherents who are at work? How can religion be an actor? What looks like a distracting counterquestion will actually help us solve the problem of instrumentalization. To restate our question, then, is it in fact people who are at work, when we ascribe deeds to religion itself?

The Anglican church historian Henry Chadwick (1920–2008) offers an apt answer.[20] Drawing from extensive research on ancient Christianity, Chadwick contends that members of the early Church knew that Christian truth cannot be derived from one single source. Rather, it thrives on the interaction between three sources of authority: Bible, bishop, and belief. True faith is not found in any single one of these three realities alone, but in their constant interrelation. They need to confirm and, when necessary, correct one another. Although *scripture* is considered sacred, it must first be selected, ordered, and recognized as such. *Ministry* judges on questions of the formation and interpretation of the canon but is itself subject to the judgment of the other two. *Faith intuition*, which is not a fixed entity per se, is present in practice. It is the believers' sense for what is Christ's full profession, and what runs counter to it. This relationship can be described as the continued tripartite interaction between textual-canonical authority, institutional-personal authority, and an intuitive-communitarian authority. How does this insight apply to the relation between religions and traditions?

The discovery of these three sources in Christianity poses, first, the question of whether something similar is found in other religions. Muslims may say that there are three material sources among the "roots" (Arabic, *uṣūl*) of jurisprudence: Qur'an, Hadith, and consensus. If consensus is taken to mean that the scholars have to agree and the Hadith is taken as a living tradition, Islam does know a threefold combination similar to Christianity's "Bible, bishop, belief" model: scripture, experts, faith community. Similarly, Buddhism subscribes to threefold "refuge" in the "three jewels": Buddha (the founder), Sangha (his community), and Dharma (his teaching).

These triple formulas imply that *the individual believer* has his or her role but is not decisive in any of the three areas (Bible, bishop, and belief). We previously asked whether a religion can liberate itself from the grip of instrumentalization. Do only people restrict or liberate religions, or do religions have a life of their own? Because the early Church recognized scripture and community intuition as doctrinal authorities, it also acknowledged that belief has a life of its own that cannot be fully controlled by the human person.

This historical insight makes clear the *role of tradition*. As a non-codified stream, it leads away from rationalization and instrumentalization. Where religion is subjected to someone's rationality, it is likely to become reduced to formalities, and thus has the potential to abolish itself.

As ideal types, the "organic vitality of tradition" versus "artificial rationalization" may be useful. Here are four examples.

> *Christine, twenty-one years old, says, "You know that I love being a Reformed Christian; but I admire Catholic liturgy: one can really plunge into it."*

That is a meaningful observation. Although she likes her own church, she feels that its services can be exhausting. She compares it to a more expressive liturgy, which one can experience almost half-consciously. One can be part of it without having completely understood it and discover something new in it each time. Perhaps one might ask, for instance, why the priest puts a particle of the consecrated host into the chalice before communion. Or, why does one put up a Christmas tree? It is enlightening to explore these questions, but not necessary for celebrating religion.

> *Albert von Le Coq (1860–1930) was a Prussian explorer of Central Asia. He reports that the Muslim Turks whom he regularly visited recited the first Sura of the Qur'an. The Sura, the Fātiḥa, was something like their holy of holies. When they told him they didn't know what the Arabic meant, he translated the text into Turkish for them. Horrified, they must have answered: "Başka yok mu—nothing else?!"*

In such a case, a literal translation may be disenchanting, thereby altering the text's beautiful sound, the mysterious strangeness, and its fervor. This is philological enlightenment. Theological enlightenment is such when it becomes new, when one is immersed in understanding, open to astonishing discoveries.

> *In Germany, some Catholics react against those Santa Clauses who arrive on the night of December 5, without wearing the miter. That "Coca Cola Santa Claus" is, they say, not the holy bishop, but simply something pagan.*

This may be historically correct, but anti-Santa actions are in danger of becoming puritanical. Even the miter that he wears was pagan first. It started life as an ancient Persian priest's headdress. One cannot purify everything. Accepting the stream of tradition should sometimes carry one and enable one to entrust oneself to it.

Some of those who have already acquired one or more for-eign languages experience a kind of claustrophobia when they try to learn Esperanto. Something seems to be wrong. Many abandon the project sooner or later.

Family customs and local habits, but also religious activities, follow patterns of tradition. Even quasi-religious—religioid[21]—activities specific to some group, such as sports rituals, display such patterns. It is typical of a stream of tradition that it is too large to be overseen, contained, or managed. It is often reassuring to know that it has not sprung from a single human brain. That however may precisely be the reason for the oppressive feeling that may befall you when learning Esperanto. A historically developed language transmits centuries of human attempts at expression. Learning it may feel like wandering through a fascinating castle holding ever new discoveries. By contrast, some people, when they learn Esperanto, sense that they have only reached the limited space of the inventor's (Dr. Ludwik Zamenhof's) skull.

Salafism

The elimination of tradition, and militant radicalization, play together in the religious sphere. This connection can be studied in the light of a current movement, which will allow for a further refinement of political religion's descriptive categories. Reform movements regu-larly work through recourse; that is, they want to interpret, criticize, and reorient the present by means of some model of order. That paradigm lies "before us" in a double sense. It dates from a previous time, and it is the model people should have before their eyes. Such a paradigm of order can be a text, read as instruction. Or it can be a group of people, presented as ideal and worthy of imitation.

One such reform movement is Salafism. It is a sort of politically instrumentalized Islam. Salafists claim they want to (and are able to) revive the Islam of the first Muslims. Hence their Arabic name: *salaf* refers to the "ancestors." If they are used as a paradigm of order, they can be described as *ṣāliḥ*, "righteous." This avant-garde of the early pious, the *salaf ṣāliḥ*, lived out "real" Islam, the Islam to which believers must return. Everything later than those ancestors amounts to apostasy—so runs the Salafist claim.

How do the Salafists try to reconstruct early Islam? One cannot find out through today's religious community. Rather, for those who appeal to the *salaf ṣāliḥ*, present-day Islam has for the most part become a victim of later distortions: of tradition or as it is called, "innovation" (Arabic, *bid'a*). It is through texts that one accesses original Islamic life. This includes the collections of Muḥammad's words and deeds, Hadith, as well as the Qur'an. Salafism is not one single, let alone centrally organized, movement. Salafism is, rather, an outlook.

The *Salafīya* throughout history. *The prehistory of Salafism can be represented through the experiences of Muslims from three different eras. They all belonged to the Ḥanbalīya, the smallest of the schools of legal interpretation. According to the Ḥanbalīs, valid legal decisions are based only on three sources: Qur'an, Hadith, and consensus. What they want to exclude thus is autonomous legal interpretation.*

Ibn Taymiyya (1263–1329) was the first to claim that true Islam is found only in the practice of the first three generations. Everything after these, he declares as illegitimate innovation, as bad tradition.

His teaching was reclaimed by Muḥammad ibn 'Abd al-Wahhāb (1703–92), who, from 1740 onward, called for a cleansing of Islam, again through a rejection of tradition. (It should be noted that this did not occur at Islam's intellectual centers, but on the educationally disadvantaged Arabian Peninsula.)

In 1909, Muḥibb ad-Dīn al-Ḥaṭīb, a journalist from Damascus (1886–1969), started selling and publishing books in Cairo, naming his shop Maktaba as-Salafīya: "The Forefathers' Bookstore." Here, talk of the salaf became programmatic. Over the years, al-Ḥaṭīb's political stance changed. He sympathized with the Wahhabis, the followers of Ibn 'Abd al-Wahhāb. Al-Ḥaṭīb admired them because they became more and more powerful in the emerging Saudi Arabia, shaking off the Ottoman rule. They in turn were interested in texts published by al-Ḥaṭīb. Therefore, he was able to open a store at Mecca. So, in his context is found an early connection of the terms Salafism *and* Wahhabism.

Salafism wants to simplify things. It therefore misses what the Muslims of earlier generations knew: the traditions were always read critically; that is to say, with a skeptical lens, to see whether or not what is being transmitted to us is reliable. They also saw that the Qur'an has begotten a whole family of Islamic sciences that do not treat the Qur'an as a manual. Rather, they saw it as a recitation that effects and expresses devotion to God, as opposed to providing operational instructions for today.

The Salafist attitude is not necessarily violent, but it is fundamentalist in the strict sense. For it hopes to heal present confusion by securing access to the original: that is, to the text and its first followers. Such a naïveté lacks historical sense; but it expresses how desperately people wrestle with contemporary problems. This desperation may lead people to claim that everything later than the pious beginnings has to be eliminated from Islam as a deviant "innovation" and may explain the easy transition to violence, even the violence directed toward fellow believers. It is, then, quite apt to see Salafism as a variety of puritan reductionism. What is true, and what is worth promoting, is only that which corresponds to pure religion. And that actually means "pure, as we define it today." Again, in the case of radical militancy, the reverse conclusion is that everything else is to be destroyed.

CULTURE AND RELIGION: RECONCILIATION REQUESTED

When examining modern religions, the cultural perspective is a helpful tool. It helps us perceive the problems of both the "culture-less" radicalizations and the "religioid" productions of culture. Religion and culture need one another. Otherwise, they become unilinear and unquestioned, developing into an ideology. What a culture and a religion have in common is that neither is fully in people's hands. Whoever tries to completely reshape a culture or religion destroys it; but they need each generation's creative participation. Human beings must both receive them *and* lead them on. How can this relationship be understood more precisely? That relation can be seen more clearly in the light of three models: compatibility, civil religion, and spirit.

Compatibility: Keeping Up with Modernity

Religion and culture can harmonize on different levels. One example is seen when a religion's representatives show that its basic texts are compatible with a current cultural value. Islam's first step toward an administrative structure is the *Constitution of Medina*, as the document was later (incorrectly) called. It may date from 622, shortly after Muḥammad's exodus to Medina with his followers. The ethno-religious situation was different there, for there was more diversity than in Mecca. In Medina, there were also Jewish tribes. The Medinans had invited Muḥammad to unify them. He soon stipulated a regulation concerning the rights of the various clans. The text is probably authentic, since it does not reflect later stages of linguistic or legal development. The so-called *Constitution* grants equal rights and participation to the Jewish people. It calls the entire (heterogenous) community, as opposed to one particular religious group, the *umma*. The document starts as follows:

> This is a writing [*kitāb*] of the Prophet Muḥammad, the Messenger of God. [It regulates the relationships] between the faithful and Muslims of Qurayš [Mecca] and Yaṯrib [Medina] and those who followed them, who joined them and struggled with them [*ǧāhadū*]. They are one community [*umma*] to the exclusion of [other] people.

Meccan emigrants, and all previous residents of Medina, including Jewish residents, are part of the *umma*. The text then lists each clan separately; but is the *umma* not a religious community? How can the Jewish people be part of it? In those early years, their way of recognizing Muḥammad was not yet fully formed. While they accepted him as a secular leader, they rejected him as the herald of true religion. They sensed that his desire to reconstruct all the "religions of the Book" was really intended to promote a new religion contradicting Jewish identity. This is why the majority of them would not accept his religious proclamation. It is also why Muslims later no longer regarded them as belonging to the *umma*.

According to the *Constitution of Medina*, however, the Jewish people still belong to the *umma*. But not "the (other) people": meaning all not recognizing Muḥammad as their leader—or rather those who do not recognize him *yet*. In the following years, it became clear that those other people might become *umma* members. But in those later years it became also clear that those who do not join the faith, such as Jews and Christians, are outside the *umma*. This is the second phase in interpreting the persistence of nonadherents in the newly established theocracy. All the nonmembers of the *umma* are considered as "not-yet-members." To this day, Muslims hardly view Islam as one religious option among others, but as the one truly human form of life, the one truly divine form of religion, so that in the long run, all will recognize this.

This is reflected also in the ambiguity of the word *muslim*. On the one hand, it can be taken to mean a "member of the religious community based on the Qur'an." On the other hand, it literally means "devout." That is why according to the Qur'an, already Abraham was a *muslim* (Sura 3:67). This, of course, leads to another question: After the proclamation of the Qur'an, does every truly devout person have to become a member of Islam? Are all others consequently unbelievers? What about their legal situation under Muslim reign?

Recently there have been significant developments on these issues. On January 27, 2016, some 250 Muslim leaders came together to sign the Marrakesh Declaration (in Arabic, *I'lān Marrākaš*). The immediate occasion was to celebrate the *Constitution of Medina*'s fourteen-hundredth anniversary (using the Islamic lunar calendar). The importance of the constitution, as the signatories perceived it, was that it "guaranteed the religious liberty of all, regardless of faith."

Religious freedom is a meaningful term only when different religions are understood to be fundamentally, and permanently, different. That was probably not the case during Muḥammad's early months in Medina. The expectation then was that the Jewish people would soon accept Muḥammad's proclamations as what already Moses and David had in mind. Still, the constitution does grant them equal rights. So, it is historically understandable, it is legally and theologically pertinent for the leaders at Marrakesh to "call upon Muslim scholars to develop a jurisprudence of the concept of 'citizenship' which is inclusive of diverse groups. Such jurisprudence shall be rooted in Islamic tradition and principles and mindful of global changes." In doing so, they subscribe to a term used in the French Constitution of 1791, *citoyenneté* ("citizenship"), its Arabic counterpart being *muwāṭana*. The French Constitution bestowed equal rights on all citizens and expressly guaranteed to every man (*homme*) four liberties: movement, expression (which included religious freedom), assembly, and petition.

How should the Marrakesh Declaration's argument for conceptual compatibility be assessed? Since many signatories were internationally known, and since they argued from a historical basis, the statement has leverage. This is true both for the global unification of Muslims, and also for how religious diversity will be handled in the future. This is not, however, the final word on the subject. Citizenship alone is not the ultimate aim of human life. Religions must use their prophetic voices. How do religions help form critically constructive citizens by shaping consciences? How can citizenship tend to new forms of exclusion? Here is an example. Turks say that in the early decades after their cultural revolution of the 1920s one newspaper's unwittingly comic headline read, *Halk plajlara akın etti, vatandaş denize giremedi*: "Beaches stormed by people: Citizens unable to sea bathe." By this line of thought, those designated as "citizens" formed a small élite, who find the rest of the population as disturbing as a seaweed plague. A new caste system could easily sneak in, one discriminating between the secular-minded "citizen" and the common people who are still shaped by dated things like religion. If a religion seeks enlightenment, it may lose both its creativity and its credibility. The appropriate interaction between modern challenges and religious tradition must not consist of the latter simply approving the new. For a religion to be a true light of the world, it must shed a critical, creative light on today's transformative processes.

Civil Religion: Nation under God

Frankfurt am Main. *Navid Kermani's (1967–) parents are Iranian. Born in Germany, he is an Islamic scholar and writer. He considers himself Muslim, but not an official representative of Islam. When he was awarded the German Book Trade's Peace Prize in 2015, he gave a memorable speech at Frankfurt's Paulskirche, a former church that symbolizes the birth of democracy in Germany. At the end of his speech, he took a risk by inviting his audience to perform an extraordinary gesture. "But really," he said, "it is not that unusual either; after all, we are in a church." Kermani called* *to refrain from applauding, but instead to rise and pray. "And if you are not religious," he suggested, they could stand for a moment with the persecuted Christians, of whom he had spoken, and wish them well. After all, he insisted, "what are prayers other than wishes addressed to God?" Here, in a nation whose largest religion is Christianity, a Muslim opened the door to a postdenominational civil religion: an invitation to live out one's faith, without taking any space from nonbelievers.*

In addition to attempting historical compatibility between key concepts, there is a second way religion and culture can go together. It is summarized under the label of "civil religion." In his 1961 inaugural speech, President John F. Kennedy (1917–63) declared, "The rights of man come not from the generosity of the state, but from the hand of God." Kennedy's speech ended with this exhortation: "Let us go forth to lead the land we love, asking His blessing and His help, but knowing that here on earth God's work must truly be our own."

Some Europeans consider such wording trite or pithy, but in the United States it is standard. Americans appreciate public gestures of faith as supporting a pluralistic polity, a "civil religion." Its signals, or what sociologist of religion Émile Durkheim calls "symbolizations," may include a linguistic formula (e.g., the Constitution's reference to God); objects such as crosses in public places; the weekly and annual rhythm of Sundays and holidays; even a special liturgy in the wake of a national disaster.

Do these symbolizations cancel the separation between Church and state? In the United States, the question was debated in detail and clarified in law. In 2010, the Supreme Court ruled that phrases like *One nation under God* or *In God we trust* do not favor any particular religious profession. They are, rather, "ceremonial deism." Thus, civil religion does not contradict the First Amendment, which states, "Congress shall make no law respecting an establishment of religion, or prohibiting the free exercise thereof." Is civil religion, then, no religion, a mere ritual? Perhaps not. While *the state* may consider a particular phrase or expression as purely ritualistic, not favoring any specific religion, still, a public rite can express *the people's* support of religion.

Civil religion is then clearly distinguishable from both *state* religion and *church* religion. "Church religion" can mean the faith life communicated and defended by institutional religious communities.

State religion: *The political authority finances and protects one particular form of faith.*

Church religion: *Institutionalized religious communities communicate and defend their faith life.*

Civil religion: *The population appreciates public faith gestures as supportive of a pluralistic polity.*

In this, the difference between the United States and Europe is obvious. One might ask why Europe's cultural and legal atmosphere are so fundamentally different from the American civil religion. For instance, while crucifixes do hang in German and Italian courtrooms, official state speeches do not invoke God's blessings on Germany or Italy. Why not? History provides an answer.

"Free church" refugees are part of America's founding narrative, but civil religion, as imprinted on its currency, is largely a consequence of the Cold War. A "believing" nation wanted to position itself against "materialistic Communism." In Europe, on the other hand, during the age of nation building, churches were already well-established institutions. They were therefore in a position vis-à-vis the new nations. Such a juxtaposition has consequences to this day. The institutional Church can assert claims against the state in the name of the faith and the faithful. However, because its public profile is so visible, religion might not have as strong a grip on the people. Furthermore, anti-Church ideologies emerged, presenting themselves as religious, or as political scientist Eric Voegelin called them, as "political religions."

In contrast, civil religion is more of an atmosphere in the population manifesting itself in political rites, especially those that build community. Though the constitutional situation grants religious liberty, many expect such displays from their government.

It was in this sense that sociologist of religion Robert N. Bellah (1928–2013) introduced his use of the term *civil religion* in 1961 during a lecture tour in Japan. Bellah was addressing a question of great importance for his Japanese hosts, the question of whether a society with no state religion can retain a reliable ethos. Bellah felt that this had happened in America; indeed, he believed it might serve as a model for other countries. A faith-based culture considers the actions of its politicians within the context of transcendence. Americans, he insisted, live with ideals of peace, justice, and truth. That ideal, not worldly success, was for Bellah the standard by which American voters judged their leaders. Of course, those leaders would always fall short of the ideal. Hence a tension arose between definitive truth and societal reality, a salutary tension that became the guarantee of morality within the political system. Bellah later revealed what he had really intended by his proposing these concepts to East Asia; he wanted "to try to explain to the Japanese what this relation of religion and politics is all about. It was a direct response to the John F. Kennedy inaugural."[22]

When European politicians call for civil religion, they typically do so with a vague reference to Judeo-Christian values, a slogan, camouflaged as religious, that gives new meaning to the concept of culture. It presents society as having lost its fundamental consensus and its social imaginary, doomed to disintegrate—a condition some depict as a horrifying "multiculturalism." Islam is made the source of all problems and what the apostles of "values" offer as remedy is a "dominant Christian culture." This is questionable both in terms of content and form. For one thing, a specific religion cannot be identified with a particular culture. The Christian sense of solidarity challenges patriotic and meritocratic views; but these are represented as part of the West's dominant culture. The call for a Christian dominant culture is also formally misguided if it is up to politics to take care of it. Here, the request becomes totalitarian. While Christianity does seek to shape society and life, even at the legislative level, it seeks to do so by persuading people, not through state power. One cannot legislate or sanction a dominant culture, only let it grow. Christian world shaping is what the proclamation of God's kingdom is all about. It can seize people's hearts, form people's consciences, change people's thinking, and thus transform social structures. But it is a change in which people are always aware of the provisional and imperfect character of their own constructions. They always need improvement. We cannot *produce* God's kingdom.

Spirit: God as Community

At the basis of the civil religion model, with its distance from religious institutions, from the "Church," lies another model of reconciliation between culture and religion: the paradigm of the "spirit."

"Spirit" can be understood as that creative dynamic that urges us toward self-transcendence. That is biblical tradition, which clearly inspired Georg Wilhelm Friedrich Hegel (1770–1831). "Spirit" is the basic dynamic of Hegel's thinking. How does he apply his fundamental intuition to the relationship between faith and society?

In 1827, Hegel lectured in Berlin for the last time on the philosophy of religion. He connects, as he so often does, his own development of a concept with the development of world history. Where human beings have accepted God both as general concept and as particularity (as a proper name), Hegel sees the spirit at work. Now the religious community has been formed, Hegel writes, "Thus the community itself is the existing spirit, the spirit in its existence, God existing as a community."[23]

Things do not end, however, at the stage wherein God exists as community. The community's dynamic is the spirit. It therefore always goes beyond itself. Spiritual reality and secular reality must be reconciled. For Hegel, the "Kingdom of God, the Church, has, thus, a relationship to the secular."[24] Because this relationship can be realized in different ways, Hegel sees three phases of Christian presence in the world: the monks' church, the church of power, and morality. Just as he employs the terms *spirit* or *community*, so Hegel's usage of *morality* (*Sittlichkeit*) is deliberately ambiguous. It can refer to the individual's conscious behavior, to the customs, or to cultural atmosphere. Morality consists for Hegel of a society in which the principle of freedom has penetrated the secular sphere. In this phase, people's typical relational forms are familiar, self-employed, and legal. Those forms of life, however, are no arbitrary human inventions. Rather, Hegel sees them as "divine institutions." Now he has his criteria at hand. Hegel draws a contrast between institutions that really come from God, and institutions that try to legitimate themselves by appealing to God but are in fact mere human constructions. For Hegel, life in the religious orders and theocracy are cases of only pseudodivine structures. Truly divine institutions, in contrast, are family, work, and rule of law. In those three forms of life, he sees a different atmosphere at work, not submission as in religious life or a theocracy. With those three divine institutions: family life, autonomous work, and a just legal system, people identify themselves by "an obedience in freedom."[25]

Spirit and Church: A New Testament Dynamic. Hegel's philosophy of spirit is not his private fabrication of concepts. He is rather in vital contact with biblical testimony and the Church's doctrinal development. (After all, he studied theology five years for his licentiate in Tübingen.) How far is Hegel's understanding of the spirit related to the spirit, as understood in the Christian tradition? In seven biblical spotlights, one might reconstruct how a reading of scripture may lead to Hegel's philosophy of the spirit.

1. In the Hebrew Bible, it is God's breath, the wind (*rûăḥ*), that creates life (Ps 104:30), a life of self-transcendence (Judg 14:6). Greek-speaking Jews translated *rûăḥ* as *pneuma*. By that, they were using a fundamental element of the Stoic worldview: the cosmos gets its dynamism and unity from the pneuma that pervades it. The pneuma keeps the universe in its all-ordering, all-defining tension.

2. This fits well with the biblical view that history is under God's guidance. God's wisdom lives in all creatures. God's spirit is the force that leads people to act freely and transcend themselves without compulsion. What is happening through their actions is God's history. Therefore, neither the people of the old covenant nor of the Church are a "contrast society," in the sense that there some people become a testimony to God through their community relationships only. Rather, being the elect for now, they serve the others, who will also belong (Isa 2:2). For being inflamed by the spirit (Rom 12:11) means intending good for all people (Rom 12:17; I Thess 3:12; 5:15); and already the prophets promise a future in which God's people will receive the spirit and will therefore follow God's laws (Ezek 36:27): a new form of covenant with God, in which the Torah is written on the heart of the people (Jer 31:33), indeed, all peoples will gather as the holy congregation in Jerusalem rather than obeying their own evil hearts (Jer 3:17).

3. It is then also the spirit who will glorify Christ (John 16:14). Indeed, the spirit will worship Jesus in such a way that he is glorified in the community (17:10), because the spirit can seize and fulfill human

beings (Num 11:29; Acts 2:4). Then no longer they but the spirit will be speaking (Mark 10:20).

4. "Spirit" is not only divine power, but also human power (Ps 51:17; I Thess 5:23), and not only individually: "spirit" is also a group's motion (Isa 19:3).

5. One of the New Testament lines of describing the Church already points at the dynamics of going forth: the people that always transcends its own borders (2 Cor 4:15; Acts 15:14, 21). Likewise, the biblical word for "church," *ekklēsia*, does not indicate some secret meeting of the in-group, a conventicle: it rather refers to the public community, the political assembly. The eschatological Jerusalem will, according to Revelation 21:22, have no more demarcated temple, since God himself will be the temple. That is relevant for the relation of the Church as definable entity toward the world. The Johannine Jesus indeed announces the new time to have already begun, in which worship is no longer to happen in a particular place but "in spirit and truth" (John 4:23).

6. God's spirit creates "in wisdom." Likewise what happens now in creation happens "in wisdom" (Ps 104:24, 30; Jer 10:12; Job 33:4). And wisdom is God's way of acting not only in creation, but also in his guidance of history (Wis 10:18) and salvation through the cross (I Cor 2:7).

7. Therefore, the Greek church authors—first, Origen (184–253)—can identify the cosmic and personal "reason, mind" (*nous*) with the biblical "spirit" (*pneuma*).

When Hegel sees Christianity as free obedience to God within the hearts of all, he can, then, legitimately appeal to early Christian testimonies.

What Hegel is describing with his third presence, the presence of the spirit (free obedience), is that in his German Protestant environment, Christian faith has, or at least should now become the decisive worldview. Church as a visible, distinguishable community, then, has become society: spirit in the world. When Hegel foresees that the Church visible within society will become obsolete, he in fact expresses the hope that all people will become "evangelic"—that is, guided by their consciences, which will be shaped by the gospel.

At this moment, the fundamental twin questions of political theology can be answered. First, can the Sermon on the Mount guide governments? Second, should the state be just or merciful?

Let us look at the second question first: Is the ideal a just state or a merciful one? The two guiding values can be defined as follows: justice is the comprehensibly appropriate response to *the actual situation*; mercy is the orientation toward *the possible future*. The state must guarantee a reliable legal framework in which citizens are free to act mercifully. The more a society is convinced that mercy is true justice, the more the state itself can act mercifully. Thus we begin to discuss the other question, the political practicality of the Sermon on the Mount. It proclaims the outbreak of a greater justice, namely of mercy (Matt 5:20).

The more a *society* is convinced that mercy should shape the world, right down to basic structures, the more the *state* can act mercifully. This becomes clearer when we remind ourselves of the social imaginary. Political orders live on shared convictions. Where mercy has become such a state-founding dynamic, the state is also obliged to act with trust, for the benefit of the doubt, both internally and externally. Therefore, one can very well "do" politics in the spirit of the Sermon on the Mount; but only if there is a corresponding conviction in the population, the spirit of mercy. In this case, the Sermon is no longer a catalog of demands on a society that actually wants to shape its world differently. Rather, it is sensed, understood, and effective mercy. It is an internalized form of life rather than a heteronomous norm of life.

Realistically, however, let us acknowledge that the spirit is unlikely to be realized in this way, at least for the foreseeable future. A more realistic ideal (to put it paradoxically) can still employ the concept of spirit as social atmosphere. Due to human limitations, however, there will be hardly any agreement on contents. What is possible, is to agree to disagree, an accordance on the form of dispute, the willingness to understand each other, a culture of dialogue. In it, the various human interests, all of which need improvement, must purify and enrich each other. Martin Luther had called for a helpful distinction in society's debates; while the people quarrel over questions of faith, the state has no decision-making power there. Physical force, however, is exclusively in the hands of the state. "Let the intellects fight away themselves, but keep the fists still," wrote Luther to his prince. It is up to the sovereign to intervene in the case of violence.[26] This principle is valid still today. Different religious beliefs and worldviews will always be in conflict. It is up to the state, which itself does not opt for any particular party, to secure the framework whereby the culture of debate remains nonviolent.

From World to Spirit: Looking Back and Looking Forward

It is time for an interim evaluation. We examined the relationship of religions to the world. We asked how they want to shape the world and what social form best suits them. To understand religion as something like culture has proved helpful. For a religion is a world of its own, ever further explorable and already alive before any exploration. It must not be artificially remodeled, and above all it must not become cultureless. Then religion would lose its critical role. Such a religion risks becoming meaningless, if not violent. In answer to the question of whether religion should be reconciled with culture, we presented three models of reconciliation: conceptual compatibility, civil religion, and societal spirit. These are three paradigms of religions facing modern challenges such as the universality of human rights, faith diversity, and free subjectivity. However, all three models share a weakness when religion is no longer a critical force. Where religion endorses modern concepts (compatibility), without offering its own specific ideas; where religious consciousness is treated as general consensus (civil religion); where religion becomes general consensus (Hegel's "spirit"), the result is a religion boringly cultivated. Such a civilized religion despises prophets as troublemakers.

By contrast, the Bible looks critically on the world as it is. Indeed, it does not see it as the beautiful cosmos of an abstract contemplation. In Israel's experience, the world is a course of events, and a disappointing one, for that matter. The present order does not last, does not keep what it seems to promise. The world of faith lives in contrast with the cosmos as it is. In the light of faith, the world becomes visibile as mere provisional presence before the desired fulfillment comes.

Our first proposal had been to extend Troeltsch's religious social forms (church, sect, mysticism) to include "culture." Slowly, however, the proposal's danger now becomes apparent. If religion is lived as culture, its novelty does not come to the fore. If a religion convinces you that your experience is an unprecedented change of perspective, then you enter into a new world. Is religion then not refounding your identity? Only when we have taken up this objection can we return to the question of religion's social form.

IDENTITY

Previewing the Second Chapter

The counterpart to a "cultural" understanding of religion is a kind of exodus to a promised land where religion heralds a new life, a new self, and a new identity. Within this context, processes of religious radicalization are to be studied, particularly their contributing factors. What do, again, the religions have to tell us about that? Just like the word *culture*, the term *identity* is not used in scripture. With the decisive dynamics our religious traditions propose, we can clarify the issue of identity. Instead of talking about identity as something static, or possessive, our scriptures work with "conversion" and "vocation." Conversion, understood correctly, is not a turning away from the past, but the readiness to let everything, including one's own past, be placed within the context of vocation.

But conversion and vocation would be fundamentally misunderstood if they were seen as something purely individual. At the end of the chapter we will see that the specific identity mediation of faith takes place in communal worship. This also offers an opportunity to test the concept that the Church is the sacrament of unity for all.

An examination of the foundational messages will show how the Hebrew Bible communicates a life in presence of history; Jesus communicates life in the kingdom of God; and the Qur'an, life in a community that cares for others. In different ways, then, we see religion as the foundation of a new identity.

2

Religion as Foundation of a New Identity

How could a human being be God, and then become humiliated, and have a humiliating death? I was always very confused, and never prayed to Jesus. When I did pray, I would pray to God. When I was young, I didn't really pay much attention to these thoughts. I did think about it all here and there, but I didn't know how to delve deeper, and explore these thoughts, and I didn't have confidence that I was on the true religion. Then at school, they introduced things like evolution and the big bang theory, and this just caused even more confusion. At the end, I was left not knowing what to believe in, but I always had faith in the Creator, and that He should be worshiped alone.[1]

Here a Finnish woman describes how she found peace. Her testimony is probably authentic. Although it does bespeak pity, it is propaganda for one of humanity's most pitiless inhumanities. It encourages others to join the violent extremism of the group calling itself the "Islamic State" (ISIS or ISIL). Here a convert presents her story in the militia's propaganda magazine *Dabiq*, in the section "For Women." The rubric's name already sounds both paternalistic and patriarchal. Hard men, it seems, must be moved by the magazine's bloody photos, women by warm words. The author expresses an urgent need to simplify reality; the main motive for her religious conversion was what is called "complexity reduction." Looking back on her early religious journey, she found her environment and her Christian faith confusing. That is easy to understand. The world is always different from what we would wish it to be. Adolescents sense the contrast between ideal and reality with particularly pain. On top of that, at first sight, the Christian faith appears illogical. From the start, its proclamations employ a whole series of paradoxes. They want to challenge people to rethink life. That is why early Christianity expresses itself in provocative phrases. These include Paul's "Christ crucified" (1 Cor 1:23, i.e., the world-changing king dying a slave's death), the centurion's "Truly this man was God's Son!" (Mark 15:39, i.e., transcendent divinity with immanent relatives), and Thomas's address to the risen Christ, "My Lord and my God" (John 20:28, i.e., the names of Israel's YHWH applied to Jesus). Is then, the Qur'an the source of complexity reduction? We have already seen that it cannot serve as an escape from intellectual challenges, as a primer in simplicity. It is rather an explicit challenge to think.

Identity through Conversion

What happens when people who are searching for identity say they have gained clarity on this topic? Furthermore, what happens when people, in their search, become radical and militant? Can our religions' sacred texts help us here?

THESIS

For both Bible and Qur'an, identity is God's call into his community.

THE PROBLEM OF IDENTITY

A new form of life is attractive if it makes you feel that your life previously wasn't real life. An insecure person is promised solid ground at last. The true basis of your true life, your "foundation," can conveniently be reduced to a few principles. Such a secure foundation becomes fundamentalism when it blinds one to the challenges of history. This exclusion is reached through means of three protective mechanisms.

Inerrancy. Between 1910 and 1915, a series of ninety popular theological articles appeared under the title the *Fundamentals*. They soon became a basis of argumentation for many Evangelical Christians. Those subscribing to the articles became known as "the Fundamentalists." One of the "fundamentals" proposed was the Bible was "inerrant," that is, error free, and that biblical narratives simply report facts. One of the authors, the Scottish theologian James Orr (1844–1913), treated testimonies regarding Jesus's resurrection and his miracles on the same level. A primary intent of the whole series was to disprove the historical-biblical criticism coming from Germany. No doubt some of those "critical" productions do deserve criticism. Historical critics, for example, could argue that the inscription on Jesus's cross is not historical, because different Gospels phrase it differently. This is pedantic overcriticism. Rather, those slight deviations, such as Mark's "the King of the Jews," Luke's "This is the King of the Jews," and John's "Jesus the Nazarene, the King of the Jews," are evidence rather in favor of historicity. However, it is too easy to explain the virgin birth, as well as Jesus's miracles, to be simply as factual and fundamental for the Christian faith as his resurrection. By a wholesale rejection of historical criticism one also dismisses historians' enlightening contributions. The various biblical testimonies have different contexts of origin, and different expressive tools. In order to be faithful to the original message, we have to verbalize in new terminology the facts to which the New Testament sources are witnessing. If the Bible is "inspired without error," this means, for a fundamentalist, that each passage is absolutely reliable. Thus biblical research from the perspective of the literary and historical sciences is inappropriate, relativizing, and subjectivist. The fear behind this is obvious: the smallest opening will cause the dam to break into unbelief.

Integrity. Second, fundamentalists claim that the original texts contain the answers to all possible questions. The reader need not, and should not, use different sources of knowledge for different types of questions. A collection of writings such as the Old Testament or the Qur'an, however, cannot be consulted when wondering on the origin of species. It is up to researchers on evolution to inform us on this. Conversely, questions regarding the purpose and meaning of human life get answers in the scriptures that can lead readers far beyond paleontology.

Immediatism. A third fundamentalist method of securing faith against the challenge of history is the claim that today's reader can have direct access to the world the text comes from. This can go as far as the call to live today exactly the way first-generation believers lived. What lies between the world of origin and us is, consequently, a time of deviation and decadence, which we can, indeed must, skip.

How to deal positively with such issues? The first step is a clear diagnosis of the situation.

Identity Mania

An attitude of openness in truth and in love must characterize the dialogue with the followers of non-Christian religions, in spite of various obstacles and difficulties, especially forms of fundamentalism on both sides. (*Una actitud de apertura en la verdad y en el amor debe caracterizar el diálogo con los creyentes de las religiones no cristianas, a pesar de los varios obstáculos y dificultades, particularmente los funda-mentalismos de ambas partes.*) (*Evangelii Gaudium* 250)

Pope Francis wisely used "fundamentalisms" in the plural and underlined that it is not enough to point to the others: "the Evangelicals" or the "Islamists." There is a fundamentalist tendency on the Catholic side as well. People resort to fundamentalist pillars above all when they feel, and propagate, that "our identity is endangered." Here, a respect-fully acknowledging self-distinction is not taking place, but rather a devaluation and exclusion of the other. In lack of other sources we start delineating what we do not want to be in order to define "myself" and "ourselves." What is at play here, then, is an "identity-mania."[2] What can theology contribute to the identity question? Where do Christians and Muslims find their secure foundation? For clarity's sake, let us study a particular type of identity creation.

In all Western countries, hundreds of people are currently iden-tifying, and radicalizing themselves, as violent Islamists.[3] Let us look more closely at this vocabulary. "Radicalization" is a personality devel-opment in which people close themselves off from challenges they do not want to face. Those who radicalize themselves are willing to sacri-fice everything standing in the way of their ideal. "Islamism" originally refers to the program whereby Islam determines culture and politics. Public debates now frequently use "Islamism" in its militant version, for those who, in the name of Islam, reject democratically based dia-logue and processes of reconciliation.

48

Can such radicalization be explained? Explanation is not the same as justification; nor is it a prediction. One cannot conclude that a person who experiences a certain number of issues will inevitably become violent. Nevertheless, it makes sense to find a language for the various sociopolitical and psycho-biographical constellations wherein radicalization happens. Theology will then have to help us face the problem. Now, though, a list of factors that contribute to an Islamist radicalization.

Inferiority complex. It may sound arrogant for a non-Muslim to begin with that term, but it may also help to understand the situation. Many Muslims today look upon the world with an inferiority complex. Since 1798, when Napoleon invaded Egypt, Muslims have asked themselves, "How could we, the last-proclaimed monotheistic world religion, which for centuries seemed to win the Islamic–Christian competition, fall behind? The West [typically perceived as the 'Christian' West] has overtaken us. We are lagging behind technically, scientifically, and economically." Such feelings of backwardness easily prepare the ground for quick diagnoses and magic formulas. One argument proposed is that this inferiority results from Islam being "contaminated." A return to true Islam is the only remedy, back to Qur'anic Islam.

The real reasons for this backlog date back centuries. A decisive year is 1485, when Sultan Bayezid II prohibited the introduction of printing presses into the Ottoman Empire.[4] This prohibition significantly delayed the emergence a self-examining Muslim middle class.

But for Muslims today, another year feels more painful: 1924. Shortly after the foundation of modern Turkey in Ankara, Mustafa Kemal ("Atatürk") abolished the caliphate. Since then, Islam has had no worldwide representative. Understandably, Ottoman nostalgia now flourishes just as much as promises to restore the caliphate, a kind of Islamic papacy, to give to Islamic unity a worldwide visibility.

Isolation. Young people sometimes simply feel alone in their environment. Those who sense they belong to a minority, or lack success, will easily see themselves as facing a hostile world. The "other" is then perceived as uniformly condescending, exclusive, and living without values. Other experiences can also lead people to feel they were left alone—say, for example, a lack of affection and intimacy at home. The prospect of at last finding a "true family, real brothers and good sisters" is tempting.

Integration. Problems of integration play a role in many stories of radicalization, in two senses. On the one hand, Muslim migrants may despise their parents' or grandparents' achieved integration into a new society and perceive it as a sort of submissive assimilation. A Westernized Islam is then seen as a betrayal of God's religion. On the other hand, the decision to participate in a militant movement now seems to guarantee what was previously lacking: acknowledgment, admiration, and a sense of belonging to a group providing both pride and order.

Insignificance. An ISIS rallying cry may help explain a young person's feelings when facing the possibility of radicalization. The group's declaration states, "Live for nothing, die for something." That is to say, if you feel your life is devoid of orientation and meaning, now you can finally provide it with a desired purpose. This is achieved by switching "from zero to hero," by the prospect of dying a glorious death.

Integralism. One may feel incapable of confronting the challenges that a pluralistic world proposes, including its sciences, cultures, and concepts of meaning. Religion must have all the answers ready: from the origin of the world to the organization of this day. In the case of Islamic radicalization, "Islam" itself is the supposed all-inclusive solution, the sure answer to any problem perceived (or invented). The advertising material for movements such as the so-called Islamic State is professionally produced, but is mere propaganda, lacking differentiated analyses of historical constellations and current geopolitics. The "bad guys" are one thing: bad. And the solution to all problems is above all else simple.

Injustices. Islamist propaganda is often blatantly anti-Semitic. "Anti-Semitism" refers to the racist hatred directed against the Jewish people. It may be true that the actions of individual Israeli soldiers, as well as democratically elected representatives of the State of Israel, deserve criticism. The Western world rightly recognizes Israel's right to exist; but injustice committed in the name of Israel should not be overlooked or explained away. Muslims who identify with the Palestinian side of the struggle often perceive such restraint as a sign of the Christian-Jewish Occident's corrupt double standards. To contribute to the elimination of Islamically motivated violence, we must also see present injustices, address them, and act accordingly. Many radical Islamic movements see themselves as the only legitimate voice for denouncing an inhumanity that is otherwise politely concealed. This also applies to organizations such as Boko Haram, as regards the history of colonial repression in certain African regions.

Islam itself. Several Qur'anic formulations and several events in Muḥammad's life can be used to justify violence in the name of God, "for God's sake," as the saying goes.[5] Obviously, this is not to say that Muslims are *obliged* to employ violence, nor is it to say that religious violence would not exist without Islam. Religiously motivated violence is not an Islamic problem alone. However, part of the solution is a critical contextualization of one's own religion's foundation: of its early history and its foundational texts.

Infighting. Even though propaganda can create the impression of a uniform Islam, one of the main reasons for the emergence of groups like the "Islamic State" is Islam's inner fragmentation. It dates from the parting of the ways of the early community into Shiites and those later called Sunnis. Shiite Iran is a local player of growing importance, soon to be a global player. Against it, the entire Sunni world is now waging a proxy war in places like Syria and Iraq. The underlying question has always been, Who is the legitimate successor to Muḥammad?

Ignorance. The less people know about their own history, the easier they can be seduced into ideology. But history does not provide instant security; it can lead to a salutary uncertainty. It is crucial for believers to know their religion's history of internal variety, especially compared to contemporary appeals for previous uniformity. It is instructive to see how serenely Islam dealt with other religions, especially at times when it was self-confident and successful. Conversely, one should remember that in eras when Islamic states flourished, a diversity of opinion was also thriving therein.[6] Various Islamic doctrines were in conflict with each other: in a conflict of arguments, producing sharp minds, not in armed conflict producing death.

Idealization. The image of the forefathers (*as-salaf*) utilized by the Salafists is only one example of the way most radical ideologies work. They argue that ideal conditions can be established. Indeed, a fundamentalist, ahistorical propaganda typically claims that the ideal condition once actually existed. "Everything was better in the old days," the saying goes.

Identity traps. To be a believer while facing the conditions of modernity is a considerable challenge. The sheer diversity of opportunities offered is confusing. The Finnish woman on the path to radicalization seems to have experienced precisely that. Her Christian belief, she remembers, was no longer a matter of course, and if it does not go without saying any more, it loses its protective warmth. "Ambiguity tolerance" is needed, the ability to live with ambivalence and continue without panic after all proof of logical certainty is lost. Fundamentalisms, by contrast, are aptly called "modern anti-modernisms":[7] they work through complexity reduction, which is appealing when one is confused. A quick solution, novel and actionist, promises to convey self-confidence through a sense of global belonging. Such a religion is "identitarian" in nervously defending its identity markers under the claim that they provide clarity. Identitarian religion is, then, the opposite of a tradition whose adherents know that it is mysterious, imperfect, and in need of a patient, growing, generous faithfulness.

Ingénieurs (engineers). Do violent movements find their recruits among the undereducated? That is possible; but strikingly often, radicalized Islamists are young male engineers. How to explain that? For a traditional family, having an engineer son is a remarkable gain of prestige. This places enormous expectation on the man. Will he have the success, and achieve the reputation his family is (in his view) hoping to gain? Also, speaking in "ideal types," the engineer's approach would be to find direct solutions for direct problems. To reduce life to binary automatisms of problem and solution is what Pope Francis calls "the technocratic paradigm" of our times.[8] When, however, life's challenges include questions of meaning, personality development, broken history (in one's own life or religion), a different attitude is required. No engineering solution will solve the problem here. No, it takes patience, a sense of humor, intuition: the makings of wisdom.

Impatience. The inability to endure uncertainties can lead one toward actionism. Are religious converts safe from this? Radicalizing Muslims, for example, have their prayers to teach them patience, don't they? It is true that radicalizing Islamists also perform their duties of worship. Increasingly militant Muslims are typically meticulous about their ritual prayers; but those are fast rites. What is lacking in such lives is the experience of long, and perhaps even boring, liturgies. In them one might experience that positive developments are often protracted processes. Within the course of history, "God's rhythm" takes time.

Institutional distrust. People anxious for security tend to see the representatives of their own tradition as cowardly hirelings, as lazy, well-paid bureaucrats, who no longer dare to speak God's harsh truth. A cynical outlook regarding one's own religious establishment is called "institutional distrust." For many youngsters attracted to radicalism, their official imam no longer sounds the divine decree. Consequently, they do not listen to him, but develop their own Islam in conscious dismissal of those whom they consider to be bourgeois weaklings.

Intuitions lost. With the rejection of inherited intuitions and traditional customs, received wisdom that has appealed for humane moderation seems irrelevant when compared to propaganda's virile enthusiasm. An adolescent caught up in his hormonal heroism may feel threatened by what used to carry him because it now seems to slow him down. Proverbs, intuition of what is truly human, a willingness to listen to one's own scruples; all this is now seen as mere defeatism to be pushed aside.

Internet. The new lifestyle that takes the place of the old wisdom can be conveyed by a fascinating preacher in a local mosque. Purely virtual encounters are also possible, through the Internet, the prime place of radicalization. In one's echo chamber, voices that might cool down your passion can be locked out easily. You choose your fellows. Now the most vicious violence can be staged as aesthetic and thus attractive.

Intentional hatred. On July 26, 2016, in the small French town of Saint-Étienne-du-Rouvray, Father Jacques Hamel, age eighty-five, was murdered. He was celebrating Mass when two Islamists cut his throat. The barbaric attack goes so clearly against all that is human and religious that one wonders, Is that not also against the logic of the so-called Islamic State? Does it not fear to lose its last credibility, its last half-hearted sympathizers? Those, however, who want to understand the logic of Islamist terrorists have to comprehend the fact that they do not want to be understood by the public. They *want* to be hated. That hatred is part of their worldview. Hatred confirms that the world of the unbelievers—atheists, adherents of other religions, but also moderate Muslims—are "against us." Thus, all further brutality requires neither justification nor self-conquest.

Irrational addiction. Our list of radicalization factors accounts for nearly two dozen entries. Each one raises the question of what to do about it; but before considering technical solutions, one must consider that persons going through the process of radicalization tend to act like addicts. Advice doesn't help them, because they are controlled by a craving stronger than reason. Because of its similarity, radicalization should also be treated as a sort of addiction. An advice, even a threat, no longer reaches such people. It might actually strengthen their "black-and-white" type of thinking. Advice is interpreted away as a dissenting voice that wants to distract them from the way of God. Attempts at reeducation are now too late. More promising are programs of prevention; and more important than instruction on the dangers of addictive patterns, is dealing with people's psychosocial void. The young often grow up without sensing their meaning in life. Prior to planning measures, the question of identity must be posed. What can the foundational religious texts offer, what can theology contribute here? Before tackling this, a last factor of radicalization needs to be identified, which will lead us to the Islamic textual tradition.

Initiating the apocalypse. The Islamic State envisions a war scenario. The jihadists want to fight history's final battle, which will then cause the Last Day to arrive.

Studying a Hadith: The Apocalyptic Battle

That definitive battle is supposed to take place in Syria, more precisely, North of Antakya or Aleppo. Here is the relevant Hadith, which we will study in detail:[9]

> **[1]** Abū Hurayra reported that the Apostle of God—peace be upon him!—said: **[2]** "The Last Hour would not come until the Romans would land at al-Aʿmāq or in Dābiq. **[3]** An army consisting of the best of the people of the earth at that time will come from Medina [to counteract them]. **[4]** When they will arrange themselves in ranks, the Romans would say: 'Do not stand between us and those [Muslims] who took prisoners from amongst us. Let us fight with them'; **[5]** and the Muslims would say: 'Nay, by God, we would never get aside from you and from our brethren that you may fight them.' **[6]** They will then fight and a third [part] of the army would run away, whom God will never forgive. A third [part of the army], which would be constituted of excellent martyrs in God's eye, would be killed, and the third who would never be put to trial would win and they would be conquerors of Constantinople. **[7]** And as they would be busy in distributing the spoils of war [amongst themselves] after hanging their swords by the olive trees, the Satan would cry: 'The Messiah has taken your place among your family.' **[8]** They would then come out, but it would be of no avail. **[9]** And

when they would come to Syria, he would come out while they would be still preparing themselves for battle drawing up the ranks. [10] Certainly, the time of prayer shall come and then Jesus son of Mary would descend and would lead them in prayer. [11] When the enemy of God would see him, he [the enemy] would [disappear] just as the salt dissolves itself in water [12] and if he [Jesus] were not to confront them at all, even then he [the enemy] would dissolve completely, but God would kill them by his hand and he would show them their blood on his lance."

Obviously, a comment is due. A Hadith (derived from the Arabic *ḥadīṯ*, meaning "message") typically claims to report a historical event of Muḥammad's life. Those messages were first transmitted orally. Later they were written down and compiled into Hadith collections. In the case of the Hadith we are studying here, the compiler is a ninth-century Muslim scholar named Ibn al-Ḥağğāğ.

[1] Hadiths always begin with an *isnād*, that is, the chain of transmitters indicating the message's origin. In our case, the source is Abū Hurayra, the most frequently quoted narrator of prophetic traditions in Sunni Islam. He had become a Muslim already before the first Muslims emigrated to Medina in 622; but he only moved to Medina in 628. The usage of the title "Apostle of God" and the eulogy are standard Islamic practice. [2] The "Romans" mentioned—*Rūm* in Arabic—are the Byzantines, just as in Sura 30 (which is late Meccan). The two places mentioned are located exactly between core Arab-Islamic areas and Greek-Christian territory. We have already met one of the two place names, Dabiq, which now serves as the name of the ISIS propaganda magazine. [3] The Muslims, forming the best army of the people (*ahl*) of the Earth, are moving against the Western enemy. [4] It turns out that they are entering a battle that is already under way [5] and that they have rushed to help their fellow believers. [6] If someone deserts now, he has committed an unforgivable sin. The fallen fighters however are thus, in Arabic, *šuhadā'*: martyrs. Why? Because those who die in a religiously motivated war suffer martyrdom, according to Islamic understanding. For that kind of martyrdom, being unarmed is not required. The victorious last third of Muslims is never "tried" (the Arabic verbal root is *f-t-n*). The verb can also refer to the intra-Islamic faith divisions. The surviving faithful achieve their goal, the conquest of Constantinople

(in Arabic, *Qusṭanṭīnīya*). In fact, the city is only taken by Muslims in 1453, by the Ottoman Turks. **[7]** The spoils do not belong to God alone, as was the case in ancient Israel's "holy wars." While distributing the spoils, the Muslims are exposed to a new temptation. Satan claims that Christ has become caliph (*ḫ-l-f*) of their people (*ahl*). **[8]** The description is now unclear: It seems that at least some of the troops leave (*ḫ-r-ǧ*) the camp in desertion but they are unable to harm the faithful; **[9]** and as the faithful return southeast, Satan abandons his attempted temptation and also leaves the camp (again, *ḫ-r-ǧ*). **[10]** What now happens is predicted for the eschaton also elsewhere: Jesus proves himself a true Muslim and prayer leader (*'-m-m*) of the faithful: an imam of Islamic ritual prayer. **[11]** Satan has no more chance and disappears completely. **[12]** If Jesus had not eliminated Satan, God would have done so. God will show the Muslims the lance with Satan's blood. This serves as demonstration that Satan is really dead and possibly also that the eschatological Messiah is indeed Jesus. It may be the crucifixion lance.

The key point is here, that till today Muslims can imagine themselves as faith fighters against the Christian imperial army on the basis of a reported prediction by Muḥammad. But would that be Islam?

THEOLOGY OF CONVERSION

Let us now, as promised, turn to a theological discussion of identity. Neither Bible nor Qur'an work with a concept like identity, let alone something like "identitarian reconstitution." Both of them know very well, however, of identity transformations and changes. They speak of "conversion." Conversion terminology in the scriptures of Christianity and Islam is worth investigating. A verse from the Gospel of Matthew may set the tone (the whole scene around the verse will in fact guide our investigation for a moment): "From that time Jesus began to proclaim, 'Repent, for the kingdom of heaven has come near'" (Matt 4:17). In order to understand what is going on here, we must look back. The entire history of Israel is vibrating in those words.

Israel: Return

Whenever Israel's writings want to designate a change, or recovery, of identity, they speak of "turning around" (Hebrew, *š-w-b*). There is a theology of identity formation at work behind this; its basis is that things are moving, and that the world is history guided by God. That is why, in the light of the biblical concept of conversion, we can develop an entire theology of time. Only in the light of such a theology does the biblical identity theme receive its profile.

Before Us

"The LORD has done great things for them" (Ps 126:2) is Israel's grateful profession. Hebrew has a word for the past, which also means "it is ahead." What has gone before us is in front of us: *qædæm*, literally, "opposite." We have not left our past "behind." What happened "before" is indeed before our eyes: English, too, can use a word that means "in front of" to say "predating," the word *before*. Latin has a similar idea: look how close (confronting) *anti* is to (predating) *ante*.

A Past Retrieved

The early days are at the same time past and future: that becomes especially clear in Hosea. At first the prophet seems only to call back Israel into its previous time. It was the time of first love, though not easy. The return turns out to be twofold: in good thoughts, "return and reflect on the origin of your election!"; and in threatening words, "you will return to slavery again!" Both calls, however, are calls for repentance and purification. In each case, the return is a renewal of the exodus. Israel can only become God's people again if it remembers its origin in the desert's hardship. It must live the new exile, remembering the first exodus.

> 1 When Israel was a child, I loved him,
>   and out of Egypt I called my son.
> 2 The more I called them,
>   the more they went from me;
> they kept sacrificing to the Baals,
>   and offering incense to idols.
> 3 Yet it was I who taught Ephraim to walk,
>   I took them up in my arms;
>   but they did not know that I healed them.
> 4 I led them with cords of human kindness,
>   with bands of love.

I was to them like those
    who lift infants to their cheeks.
    I bent down to them and fed them.
5 They shall return (*š-w-b*) to the land of Egypt,
    and Assyria shall be their king,
    because they have refused to return (*š-w-b*) to me.
6 The sword rages in their cities,
    it consumes their oracle-priests,
    and devours because of their schemes.
7 My people are bent on turning away (*š-w-b*) from me.
    To the Most High they call,
    but he does not raise them up at all.
8 How can I give you up, Ephraim?
    How can I hand you over, O Israel?
How can I make you like Admah?
    How can I treat you like Zeboiim?
My heart recoils within me;
    my compassion grows warm and tender.
9 I will not execute my fierce anger;
    I will not again (*š-w-b*) destroy Ephraim;
for I am God and no mortal,
    the Holy One in your midst,
    and I will not come in wrath.
10 They shall go after the LORD,
    who roars like a lion;
when he roars,
    his children shall come trembling from the west.
11 They shall come trembling like birds from Egypt,
    and like doves from the land of Assyria;
    and I will return them to their homes, says the LORD.
      (Hos 11:1–11)

In order to better understand the passage, it is important to understand that Ephraim is the tribe of the Northern Kingdom of "Israel," which adjoins the Southern Kingdom of Judah. Therefore, the Bible occasionally calls all Israel *Ephraim*. (Just like the French, who call Germans *Allemands*, after the westernmost Germanic tribe.) Some words of the Hosea prophecy can be found translated differently in different Bibles. The versions may sound contrary. The disputed passage is the beginning of verse 5. It reads, *lô yāšûḇ æl-æræṣ Miṣrayim wə-Aššûr hû malkô*. That can mean: "No! (My love remained unanswered! Therefore, Israel) will return to Egypt; and Assyria will be his king." Or, "(Israel) will not go back to Egypt, (but a new slavery is ahead, because) Assyria will be his king." In the end, what appears to be contrary is nevertheless similar. The passage works with a "typology," that is to say, a present event is seen as an old event's fulfillment: the disaster of "Egypt" will be repeated now, with a new exile; this time in Babylonia. A new enslavement is imminent.

The Old Days Today

This Old Testament duplication of time is staged particularly dramatically in Deuteronomy. Its words put the listener back into the time of Israel's entry into the Holy Land. Deuteronomy uses several means to intensify the prophetic appeal. The book addresses the people not only in the plural, but also in the individual "thou." And between the desert history (past) and the land of bliss (future) lies the Deuteronomic "today," indeed, the Deuteronomic "now."

> So now [*'attâ*], Israel, give heed to the statutes and ordinances that I am teaching you to observe, so that you may live to enter and occupy the land that the LORD, the God of your ancestors, is giving you. (Deut 4:1)

> Keep, then, this entire commandment that I am commanding you today [*ha-yôm*], so that you may have strength to go in and occupy the land that you are crossing over to occupy. (Deut 11:8)

Thus, the whole book is superimposing the "Now" of its contemporary seventh-century BC hearers with a "Now" of the past, a flashback to the "Now" that God had once brought before Israel's eyes when they were standing between desert and Jordan. Thus the words of Deuteronomy are pedagogically dramatized *mišnê ha-Tôrâ*, "retrievals of the instruction" (in Hebrew); that will become, in Greek: *deuteronomion*, "the second Law" (Deut 17:18).

Why the Baptist Baptizes in the Desert

Right before Jesus's public ministry, John the Baptist will then call Israel to the plain of the Jordan. Even from the city of Jerusalem, people come to be baptized (Mark 1:5). What is John doing there? He restages the Deuteronomic gesture. The inhabitants of Judah are to put themselves back, even geographically, to the moment of entry into the promised land. They are to enter anew, they are to enter renewed. They are to take possession of the land again by returning to the place of entry and returning to the "ways" of God (see Deut 8:6). The sign of baptism is like a passage through the Jordan River, and is thus a new commitment to the law (Deut 11:31). But baptism is also individual and collective purification and thus the last chance to escape the imminent judgment (Matt 3:7).

JESUS: TURNING POINT

The Greek form of the name of Jesus is *Iēsous*. This is also the Greek version of Joshua, who led Israel into the promised land. In anticipation of the entry, Moses elects twelve men; and Joshua, in remembrance of the entry, elects twelve men: one of each tribe (Deut 1:23, Josh 4:2). When Jesus elects the Twelve, he is building on this.

In Jesus's proclamation, the motifs of John the Baptist can be rediscovered. But now they are programmatically reaccentuated. For Jesus,

- the imminent judgment is God's nearness;
- after the call to leaving people (come to the desert), there is call to visiting people (go to their dwelling places);
- what was previously only a demand is now an entrance opened into the kingdom of God;
- the urgent call to seize the last chance of conversion is complemented now with the consciousness of slow growth;
- to the challenge of necessary cleansing is added a healing, gifted through touch;
- in addition to the claim that everything depends on the addressee's decision, there is now the experience that the decisive factor has come with Jesus's own arrival;

- the challenge of a radical new beginning comes together with the promise that what has been there so far will not be eliminated but fulfilled.

Jesus's understanding of time can be demonstrated in three specific dynamics.

Anticipated Joy

Those who experience a painful privation and come to see it as living in community with Jesus, can already feel the joy that will, at the end of history, determine lasting life:

> Blessed are you when people revile you and persecute you and utter all kinds of evil against you falsely on my account. Rejoice and be glad, for your reward is great in heaven. (Matt 5:11–12a)

Jesus is not only speaking of a later joy; Jesus speaks of a joy one can sense now. In fact, his entire appearance is pervaded by anticipated joy. His disciples, too, have started looking forward to the kingdom. When he celebrates with others, he anticipates the fulfillment of time. His words are not just a promise for the future, as if to say, "Later something else will happen." Rather, with his words, Jesus places his audience in a different life situation they can experience now. Jesus is communicating the coming salvation. His Beatitudes are performative: they provide what they say. They are a sacramental blessing.

Lived Future

God's rule is at hand (Mark 1:15): that is Jesus's testimony. That is the certainty he communicates in words, in his healings, and in his whole way of life. "Kingdom of God" means that God is knowable and acknowledged as all-determining. "Near" means that God realizes his power not in solitary overpowering. "Near" means an opportunity now opened up, in tender care, which wants to be dependent on the creatures' cooperation. Therefore, each addressee can now engage in God's kingdom. It is to this that Jesus challenges people when he invites them to join in his community of life. This means acknowledging Jesus (Luke 12:8) and, out of anticipated joy, adopting his lifestyle: love that frees one to serve humanity. So people can already live the lifestyle of God's hoped-for kingdom. For those who are called to do so, that includes the specific forms of life of apostolic poverty and celibacy.

Recovered Origin

The newness of God's kingdom does not blot out the old. Rather than abolishing, Jesus speaks of "fulfillment" (Matt 5:17). The new order realizes the Creator's original intention. That order was what God had set in motion originally: "But from the beginning of creation, 'God made…'" (Mark 10:6).

For Jesus, conversion is therefore a key dynamic; but it is part of his specific concept of time. He offers God's future to people. They can now engage in the anticipated (i.e., already experienced) fulfillment of history; so much so that this fulfillment transforms, turns, converts, their lives; and the new style of the kingdom is at the same time the restoration of the origin, a "return."

PAUL: INTEGRATION

What can the New Testament's earliest author, Paul of Tarsus, contribute to our understanding of conversion? The New Testament does not speak of his transformation specifically as a "conversion." It is true, Paul can sharply contrast his life "before" with his life "after" (Phil 3:7). But when he reflects on his transformation, he does not stick to oppositional terms, as his epigones will tend to do. His conversion is vocation; it is gift. And even if there is a sudden break in his life, that life still remains a journey of growth and, above all, an absorption of the old. This can be observed in his letters, which testify that many of his linguistic expressions develop over time. He reaches new viewpoints. He applies both his Greek and his Jewish education (in sapiential, textual, and methodological knowledge) when formulating and justifying his Christian testimony. The understanding of conversion that becomes visible, in the light of Paul's life, is that a true conversion is neither a simple return to the old, nor a complete transition to the new. A true conversion is, rather, from the particular to the whole. All reality, life, and our whole history thus come into perspective.

FOUNDING A NEW *CIVITAS*

We have been looking at the Bible and its various strategies of founding what we today call new identities. Is the Qur'an, too, trying to create a new identity? How does the Qur'an handle the challenge of identity? These questions can be answered with the help of Qur'anic chronology. As noted earlier, one can state with plausible certainty *when* each of the proclamations later collected in the book of the Qur'an left Muḥammad's mouth. Both traditional Muslim and contemporary critical Qur'an research use a chronological scheme when reading the Qur'an. Let us, thus, first look at an early Sura, called "The City," proclaimed around the year 612. It truly creates a new identity: a new *civitas*, we might call it. Afterward, a Sura will be studied that takes the first place in copies of the Qur'an today, but was proclaimed later than "The City," perhaps in 615. What can be observed there, is how the Qur'an is founding a congregation. That other Sura will, like "The City," have striking similarities to biblical texts, but the Qur'an uses the material in a particular way, different from the Church's reading of the Bible. Finally, a passage from the time shortly before Muḥammad's death will be quoted. It introduces an important distinction by saying that not every alleged conversion deserves this name.

Studying the Qur'an: Sura 90 (al-Balad)

In his first years, Muḥammad had been teaching to perform the ritual prayer in the direction of Jerusalem. That was what he knew from the Jews. During the Diaspora, they turned in prayer toward the city, which at that time was lost to the people of Israel. For Muḥammad's first followers, too, Jerusalem seemed unreachably far away. But the distant city provides orientation: direction of prayer, and order of life. Only when another city has become the (transitional) center of the community around Muḥammad, and when his task becomes, with increasing clarity, the foundation of a pluralistic polity, does the direction of prayer change (Sura 2:142). Now, in Medina, they are orienting themselves toward their old home, to Mecca. Long before, however, Muḥammad was visible at the Meccan sanctuary, the Kaʿba, gathering a small congregation. There, he sounds a cry of fundamental rejection: "No!" For the new message he proclaims is in decided contrast to the activities at the sanctuary. No one, he feels, should worship figures from the ancient Arabian pantheon. Hence the resolute "No." If it is not a mere "Wow!"

Sura 90—*al-Balad*: The City

In the name of God, the Merciful Mercifier!

1 No! I swear by this city

2—where you are free of obligations—

3 [I swear] by someone who has begotten and by what he has
begotten.

4 We have created the human person in toil.

5 Does he think that no one will have power over him?

6 "I have squandered great wealth," he says.

7 Does he think no one observes him?

8 Did We not give him eyes,

9 a tongue, lips,

10 and point out to him the two clear ways?

11 Yet he has not attempted the steep path.

12 What will explain to you what the steep path is?

13 It is to free a slave,

14 to feed at a time of hunger

15 an orphaned relative

16 or a poor person in distress,

17 and to be one of those who believe and urge one another to
steadfastness and compassion.

18 Those who do this will be on the right-hand side,

19 but those who disbelieve in Our revelations will be on the
left-hand side,

20 and the Fire will close in on them.

The Sura, at first glance hardly comprehensible, can be heard as projecting a new civilization. Key insights on this point were first proposed by Qur'an scholar Angelika Neuwirth.[10]

Muslims do not give numbers to the Suras; in this case, they speak of Sura *al-Balad*, rather than "number 90." A Sura's name is usually a striking word taken from its text. Here, the headline also names the keyword: city (in Latin, *civitas*). It is worth noting that *balad* is borrowed from a Latin word, *palatium*. A *palatium* is, first, a large private house, as found on the Palatine Hill in Rome, a "palace." In its adopted Arabic form, the word does not refer to a single building, but means (in today's Arabic) "land" and in Qur'anic usage "city." One can, as already indicated, imagine Muḥammad reciting within sight of the Meccan sanctuary:

1–2 "No! I swear by this city." If this is rejection, it might refer to the polytheistic cult practice taking place around the Kaʿba. Just like Arabic soothsayers of that time, the Sura confirms its statements with an oath. What does that mean? What is heard here is as true as the phenomenon mentioned in the oath. Such oaths can refer to natural phenomena or historical-cultural ones. What is meant here is the city of Mecca.

The Sura now addresses a human being in the singular, a man. He is reminded of his experience of the city as a sheltering place, in contrast to the difficult environment of Bedouin life, where the individual is at the mercy of the threats of human revenge and natural disaster.

3 What follows is a second oath. It seems to refer to the person who has just been addressed and who is now identified as a father.

4 However, the subsequent verse teaches him a different lesson. The addressee is not really the producer of life. Rather, the origin of everything, including all human life, is the Creator (who is referring to himself in the plural). Again, the text speaks ambiguously. On the one hand, "in toil" can mean that God does not produce anything meaninglessly; his creation is, rather, well-planned, well-ordered. That is why later a Sura will teach us that "we have created heaven and earth, and what is in between, not for the pastime" (*lā ʿibīna*, 44:38). Now starts the suggestions that city life, too, which seems comfortable at first, has its own challenges for the city dweller.

5 The Bedouin, though believing himself to be completely independent and self-determined, is in reality subject to the power of God. A rhetorical question recontextualizes the life of a previously egocentric man. He is always under God's sovereignty.

6 Now the Sura alludes to a line from old Arabic poetry (ʿAntara, *Muʿallaqa* 40): "You were meant to demonstrate your heroism by being so generous that giving turns into wasting."

7 Another rhetorical question follows, allowing for a new contextualization of life; but again an initial understanding of the verse leads into the trap. The one who sees all is in fact not a fellow human being in an applauding public, which incites the boaster to ever greater irrationality. Rather, the One who sees all is the Creator, who is also your Judge.

8 He does not only see, he also makes one see: he has created the eyes. The dual forms imply symmetry. Divine creation is laid out in beautiful, clearly recognizable order. And this order is also committing. It obliges people to perception, but equally to responsibility and life in balance. God looks the human being in the face. God created for them a tongue and two lips.

9 Just as for seeing, for clear speech one also needs a pair, a pair of lips; but the tongue is only one (possibly a warning against duplicity). However, not only is the human body symmetrical. The city also has such a structure.

10 As in Sura 55, which we studied before, the present text is looking at creation, discovering its beautiful symmetry and pointing at the order (legal obligation) that follows from the order (cosmic structure). But here the gaze does not rise into the sky and out into the sea. Sura 90 is, rather, zooming in on the creature that is the text's "thou," the human being. And now the point is no longer only to *obey* an order, but to *erect* it: in the symmetrical city, the *balad*, the *polis*. Make the *civitas* a place of civility, it seems to say.

11–12 The listener is now asked whether he is aware of God's giving "guidance" (*hudā*) to all. God puts before us an easy way and a difficult path, just as in Psalm 1, or in the case of Jesus's "narrow gate" (Matt 7:13).

13–16 But civilization's new challenge is not an adventure to be faced in solitude. The test no longer calls for courage in nature, but for social competence; the text takes up a directive from Isaiah 58. What Jews and Christians hear as obligatory prophecy also applies to Muḥammad's listeners: care for the poor!

17 Already for reasons of form, this verse can be recognized as a "Medinan insertion," because it is so long. Into the praying community's recitation material, an addendum can be included in a later time and from another social context. Here now, after the establishment of the *umma* in Medina, not only individually provided care for the least is required, but also active community affiliation.

18 This verse may be a reference to the eschatological tribunal mentioned in Matthew 25:31. Both Qur'an and New Testament put the acquitted to the right side. However, the Gospel reveals that any act of mercy for your needy neighbor is an action taken toward Christ himself, who identifies himself with the "least." The Qur'an does not simply quote the Bible, does not simply copy, does not simply allude to it.

The Qur'an is the Bible reread. The Qur'an reaccentuates the biblical proclamations. The reference to Christ has deliberately been dropped. Care for the poor, yes, but not for any christological reason!

19 In the end, the Sura shows what the human world is: not an incomprehensible sequence of events, not a meaningless sum of things. Rather, everything is "sign." Signs can be read. Every single verse of the Qur'an is such a sign, too: the word for "Qur'anic verse" is also "sign" (*āya*)! Divine communication is happening everywhere, because God's existence, authority, and will can be known in nature. The communication requires a corresponding behavior in active faith; those who do not comply, says the final threat in verse 20, will face hell's painful punishment: "Fire will close in on them."

If this interpretation is correct, in this Sura we witness a transition from the heroic Bedouin's individualism to the socially and eschatologically committed *balad* citizen's individual responsibility. The new proclamation founds a new *umma*, as it will be called later, a new people. So here, we have before us the founding impulse and the basic orientation of Islam: a new civilization, marked by the acknowledgment of God and fellow human beings.

Religion, or Culture?

Sura 90 presents a religion that is both community based and transformative. Religion here comes with the claim to found a new community identity. The new foundation through religion, however, is not marked by the artificiality of an invented new culture. Neither the Sura about the "City" nor indeed any other Qur'anic passage claims to present something new. The Qur'an wants to be a reminder (in Arabic, *dikr*, Sura 80:11). The Qur'an calls people back to the faith and life of the prophets. It wants to remind us of things that people with open eyes can recognize by simply looking. The new *civitas* is, in fact, the old. It does not pretend to be a contradiction to biblical prophecy, but instead its continuation, its restoration, and its completion. This is the Qur'anic synthesis of religion, as the foundation of a new identity, and of religion as culture. Religion is a call to both the individual and the community. It is new insofar as it overcomes later distortions of the original. The Qur'anic religion, is thus, classical. Islam has always experienced its own tension between new and old.

THE POLITICS OF CONVERSION: "PEOPLE"

Crucial to the biblical understanding of conversion is that it describes the process as a return. Conversion is not only a matter of the individual, but also of the community, of the people. If we see this, we can also see that Jesus's proclamation is, from the start, political in the sense that he is reestablishing God's people. But what is a people?

"People's Republic," "popularity," "popular science," "populism," "popular referendum," "folk tale," "Volkswagen." If one listens closely, the word *people* seems almost omnipresent. It can be used programmatically in different, even opposing movements. Classical Greek offers four markedly different words that English renders as "people." Greek allows one to distinguish various ideas about "people." This may help to create some clarity. Of course, such clarifications tend to exaggerate the differences. In real life, the borderlines among different meanings are blurred. In order to indicate the possibilities, however, let us present four Greek words for "people," each with its critical counterdynamic.

- *Okhlos.* "Crowd" is the mass: erring, surging, pressing. The shepherd (Mark 6:34) is called in to guide them. The counterpoint of *okhlos* is order.
- *Dēmos.* In the "people's assembly," a spirit of communion manifests itself, "demo-cratically" deposing false leaders (Acts 12:22). Its counterpart is dictatorship.
- *Laos.* "Nation" implies election by God. The Hebrew Bible speaks of ʿam YHWH: "the Lord's people." It comes into being because of God's free choice (Ps 33:12). God chooses to be represented in one people against "the peoples" (*ha-gôyîm* in Hebrew, *ta ethnē* in Greek). Such an election needs no justification, say, in the merits of those thus chosen; and the life after divine election turns out to be no mere pleasure. God assigns a new task to the elect nation, but the election seems to overburden the elect. That is why the Bible juxtaposes election with judgment; and for the people of God as well as for the other peoples, the debate remains: Why did God decide for this specific dwelling place; why is God not equally accessible everywhere? Rather than rationality and universality, in

68

the concept of *laos* one can sense love's mystery. The beloved feels grateful humility and a call to serve the others. *Laos*'s opposite is, then, self-referentiality, be it individualistic, nationalistic, or chauvinistic.

- *Ethnos*. The fourth word for "people" can be translated more precisely as "tribe" or "folk." In today's discussions, *ethnos* is used above all in critical cultural anthropology, which sees how universalizations tend to end in uniformity, and so ignore the wisdom of the original folk spirit. Such standardizing attempts can be made by a "priestly" class through theological objections to syncretism or in the name of universal reason. Thus the concept is the antithesis to rationalization. Yet a danger also lurks in the concept, the "racist-nationalist" and the "demagogic-populist" danger. A particular group might declare certain "others" to be excluded from the people's "We," such as the "elite" or the immigrants. Then, the concept has lost its openness to polyphony, undefinable intuition, and growth. It has become the instrument of power for exclusion, and it is now an antonym of "the others."

The full impact of the "people of God" discourse can be felt only when we understand where it began in the Old Testament. Thus we will see that the biblical *laos* clearly has a *dēmos* dynamic, a power against the powers that be. The very phrase *people of God* originated in a prophetic critique of Israel's Northern Kingdom. It was ruled by dynasties that shouldn't have been in power. A self-protective apparatus, a "state," ruled. Prophets proclaimed that Israel's Lord was neither a state's god nor a dynasty's god; rather, he is God of a "people."[11] God has already chosen this people by calling it out of slavery. So now, the process of becoming a people is being antedated into the times of the patriarchs. An eighth-century description lets Moses (centuries earlier) receive the divine promise:

I will take you as my people, and I will be your God. You shall know that I am the LORD your God, who has freed you from the burdens of the Egyptians. (Exod 6:7)

The idea of God thus arises as a relativization of the institutions. Justification of "our" identity is neither our land ownership, nor our state, our representative administration, but that God has liberated us to be God's people. God's power and our relationship with God do not depend on our political status.

The people's foundational history, divine liberation from slavery, is not an ethnocentric justification for doing what others are not allowed to do. Ethnic belonging is not a license for selfish behavior. Rather, historical memory is an obligation. Deuteronomy especially clarifies this. The founding history of the people becomes the basis for ethical obligation: you must grant rights. Particularly impressive is the following passage:

> If your kinsman, a Hebrew man or woman, sells himself to you, he is to serve you for six years, but in the seventh year you shall dismiss him from your service, a free man. When you do so, you shall not send him away empty-handed, but shall weight him down with gifts from your flock and threshing floor and wine press, in proportion to the blessing the LORD, your God, has bestowed on you. For remember that you too were once slaves in the land of Egypt, and the LORD, your God, ransomed you. That is why I am giving you this command today. (Deut 15:12–15, NAB)

In this, there are five conversions, five relational transformations:

- *Becoming relatives*: the shared experience has turned you into a family. The "kin" is clearly not just the one who has the same mother as you; that would be stated explicitly (cf. Deut 13:6).
- *Empathy*: Because you know life on the other side of ownership, you must also respect the rights of the poor.
- *Gratitude*: Because you were gifted by God, you must be generous yourselves.
- *Task*: Because this foundation of a people is creating a new model society, justice must be practiced.
- *Collective personality*: Thus, the people become one individual that can be addressed in the singular

(as does the text here); they have become a "corporate personality."

The Hebrew Bible's dynamics of "the people" resonates again when Jesus proclaims the "kingdom of God." Jesus is thus witnessing to a triple breakthrough. The people's true ruler should be no human king, but God (Ps 24:8). Israel's God should rule not only over one people, but over all gods, all kings, all peoples (Isa 44:6). This change is not expected for later, but now this new way of life is breaking through (Matt 4:17).

A late New Testament letter says that Jesus Christ created, by his self-giving, a pure people (Titus 2:13; see also 1 Kgs 8:53). Such a formulation is a title of nobility for Christians; they are allowed to share in God's election of Israel. In it, though, there is a deadly danger, too. If those cleansed to be God's proper people no longer feel that they have received an undeserved gift; if they forget that they have been chosen to belong to the already existing covenant and people, they put themselves in the place of the first elect. Then, the surprise gift has become a possession. Then, the role of the old covenant is no longer acknowledged. Then, the amazement, humility, and joy caused by such unexpected grace turns into the arrogance that leaves no room for another way of belonging to God.

Where does this narrowing come from? We have to briefly study the history of the impact of "people" as idea. Toward the end of the Middle Ages, a Latin concept of "people" was recharged with new meaning, the concept of *natio*. Which Greek word for "people" does it represent? The *nationes* were already known from the "Vulgate," that is, the classical Latin translation of the Bible. *Nationes* was there rendering the *gôyîm*, the *ethnē*, the Gentile peoples. But Latin had two other words for "people," *populus* and *gens*, which were more commonly used. *Natio* was a fairly rare word by comparison and was therefore less legally defined. That is why "nation" now lent itself to a new idea: to express the community of those who feel united, and distinguished from others, by a language other than Latin. That referred especially to the *natio Germanica*, or *Alemanica*.[12] It is helpful to remember that *natio* is formed from the verb *nasci*: "to be born." Birth suggests "descent." At the same time, however, the biblical background of the nation idea kept the consciousness alive of a particular people's purpose and destiny.

This predefined the double-edged legacy of a group's feeling itself to be "a people." A group can sense a God-given purpose, and thus be moved to be helpfully humane. But they can also, in sharp contrast to God's idea of being called out of slavery into new service, now consider themselves as a sort of "master race." Then, a vocation has become a possession, leading to condescension, and even to discriminatory nationalism. The twentieth century has seen the murderous potential that lurks in the idea of a nation. We can now see how truly political the concept of "people" is. We were able to sense how it resonates in Jesus's proclamation of God's kingdom, and why it needs to be understood not only in the context of identity and conversion, but also of vocation.

SYNOPSIS: CONCEPTS OF CONVERSION

For the Hebrew Bible, conversion involves a return to God. For Jesus, people are enabled to live that return, because God has already made God's future accessible. For the Qur'an, conversion means surrendering to God's guidance toward the original human civilization.

Common to all of them is an understanding of conversion as an entry into the history of the living God. In this moment, however, the danger of conversion can manifest itself. Faced with an unsettled situation, one might obtain clarity through a fundamental change. Before that, life seemed disorderly, even meaningless, because it was simply earthly. Now, conversion has turned it into a divine project; now it has direction, even an incorruptible meaning. However, clarity thus obtained through the authority of the Absolute can become imperceptibly the absolutization of one's own goals. How do we get beyond this?

Conversion by Vocation

Religious identity cannot be based only on someone's own decision. Conversion is mere ideology if it is based on human initiative alone. Scripture shows us that conversion, an entry into God's history, happens because God himself is calling. True, the voice of God can always be confused with human interests, be they one's own or other people's. If, however, a truly religious conversion comes from God's call, we need to study conversion as vocation. What does the Bible say about vocation?

THESIS

Identity cannot be created by a one-time conversion, nor can it be possessed or restored, because it is historical. Identity, therefore, cannot be founded on any tangible foundation. It always requires new openness because it must be received from a personal relationship, as a vocation.

Vocation transforms a conversion into a relational process. In order to explore this, we must examine New Testament imaginaries; after all, the idea that conversion comes from vocation is a biblical notion. We will, for a moment, use a meditative approach. Later, we will also make theological and philosophical considerations on this.

VOCATION, A PERSONAL RELATION

When we were trying to understand the biblical dynamics of conversion, the guiding motif was Jesus proclaiming the kingdom of God. That proved helpful because in Jesus's ministry, proclamation and call are closely linked. In the Gospel of Matthew, immediately after Jesus's general call for conversion, we find three verses that explain the range of vocation dynamics. Let us look at them in detail, beginning with this passage: "As he walked by the Sea of Galilee, [Jesus] saw two brothers, Simon, who is called Peter, and Andrew his brother, casting a net into the sea—for they were fishermen" (Matt 4:18).

Already this inconspicuous verse sheds helpful light on the identity problem. The scene gives an insight into shaken identities. The place is even geographically telling; we are in the border districts between the Holy Land and the Gentiles' regions. The names of the two brothers, too, reflect this border existence. Though from the same parents, they have strikingly different names. The younger one has a Greek name: "Andrew" ("manly" or "brave"). The identity of Israel seems challenged by the culture of the Hellenistic world. In having named, however, their elder son by the Hebrew name Šim'ôn, Simon, the parents evidently recalled the nationhood of Israel. Simeon is one of the first sons of Jacob (who, so to speak, is Israel's DNA). Simeon was one of the twelve tribal heads, a cunning and successful warrior (Gen 34:25) and later the honored hostage of his own brother Joseph (Gen 42:24). People at the time did not choose names for their children simply because of their acoustics.

IDENTITY

Jesus "calls" Simon by another name, "Peter." He is now meant to be "rock," providing security in an unshakable foundation. People who, in confusing times, think they can get solid ground under their feet by relying on the word of scripture are facing the fundamentalist temptation. Are they trying to establish all certainty onto an old formulation (understood, of course, with a new consciousness), or are they trusting in God's call, to which scripture merely testifies? For the New Testament, the foundation of faith and life is neither a thought nor a book. It is Christ. He is the truth (John 14:6). This quote makes the situation particularly clear: "For no one can lay a foundation other than the one that has been laid; that foundation is Jesus Christ" (1 Cor 3:11). For the Old Testament, too, the unshakable rock, the safe refuge, is not a people, nor a writing, let alone some dogma. Safe refuge is God himself. He is the rock (Deut 32:4). Scriptural faith is therefore not a fundamentalism that seeks to safeguard certain beliefs, but a life of faith that derives its identity from a living relationship. Thus, identity comes forth from vocation, from the future opened by God.

A vocation is being prepared here that will pull the disciples-to-be out of their everyday business. Religious calls for conversion are especially attractive when they promise a strong and new identity and at the same time claim to be in connection with the traditional, in line with who we are "really, by origin." How can a lost home be restored?

> As [Jesus] walked by the Sea of Galilee, he saw two brothers, Simon, who is called Peter, and Andrew his brother, casting a net into the sea—for they were fishermen. And he said to them, "Follow me, and I will make you fish for people." Immediately they left their nets and followed him. (Matt 4:18–20)

This scene is programmatic for all Christian faith. Christianity is based on vocation (Rom 1:6). People are called personally and placed in a new task. A divine vocation creates new identity. That is already true of Israel. It is called out of slavery into freedom. This will make Israel God's testimonial people. Israel now feels its calling, its identity. And together with this, its mission. They sense their "destination," their "destiny." The call into identity is at the same time a name that gives one a place in the whole and an orientation toward the future.

74

While the task given to the disciples by the sea is new, it is also an explicit continuation of what has been there before: fishers of fish will become fishers of humanity. The new identity does not replace their former life but fulfills it. Those who are called have something to offer. It is not eliminated but used in a new context. Matthew narrates the appointment of the Twelve, the prototype of ecclesial ministry. In Paul, the same dynamics hold true of every Christian. You are a Christian because you were, and are, called to be such. Already in the New Testament's oldest testimony, Paul reminds his addressees how he admonished, encouraged, and invoked them "that you lead a life worthy of God, who calls you into his own kingdom and glory" (1 Thess 2:12).

The early Church's understanding of vocation, and thus, the Church's self-image, has stood, from the beginning, in a fourfold tension; a tension that Christians apparently processed well:

- Christians felt called into salvation; but what about those who do not believe?
- Christians saw that some of them professed the faith, but did not live up to their salvific calling. So, is God's call inefficient?
- Christians recognized vocation as someone's appointment for life and ministry in the community; but is there no vocation for life and service in the public sphere?[13]
- Finally, there were vocations to various functions in the Church, to "ministry": to the *oikonomia* and *diakonia* of apostles, prophets, evangelists, pastors, and teachers. This may come as a surprise and disappointment: Why does the Church, in which there are "no longer slave or free" (Gal 3:28), no separations, no preferences and subordinations of its members, now reintroduce its own hierarchies?

THEOLOGY OF IDENTITY

The New Testament Church expresses her new identity in a remarkable terminology: Christians experience themselves to be one body; indeed, as the one body of Christ. What does that mean?

New Testament Identity

Together. First of all, the body experience solves the problem of whether the Church is in fact simply a new edition of a temple hierarchy. Indeed, there are functions of leadership, administration, and representation; but they are gifts of God's grace like any other gift of the Spirit in the life of the Church. Each and every function is a necessary part of the body, with its own dignity. Indeed:

> God has so arranged the body, giving the greater honor to the inferior member, that there may be no dissension within the body, but the members may have the same care for one another. If one member suffers, all suffer together with it; if one member is honored, all rejoice together with it. Now you are the body of Christ and individually members of it. (1 Cor 12:24b–27)

What we see coming into being here is a community of mutual empathy and service; but it does not level differences: it welcomes individual diversity.

In Christ. The first Christians regularly verbalize their foundational relation as being, living, resting "in Christ." The Risen Jesus is for them at the same time resting place and challenge.

God keeps calling. If Christians say they live "in Christ," one might object that this is precisely not expressing a personal relationship. If I am in Christ, or, if "in [God] we live and move" (Acts 17:28), there seems to be no interpersonal relation, no alterity. The New Testament teaches its listeners by contrast also to see God as now personally active, as calling. Already Paul's earliest letter speaks of God as the "calling one" in the present day. God (Paul writes shortly before the end of the letter) will reliably keep safe those he has called: "The one who calls you is faithful, and he will do this" (1 Thess 5:24). Identity is, then, not something that you can store up for all times. It comes from the ever new relationship with God in prayer. God has a "will" for God's people (1 Thess 4:3; 1 Cor 1:1; Rom 12:2). What God's will is for our daily decisions needs to be found out in humble listening.

Corporate personality. The idea that many persons together have, again, a kind of a person's life is, for the early Church, a familiar experience. The great English Old Testament scholar H. Wheeler Robinson

(1872–1945) has found the apt term for this: *corporate personality*.[14] Already the Hebrew Bible designation of a people with the name of a single person, Israel, indicates this form of group identity; but even that man, Israel, has his name and identity from an encounter with, and calling by God, and indeed from a most individual one (Gen 32).

Citizen of Heaven: Augustine's Tension

The New Testament assures Christians that their real home is not on earth; they belong to the citizenship of heaven (Phil 3:20; Eph 2:19). Augustine develops this idea. As Rome is sacked by the Visigoths in the year 410, critical questions arise against the newly adopted religion, that is, against "catholic" Christianity. Paganism is stirring again. Have we become losers because we neglected, for Christianity's sake, Rome's traditional protective gods? What the defeat made clear at any rate, was that the Roman Empire is not the kingdom of God. Here Augustine offers a new theological solution. It rests on the anticipatory tension that lies in the proclamation of Christ: the kingdom of God is near. You can enter it; but it is not yet sufficiently visible to convince everyone Christ has not yet come "in his glory" (Matt 25:31). Thus, Augustine can say the *civitas terrena*, the earthly state, is a necessary ordering power according to God's will (Rom 13:1); but it must by no means be identified with God's state, the *civitas* of heaven. All earthly things are thoroughly permeated by nondivine powers. Thus God's state has its only present reality in this form: individuals live in correspondence to God's will.

Here, then, a Christian classic, Augustine's *City of God*, has kept up the basic tension of Christianity instead of dissolving it in one direction or the other, as if the Church were the kingdom of God, or as if the kingdom of God were something to happen only at the end of history. For Christian identity, this tension is essential. Christians live, so to speak, in the past, in the future, and in the present at the same time. Is that incomprehensible? Perhaps not. Pope Francis has repeatedly shared his views on European identity, on the history that the continent has in common with Christianity. European history is, however, not only in the past:

This history, in large part, must still be written. It is our present and our future. It is our identity.[15]

THEOLOGICAL ANTHROPOLOGY OF IDENTITY

If it is an identity problem that lies at the bottom of militant radicalization, we have to study the concept and dynamics of identity. Is it possible to sketch out a theology of identity? That can indeed be done, as will be seen shortly. With it, we will also find a helpful concept that may even point at elements of a cure for the identity problem. Which problem?

The problem of identity can be verbalized for the moment as follows: I want to be myself. This will is constitutive for independent life. The ego strives to preserve and to realize its Self.

Such formulas, however, require further inquiry. What is the difference between "ego" and "Self"? The ego is the reality a person perceives of himself or herself in the present moment. The Self, by contrast, is the total of all the ego moments that a person has ever experienced at the end. At no point in life, therefore, is the Self already fulfilled. In history, a human being can only ever intuitively sense his or her Self; sense it in a provisional manner, with ever new additions. When others acknowledge that I have not fully realized my Self at this moment, that I am more than anything that I can now show, they acknowledge my dignity. They acknowledge that I am a mystery that is only slowly revealing itself. My Self is still coming into being. My task is to participate in that.[16]

Theological criticism of culture sometimes rejects the struggle for self-realization as un-Christian, as selfish. Self-realization, however, is not self-obsession or egomania. Rather, theology can say that the basic feature of created life is the tendency toward self-realization. Creation means God wants reality that is not God himself. From this already follows a relative independence and a tendency toward self-preservation. Self-realization is only problematic when I say that I do not need others, as if I had everything I need within myself; as if I already knew everything about myself; as if the project of my Self needed no exterior determination; as if I had, rather, to impose it by all means necessary. Then self-realization becomes self-closure. Life, however, precisely needs an opening. I have to rely on others.

The fact that my Self is not clearly visible to me, at any time in history, also explains why I might have self-doubts. One may feel uncertainty about oneself, especially in cultures that do not define people's life paths in a unilinear manner. One is constantly checking whether one is not perhaps losing oneself. It is within this context that the feeling arises that one's own identity is threatened.

Identities exist individually (as personal identity) and socially (as group identity). At the moment of a perceived identity threat, it is doubtful whether the one who I am, and the one I perceive, are identical; and whether the one I was the day before yesterday and the one I am today are identical. That is why one speaks of "identity" in relation to a Self. Am I "the same" despite a perceived distinction between ego and Self? Am I, across the changing moments, and in spite of my changing life contexts, still "the same"? Am I (to say it in Latin and thus explain the origin of the word *identity*) *idem*? In the same way, a community can ask, If we accept this or that, if we let go of this or that, are we losing our "same-ness," our identity?

Identity consists in continuity, but that doesn't mean that it is static. The refusal to move on would precisely be the kind of self-closure that stifles life. In every moment of the ego, there are elements of the Self still to be disclosed. Continuity, however, means that in the transition to any new state, I can sense myself as still "me."

Our tendency toward self-preservation can be explained as "striving for cohesion," and that in three directions: the problem of identity arises as a challenge through "the other," then through inner ruptures, and finally as the challenge of time passing. What is meant by that?

Alienation

I do not want to "be lived," but to live. That is, I wish to sense that "this is really my life." Autonomy is a part of life, but that does not mean self-isolation. Rather, it is a living ego that realizes itself in a living manner, that is, in relation to others. Human life is relative independence. Its opposite is "alienation."

Although the Bible does not explicitly mention the fear of losing "identity," it does say expressly that "alienation," separation from the source of life, makes real life impossible (Eph 4:18). And what is the Bible's solution for such an alienation? Rather than saying "stay where you are, protect yourself in your inner castle," God's call is to open oneself up and to go forth. Israel's scriptures instruct the people to love the stranger (Deut 10:19). This can be justified in terms of what is called "identification." You can identify with the stranger because you yourself were once a stranger. While the New Testament can also address the theme of past slavery, it places identification within the context of the future; one cannot protect oneself from alienation by clinging to the old. Paul calls not for an opportunistic adaptation to the transmitted world situation; rather, Christians are meant to renew their minds (Rom 12:2). The new does not stifle identity, but instead enables it.

How do the early Christians manage to see the new so fearlessly, indeed, joyfully? Christians have already come to know the new in Christ's coming. It is the kingdom of the Heavenly Father, the new era of communion, the fulfillment of history rather than its petrification or destruction. Therefore, they can look forward to it and live accordingly. To the early Christians, novelty (*kainotēs* in Greek) was not a frightening loss, but departure from slavery into free service and true life (Rom 7:6; 1 Tim 6:19). The believers' "identification" happens from the future: they are citizens of heaven (Phil 3:20).

Identity is challenged by "the other" but also by sin and by time; let us now tackle what might be termed technically the hamartological and the chronological threats.

Guilt

People can find themselves in a moment of deep shame when they ask themselves, "How on earth was I able to do that? How was it possible I sank so low; where was my conscience?" Conscience is the knowledge that goes along (in Greek, *syn-eidēsis*; *con-scientia* in Latin; Rom 13:5 et al.) and permits the ego a foresight into the true Self. Shunning shame, I do not want to believe it was me. One biblical scene is iconic (2 Sam 11—12). King David is in shock as he faces his own guilt, for he had not really seen it before. The great penitential Psalm 51, which shows David as a person shocked at his self-knowledge, does not hide the facts: the sinner is a sinner. There is no escape. He cannot discard any part of his life. How can he still live out his identity now?

At this point, human history has reached a new depth of self-awareness. The king, exposed to himself and to his God, cannot undo what has happened. He does not neutralize his individual guilt in a corporate personality, nor hide behind his status, or place the blame elsewhere. David lives out his true identity, not by denying any part of his own history, but, rather, by daring to sincerely acknowledge everything, including his guilt. And he dares to ask for healing, for God's life-giving forgiveness. The Hebrew Bible's word for "confession" (*y-d-h*) is the simultaneous acknowledgment of one's guilt as well as God's mercy. David's full identification with his act enables him to identify with a David who has not yet fully come to light: his true Self. It enables him to encounter the God who makes all things new.

Time

The passing of time also puts identity into question. Am I, are we, still "the same"? This could be called the "chronological identity shock." There is a craving for safety because the present day seems confusing and opaque to every generation. Therefore, people have always tended to recall "the old days," which must have been simpler: "If only we could get back there! There, we would be able to cope with life!" This longed-for place typically coincides with our origins. Many feel that a former condition will guarantee identity, because they were then more themselves. This yearning for a return should not be confused with the biblical dynamic of conversion. The prophetic call, rather, urges us to recommit to life under God's ever new summons. The desire to get back, by contrast, is graphically expressed in the word *nostalgia*. Literally, that is *nostos pain*, with *nostos* being the "nest," or "home, sweet home."[17]

The problem with any attempt to escape the present is that it is oblivious of history. To acknowledge history means to acknowledge that time is flowing and cannot be turned back; and just as the past cannot be brought back, one cannot protect one's future with a magic formula, for history also means that new things will happen. True, the Christian confidence consists in the perspective that in the end all will be good, that we will be living in God's eternal communion, that God will be all in all (1 Cor 15:28). But the course of events leading to this is unpredictable. Human history is not a predetermined program. Our future is open and cannot be prepared or secured against all eventualities (Mark 13:11).

In our convulsive attempts to ensure identity, the identity dilemma manifests itself. It consists of the desire to possess identity (as if you could define it for yourself), and at the same time to sense that my identity does not come from my own projection (because it could never lead me into the web of relationships where life happens). If you think that your life belongs to you, it is not that great dynamic to which you want to belong. How can we get out of the identity dilemma?

Meaning: Sense

As we have just seen, attempts to ensure identity fail. There are, however, ways to accept our present movement from one state to another, as a development of our Self, although we cannot shape it all by ourselves. We seek our own continuity-in-motion. If the individual transitions are relatively small, our sense of identity remains palpable. Thus, the *idem* of the identity can be experienced. The identity question is, however, looking for even more.

The sharper the question of identity becomes, the more a definition is required, and the more the question itself becomes an identity trap. It cannot be silenced with a formula; but it may direct our attention to the overall process where everything is happening. More precisely, this means that I want to see the logic behind history, to recognize the overall context and its justice, and I want to sense myself as participating in a moment of history. We are looking for the "grand narrative."[18] We even have a tendency to ask for the unity of universal history. In history, my Self and everything else should be able to find their place. If that is the case, meaning becomes visible.

What is the "meaning of my life"? The quest for this, using that term, goes back to a 1796 letter from Johann Wolfgang von Goethe to his friend and fellow poet Friedrich Schiller. Goethe wrote *Lebenssinn*.[19] Because of its great impact on the quest for the meaning of life, we need to explore this word for a moment.

The German word *Sinn*, close to the English "sense," really means four different things at the same time: significance, purpose, direction, and feeling. A Christian theology of identity can see all four levels together. The question of my life's significance can be answered in terms of the purpose it serves: What effect does my life have? But since the consequences of my being and doing can have, in the long run, effects different from what is foreseeable now, the question of meaning opens the view toward the whole of history. Here the question of "direction" comes into play. Christian hope can be thus explicated: all events will prove to contribute to a good outcome, and thus everything will have found its place in the communion of life in God, in God's "kingdom." But this hope is not intellectual. Thus, the fourth meaning of *Sinn* can be addressed: "flair," "feeling," "sensual perception," "intuition." Jesus already lets his friends sense the hopeful fulfillment of everything, in the kingdom that has come "near."

Now these are truly fundamental considerations, leading us from the question of identity to a theological proposal on the meaning of life; but how does that feel in everyday life?

Ömer is an Islamic theologian from Turkey. Xavier is a Jesuit psychologist from Korea. Together, the three of us had gone from Jerusalem to Rāmallāh that day. When Ömer went to perform his afternoon prayer in the main mosque, Xavier and I waited at the entrance. We saw some Arab brothers in faith spontaneously greet our friend; we saw him bowing, kneeling, and touching the ground with his forehead. After a few minutes, he is with us again. I say the usual after-prayer greeting: Allah kabul eylesin, *"May God accept it!" and Xavier asks him, "What is that for you, prayer?" Ömer seems to listen to his inner self for a moment. Then he says, "Muhammad Hamidullah's answer was, 'Just like the tree gets its force from the ground.'"*[20]

COMMUNION

Religion promises people a new identity, so that change becomes possible. It can lead to a profound humanity, but also to an atrocious inhumanity. Theologically, a change of identity has so far been studied in the light of the dynamics of "conversion" and "vocation." Bible and Qur'an offer theological input for a theology of identity, which for them is not a question of individuality. Instead, with regard to the foundation of identity, the individual is led beyond herself or himself. But not only is the individual converted and called; communities also experience a conversion through call. What is the community's role in the process of a person's search for identity? A community can provide identity, can question it; community is a common search for identity. The process of "becoming oneself" is therefore incomplete, if it looks only at the individual. That is why we also studied the idea of "the people." Still, identity creation and self-realization are presented incompletely if the person or community are merely recipients. Are they not also actively involved?

Are there processes in which identity is neither created artificially, nor attributed to external factors? There is a form of being together, in which both individual and collective activity, active and passive participation, life past, present, and future, where all this comes together in one particular experience, namely, in celebration.

Identity in Celebration

Catholic language calls by the same name both the identity-creating celebration, and the community thus founded: communion.[21] When reflecting the dynamics of identity foundation, liturgical celebrations deserve exploration, too.

How can a people communicate their identity without trying to possess it, as if they were genetically entitled to it? How can a people welcome their identity as a challenge, as a call to live toward the future of a shared humanity? A Christian answer to this is that one cannot own identity, but only celebrate it in worship, which is at the same time historical and open to the future.

Liturgical Identity

Martin Luther wrote his famous phrase *sola scriptura* in 1520: scripture alone should reign. But how can a book "reign"? Luther explains it himself. He wants the Bible "not to be interpreted by my spirit or the spirit of any other human being, but that it be understood by itself and its spirit."[22] His concern was to keep clear the contrast between someone autocratically explaining away scripture's liberating message, and that humble understanding that accepts the word as a salvific gift.

Luther relied on the word as witnessed in scripture, but he did not turn the Bible into a family's private reading material. Rather than turning scripture into a house book, he made it the parish book. Lutheranism, just as much as Catholicism, feared arbitrary interpretations and fragmented communities. From Luther's *sola scriptura*, however, some of his adherents later constructed a scriptural piety that could replace the community's sacramental celebration with private Bible reading. In fact, in other Reformation traditions, particularly Calvinism, Puritanism, and Pietism, domestic scripture study, alone or with the family, flourished as the standard encounter with the Bible.[23] Indeed, as Jürgen Habermas notes, from around 1770 on "private reading and contemplative listening" became modern Europe's "royal road of bourgeois individuation."[24] Personal Bible meditation also remained on the Catholic side, for example, both in the monastic and Ignatian traditions—a royal road of Christian identity formation. Here, however, it was embedded in a communal liturgy. Where the common sacramental celebration fades away, spiritual reading is in particular danger of becoming autocratic again. It is then precisely the "interpreting by my own spirit" against which Luther was working: concocting your own belief system, or even inventing your own divine mandate.

People who are looking for definitive clarity tend to be open to verbal communication; particularly attractive is written communication. Immediate access seems possible, without distortion. When reading scripture, one may believe that all mediators are excluded, and one is alone with God. With the beginning of writing, the text seems to guarantee legal claims in unprecedented measure. A celebration, by contrast, always contains nonverbal communication, signs, gestures, acts: it is "mystery," to use an old term for the Church's own foundational celebration. A celebration takes its time and uses an ambiguous language. It may have its own type of beauty; it is lived tradition and requires the cooperation of several people. To a certain degree, those who celebrate liturgy must rely on one another.

The founding Christian worship, the Eucharist, implies a peculiar time scheme. It can be found in the Jewish Passover celebration as well. An event of the *past* is being celebrated; in the Eucharist, it is Jesus's last Passover meal. That feast and the one who rededicated it, Jesus, become *present* to those who celebrate it today: "Here is the Lamb of God" (John 1:29). Indeed: Christ himself gives his presence to his friends (Luke 24:30), a presence "in spirit," as the New Testament says (1 John 5:6; Rom 8:16); that is, in transforming and missioning them. However, in this, the Church celebrates the heavenly wedding supper (Rev 19:9). So it celebrates its *future* form of life, the eternal communion in God.

Thus, the eucharistic celebration allows people to imagine a new world. They are inserted into a new imaginary. Things do not have to be the way they are today. There is a different life, a goal that relativizes and orients everything that people produce. The Eucharist is an ever-repeated invitation to engage in a transformation process that is neither primarily self-active nor primarily cognitive. In the celebration of the body of Christ, a new beginning can grasp people, the transformation of all creation, in order "to gather up all things in [Christ]" (Eph 1:10). What they celebrate is that they themselves are becoming the body of Christ (Eph 4:12).

The foundational Christian liturgy represents a meal. What is the basic symbolism of the *Islamic* ritual prayer? Even though Muslims at prayer may feel a special proximity to Muḥammad and his first companions, the prayer's basic intention is not to recall the foundational era. The major purpose is not to celebrate an event or anticipate paradise: it is, rather, practicing an attitude. What is being expressed, in the language of word and body, is veneration, all the way down to prostration; if performed in a mosque (*masǧid*, in Arabic, "place of prostration"), the direction is indicated by something like a throne niche. There is no food. The symbolism of the Islamic ritual prayer is not a meal but an audience. Five times a day, together with millions of fellow believers worldwide gathered around the Meccan sanctuary in concentric circles, what Muslims practice together is an attitude, of being their Lord's obedient servants (Sura 31:1–5).

A liturgical celebration, in any religion, shapes the identity of the faithful and represents it; more so than any reading. Such celebrations are representations: of cosmic order and historical events, of power relations, of the relativity of human power. The following two chapters examine how reference to the sacred (both experiential and organizational) can establish human power, and can question it. First, however, the dynamics of the preceding chapters need a synthesis.

From Conversion to Vocation and Sacrament: Looking Back, Looking Forward

To describe a faith's possible social forms, four terms have been offered: Troeltsch's "church, sect, and mysticism" as well as "culture." Our exploration of identity's problematics has now, however, led us, by way of "conversion" and "vocation," to mystery. Are the concepts of religious social forms presented so far inaccurate because they under-expose the world-shaping, indeed transformative power of religions?

Religion as Foundation of a New Identity

The Hebrew Bible, the New Testament, and the Qur'an see a new community emerging as God's way to renew humanity. Israel consists of a people whose life as minority among the other peoples becomes characteristic, but also critical, and therefore world-changing (Isa 2:2).

In its oldest conception of the *umma*, Islam does not separate between polity and faith community, but provides space for nonmembers, especially for People of the Book, the followers of other monotheistic religions. The religious social form of Islam is "civilization," in the sense of prophetic civilizing or the reestablishment of the original divine social order, cleansed of human distortions. With its proclamation of the forthcoming judgment, the Qur'an founds a new communitarian and individual identity.

The specific social form of the Christian faith is the Church. It is distinguished from the surrounding polity; it is the community of faith and the anticipation of humanity's future. But since the kingdom of God is the communion of all creation, the Church, despite its distinctiveness from contemporary society, does not make a sharp distinction between those who belong to her and those who do not. Thus the Church explicitly understands itself as God's means of transforming the world into a communion with God: as *sacramentum*. The Second Vatican Council, as is well known, has dared to formulate an ecclesiastical redefinition: "The Church is in Christ as it were the sacrament, that is to say sign and instrument for the most intimate union with God as for the unity of all humankind."[25]

If religions understand themselves as the divine means of transforming earthly conditions, what is their relation to human power? They can empower human beings to govern (as we will see in the following chapter), but religions can also relativize human power by showing that nothing on earth can produce the perfect world (the subject of chapter 4).

VIOLENCE

Previewing the Third Chapter

This chapter will address the question of power and its justification, looking at the issue from two sides. One side is physical violence and its sanctioning in the Bible and Qu'ran. We will discuss the claim that monotheism is inherently more violent than polytheism and atheism. Our counterproposal is that any ideology leaving no room for development and diversity is prone to justify violence.

In studying various legitimizations of rule, we will then apply a concept political scientist Eric Voegelin used productively. Voegelin saw all ordered human power as a form of "representation." In the light of that, we will examine political theologies with regard to their justification of power. We will also study Paul's justification of the Roman rule, and Constantine's self-justification. Jesus, too, claims authority, but we will characterize his rule as participatory and liberating. In chapter 4, the idea of representation will again be applied, when we identify Jesus's witness to the kingdom of God as a new form of power justification, which already contains a critical trait. But first we will now discuss religion as a legitimation of rule and violence.

3

Religion as Legitimation of Rule and Violence

In the early twentieth century, the conceptual templates of holy struggle and *ǧihād* came into their own as ready-to-use patterns of justification for Europe's war enthusiasm. In 1914, war fever had also seized German Catholics. Bishop Michael von Faulhaber of Speyer (1869–1952) had just been appointed as the leading Catholic military chaplain. Later, as cardinal archbishop of Munich and Freising, he stood up against Nazi crimes. He also helped Pope Pius XI formulate the 1937 encyclical *Mit brennender Sorge* ("With Burning Concern").

In August 1914, the German Empire had violated the neutrality of Belgium and Luxembourg in order to attack France on its unsecured flank, an act that pulled Britain into the First World War. At the time, Faulhaber argued that under certain conditions the New Testament permitted war. He claimed to take a middle ground between what he calls "martial" and "Sabbatist" (i.e., pacifist) positions. About the conflict that would later be called World War I, Faulhaber wrote,

---

Can it be justified before God and the history of the world that nations let the weapons decide their disputes, even though half of the world may be destroyed in it? The question is not: is this or that particular war just? In the long run, the London wafts of mist will not obscure historical truth.

The German army departed with their shields shining in steel. I am convinced that in war ethics this campaign will become a *textbook example
of a just war.*

At Jesus' captivity on the Mount of Olives, hot-blooded Peter draws
the sword, but the Master prohibits this violent attempt at liberation
with the measured order: Leave it alone, Peter, "put your sword in its
place! For all who take the sword will perish by the sword" (Matthew
26:52). This command to the world of the Gospel is to be understood
as a *religious* orientation, not as a military prohibition of the sword, in
the sense of the Sabbatists. The command was addressed to a pope,
not to an emperor. It wants to prohibit the spread or liberation of Christianity by force of arms, but not to prohibit any usage of the sword by
the state authorities. It is not for nothing that the rulers bear the sword
(Romans 13:4), and it is not for nothing that in the Church's consecration of the king a consecration of the sword is explicitly provided for.

War is a legal fact in the area of the Christian world order; into war's
identity card we also write Christ's categorical imperative: *"Give to the
emperor what is the emperor's!"* (Matthew 22:21; Mark 12:17). The Savior's word has the tone of a measured military command; it was issued
at a time when it was more than today for the emperor to declare and
wage wars. It was a harsh word because it referred to an emperor who,
without ancestral rights as ruler, laid, by the conqueror's fist, the sword
on the neck of Daughter Sion. In this courageous and majestic "Give to
the emperor what is the emperor's" lies the eternal guideline of the civic
conscience also to go and sacrifice even on the killing fields; in it lies the
expression of New Testament Christianity for the necessary, holy fight
of the peoples.[1]

Religions seem to lend themselves more easily to justifying brute force
than to justifying righteous rule. Both patterns of justification need to
be examined now.

War in God's Name

THESIS

Belief in the one God can be used to legitimize acts of violence. Neither polytheism nor atheism, however, is a better guarantor for tolerant convivencia—*but humility is. It allows us to live our convictions as a confidence that is ready to learn—that is, as "faith."*

HOLY WAR IN ANCIENT ISRAEL?

Distinguishing between holy war and secular war would be unthinkable for the entire ancient Middle East. The Old Testament explicitly connects holiness and war. The God of Israel is "the Lord of hosts" (*YHWH ṣəbāʾôt*, Ps 24:10). When biblical Israel lived under the protection of the state, they told their nation's early history as a military history. They believed that when the Lord waged war, he was so manifestly present in the camp that those called up for service lived in a state of consecration. The formula for this is "Perform the holy war rite" (*q-d-š* pi. *milḥāmâ*, in Hebrew, Jer 6:4, author's translation). Warfare becomes ecstasy. Later, what had happened could be told as follows: Warfare begins ritually, by a sacrificial celebration. An ad hoc speaker seized by the spirit (no further legitimization is needed) speaks to the troops. The call then resounds: God gives the enemies "into your hand" (Judg 3:28). The Israelites, seized by a sense of certain victory, sound the battle cry, and the enemy loses courage. Now God himself is fighting. He typically acts through miracles or an unlikely, seemingly unfit person. This proves both God's power and the enemy's weakness. The spoils belong to God alone: everything must be destroyed. Israel fights "with" the Lord. This means much more than just being on a divine mission: the actual actor is God. What is happening here is "YHWH's war" (see Num 21:14).

However, as we see later in the Old Testament, God's wrath can also flare up against his own disobedient people. When he fights "with" Israel, it now means *against* them. Prophets later offer a different perspective: the Lord will put an end to all war. The Hebrew Bible's translation into Greek, the Septuagint, will render the old term "the Lord is a warrior" by its exact opposite: He is the "Lord who smashes wars" (*Kyrios syntribōn polemous* instead of *îš milḥāmâ*, Exod 15:3, author's translation).

HOLY WAR IN ISLAM?

Also according to the Qur'an, God would be able to wage his own war; but he does not. The believers should fight "in the path of God" (2:190, etc.). This is how God wants to test people (47:4); but once the believers have won, the Qur'an declares that it was not they who shot their missiles in battle, "but, rather, God" (*wa-lākinna llāh*, 8:17). Anyone who declares "war" on the jihadis of a network calling itself the "Islamic state" is practically recognizing, under the terms of international law, religiously motivated terrorism. It is, however, Islamists' militant rhetoric that makes Islam appear as the religion of holy war. What is true of this will soon become apparent; but one should not translate *ğihād* with "holy war." In the Muslim texts, "holy" is never used to describe an action. God is holy, and sometimes land is called "sanctified." Plus, the expeditions to which the Qur'an calls believers were not war in the strict sense. The call to *ğihād* is a personal appeal to commitment. If the organized overall event is meant, there is another Qur'anic word that must actually be translated by "war," *ḥarb*. If we hear, however, that real *ğihād* is the fight against one's own selfishness, we should not overlook the fact that the Qur'an does often unambiguously describe armed action with words formed from *ğ-h-d*: that is the word used to speak of human action "for God," and "for God" means, for the spread of Islamic supremacy (see 9:81).

STUDYING THE QUR'AN: SURA 2 *AL-BAQARA*

Immediately after the emigration of Muḥammad and his faithful from Mecca to Medina, we hear,

189 They ask you [the Prophet] about new moons. Say, "They show the times appointed for people, and for the pilgrimage." Goodness does not consist of entering houses by the back [door]; the truly good person is the one who is mindful of God. So enter your houses by their [main] doors and be mindful of God so that you may prosper. **190** Fight in God's cause against those who fight you, but do not overstep the limits: God does not love those who overstep the limits. **191** Kill them wherever you encounter them, and drive them out from where they drove you out, for persecution is more serious than killing. Do not fight them at the Sacred Mosque unless they fight you there. If they do fight you, kill them— this is what such disbelievers deserve—**192** but if they stop, then God is most forgiving and merciful. **193** Fight them until there is no more persecution, and worship is devoted to God. If they cease hostilities, there can be no [further] hostility, except towards aggressors. (Sura 2:189–93)

This evidently is a passage in need of explanation.

Legitimation and Limitation of Violence

189a Already in the Meccan period before 622, the Qur'anic text reveals that the addressees have questions that Muḥammad answers in God's name (see Sura 79:42). In our case, the query is about sacred times. How should one behave during holy periods? Should one continue the pre-Islamic custom of not entering at new moon one's dwelling through the main entrance? The answer also contains the "say!," the divine mandate to the prophet to transmit this.

189b So the criterion for good action is one's attitude, which then also expresses itself ritually: not in magic practices like avoiding the front entrance, but in the encounter with God when setting out together on the pilgrimage. Now piety includes not only attitude and ritual, but also struggle. God calls personally to such involvement.

190 The call is, literally, to "fight in the path of God" (in Arabic, *qātilū fī sabīli llāh*). So there is explicitly a *ius ad bellum*; a *religio pugnæ*, to be precise (in Latin): a religious duty to fight. It is a reaction to what is perceived as the opponents' oppression and temptation. With their supremacy they want to dissuade the (so far, few) Muslims from their faith. In other words, they want to prevent people from identifying with Muḥammad's person and mission. While here the opponents are pagan aggressors, a later Sura will also call to fight against disobedient members of the other "Religions of the Book" (9:29, in what is possibly a subsequent addition to the text).

The commitment all the way to killing is being justified by four arguments:

- God is commanding it.
- It happens "on God's way," so for him.
- The goal is to give rule to the one true religion.
- The opponents were already violent against the Muslims.

The Qur'an, however, also teaches the *ius in bello* as the Latin formula goes: "law in war," that is, a regulation that is to control people's behavior during the fighting. Those who submit must not be struck any further; that would be transgression. Such a restriction is needed because even a witness to civilized humanity can, with a weapon at hand, turn into a lethal machine.

The Islamic legal scholars have argued themselves into a safe zone when they declare that the duty to *ǧihād* is not incumbent on every Muslim personally: the commandment is fulfilled if enough men are found for it, if the fight can take place at all, they claimed. What *ǧihād* wants, according to the classical texts, is not war, but the liberation of the world from unbelief—by means of armed force, though. Today, most Islamic scholars only concede a right to fight in case of defense; but the Qur'an meant "attack." Therefore, it offers welcome fuel for the process of radicalization.

CHRIST'S STRUGGLE

Israel, in its "YHWH's war" narratives, reimagines its pre-Davidic conditions. When the Qur'an calls for *ǧihād*, the tribal society on the Arabian peninsula does not have a state or ruler either. Jesus, by contrast, lives under two rulers at the same time, the Herodian Tetrarchy, which in turn is under the patronage of the Roman Empire. In his life, one or the other state's power is always palpable; but Jesus does not fight against either of them. Nevertheless, his public ministry represents a fundamental transformation of the power relations. The Johannine Jesus's answer to the Roman governor Pilate seems to reflect accurately the historical reality.

> Jesus answered, "My kingdom is not from this world. If my kingdom were from this world, my followers would be fighting to keep me from being handed over to the Jews. But as it is, my kingdom is not from here." (John 18:36)

The Johannine scene is likely to reflect the historical Jesus's view. One only has to understand that the phrase "not from this world" is anything but apolitical. It rather means this: the kingdom opened in him gets no power from earthly rulers. For Jesus, the kingdom is something that his Heavenly Father bestows, giving it to him personally. It can be relied on; one cannot produce it oneself. The kingdom of God is growing daily. It can no longer be stopped by resistance and rejection. Indeed, it involves even its enemies in its growth process. When trusting in God's transformations, one no longer tries to act through self-enforcement. That is why in Jesus's way of life, nonviolence is essential. He challenges those who join him to discover ways of action that do not imply violence, indeed that overcome violence (Matt 5:39). Turning the other cheek is not self-victimization. What Jesus proposes here is rather a new thinking and behavior: instead of merely reacting, see what happens when acting in active, creative freedom. It might change the attacker.

What is the Catholic position on violence? The early Church took up the idea of God's war—but fundamentally transformed it in the light of God's coming kingdom. Unambiguously, the language of weapons is now a metaphor for a new form of war.

> Finally, be strong in the Lord and in the strength of his power. Put on the whole armor of God, so that you may be able to stand against the wiles of the devil. For our struggle is not against enemies of blood and flesh, but against the rulers, against the authorities, against the cosmic powers of this present darkness, against the spiritual forces of evil in the heavenly places. Therefore take up the whole armor of God, so that you may be able to withstand on that evil day, and having done everything, to stand firm. Stand therefore, and fasten the belt of truth around your waist, and put on the breastplate of righteousness. As shoes for your feet put on whatever will make you ready to proclaim the gospel of peace. With all of these, take the shield of faith, with which you will be able to quench all the flaming arrows of the evil one. Take the helmet of salvation, and the sword of the Spirit, which is the word of God. (Eph 6:10–17)

On this line lies Vatican II. The Council speaks of a war-free future, knowing that humanity cannot embrace it today but must work toward it: through arguments and education, through trust building and through the creation of new institutions.[2]

For the early Christians, military service was not completely banned, but killing was strictly prohibited[3] and they did not swear an oath of allegiance (*sacramentum*) to the earthly ruler. That would have relativized their baptismal promise. God alone, no earthly sovereign, should have the final say about those believers' lives. That is why the first Christian centuries saw numerous "soldier martyrs." They did not die on the battlefield because they were soldiers, but their own superiors executed them because they were Christians.

A new challenge arises, however, when Christianity is no longer a marginal group persecuted as an enemy of the state, but has a voice among political leaders. Now the Church's basic testimony, the world-changing love of Christ, must also translate into political realities. Now it must also answer the questions whether one may wage war. St. Augustine of Hippo (354–430) no longer saw the sin of the soldiers, for example, in their killing on behalf of the lawful authority, but in their refusal of an order to kill.[4] With Augustine, the ecclesial doctrine on war also adopted the Stoic idea that war could be "just." The criteria for that, still scattered in the Augustinian writings, were brought together by St. Thomas Aquinas (1225–74) in the famous argument for a just war: (1) it must be waged at the command of a legitimate authority; (2) there must be a just reason; (3) one must have the right intention, namely peace. If these criteria are met, one may accept the evil of war and commit oneself to it.[5]

But how could an attack be justified through quotes from the New Testament? This can be seen in an event that happened almost two centuries before Thomas.

In 1095, Pope Urban II had, at Clermont-Ferrand, called the crowds to a struggle for liberation. Jerusalem was to be freed from Islamic hands. Robert the Monk (c. 1055–1122) depicted the pope's sermon as expert propaganda. First, the pope described the "Persians'" atrocities. Then, he reminded the audience of Christ's summon: "Whoever loves father or mother more than me is not worthy of me" (Matt 10:37). Immediately afterwards he again quoted Matthew: "Everyone who has left houses or brothers or sisters or father or mother or children or fields, for my name's sake, will receive a hundredfold, and will inherit eternal life" (Matt 19:29).

He then contrasted the confined, conflict-laden conditions of the Frankish Empire with the vastness of the land where milk and honey flow. When he then cited the Franks' "unique courage," offering them forgiveness of sins and the kingdom of heaven, they responded to his warmongering by shouting (in a medieval form of Latin), Deus lo vult—*"God wills it."*

Urban's brief answer to the willing audience (again, according to Robert's account) provided another New Testament justification. He said that the armed journey to Jerusalem is both the apt response to Christ's word, "Whoever does not carry the cross and follow me cannot be my disciple" (Luke 14:27), and is "a living sacrifice, holy and acceptable to God" (Rom 12:1).

Pope Urban had just instigated what would be called the First Crusade. He used the doctrine of just war already developed in Christian theology, thereby making it possible for Christians to speak indeed of holy war. No written testimony of that First Crusade speech exists. Extant renditions are late, and contradictory. However, Urban must have preached, so the sources agree, by quoting only one source: the New Testament.

Since then, we have seen in every generation other such instrumentalizations of the gospel and God's will for armed action—with or without the invocation of a "holy war." President George W. Bush, for one, was quoted as saying, "And then God would tell me 'George, go and end the tyranny in Iraq.' And I did."[6]

Such instrumentalizations have led to doubt, which on some level is helpful as a question of inquiry. But these doubts are so fundamental that we risk losing whole dimensions of the human experience. Can, for example, people really discern God's will (Rom 12:2)? That must now appear to be either dangerous or impossible. Furthermore, a religious justification of state action (Rom 13:1) now only looks like arrogance of authority.

TWENTIETH-CENTURY HOLY WAR AND *ĞIHĀD*

At the start of the twentieth century, England, France, and Russia joined forces to form the "Triple Entente." Germany, Austria-Hungary,

Bulgaria, and the Ottoman Empire formed the alliance known as the "Central Powers." In early November 1914, the Entente declared war on the Ottoman Empire. If Germany could see war as holy, so could the Turks. The Şayḫülislām, the Grand Mufti of Istanbul, soon proclaimed *ğihād*. Thus, an old legacy had been excavated, the religious duty to fight "unbelievers." But the Ottoman imperial government, known as the "Young Turks," were of a more modern bent. They no longer divided the world into religious communities; they thought in terms of nations. Still, if this war could become *ğihād*, they hoped to extend Turkish influence eastward. Iran, Afghanistan, and the Central Asian Turkic peoples were within reach. The Germans liked the religious responsiveness of their Muslim brothers in arms, who thus retrieved a forgotten source of motivation. Therefore, Berlin promoted the *ğihād* idea, and indeed so strongly that the great Dutch scholar of Islam Christiaan Snouck Hurgronje (1857–1936) finally commented that this was a *ğihād* "made in Germany."[7] Though he was not completely serious, this quotation aptly expresses how artificial the recycling of old templates for agitation is, and how dangerous.

MONOTHEISM AND VIOLENCE

At the beginning of this millennium, the Heidelberg Egyptologist Jan Assmann (1938–) published a sensational thesis. According to Assmann, the biblical Book of Exodus has given birth to a fatal innovation in the history of ideas, namely, what he calls the "Mosaic distinction."[8] From Moses onward, monotheism has been present, says the German scholar, and since then the confessional distinction between true and false has caused intolerance and religious wars.

Assmann's Adjustments

Inspired by disputes among his colleagues, and after further research, Assmann toned down and modified his thesis.[9] That happened not only because of his deepened knowledge of the history of religious ideas but also because of a number of contemporary events.

- Just as his *Mosaic Distinction* came out, several
  acts of violence happened that were motivated by non-

monotheistic religious views. Notorious are the Hindu attacks on Muslims and Christians.

- Only in polytheisms do the gods fight with each other; human acts of war can then be understood as representing this.
- It is not the distinction of true or false that forms the basis of violence, but the distinction between friend and foe.
- Assmann later said that Moses was not so much concerned with the difference between true and false; the basic Mosaic distinction fell rather between loyalty and apostasy, faithfulness and defection.
- In exile, Israel came into contact with contemporary Middle Eastern currents of thought. Only then, according to Assmann, was the main concern of faithfulness growing into the truth question; but not even here do we find a justification for violence.
- Only when the history of distinctions is available as scripture does a narrative of origin serve as marking mental camps of "them" and "us." Now it can be instrumentalized to justify inhuman behavior.

Truth, Ideology, Faith

Assmann has broadened the range of his distinguishing pairs: from true versus false, to friend versus foe, to loyalty versus apostasy. Now he holds religious writings responsible for people thinking in inimical terms; but perhaps he has not yet introduced the decisive distinction. Is it not more productive to draw the line between faith and ideology?

What, however, is an ideology? A comprehensive worldview is ideological if it is wrong—one might propose. But who decides what is wrong? More helpful may be a definition of ideology not in view of content but of form. A claim at comprehensively interpreting the world and ordering life stops being an ideology only when it becomes responsive to reality. "Reality" in which sense? Responsiveness can be tested on three closely linked levels: plurality, culturality, and historicity. Thus, a short list of questions can be applied:

- Are different approaches permitted to understand reality, including variant interpretations of one and the same worldview?
- Is there space for ambivalence?
- Are forms of life and modes of expression that are not regulated by the worldview recognized as valuable, such as the fields of beauty, the body, literature, tenderness, or a sense of humor?
- Can the understanding of reality be renewed in the light of new insights? Is there a sense for the changes in thought and language forms, so that no particular formulation of the worldview is identified with the worldview itself?
- Is tradition neither simply transposed into the present nor simply cancelled? Can earlier views and expressions be reinterpreted?

Religious belief is not automatically ideology free; but it has a good chance of avoiding the ideological trap, as long as it does not see itself as a possession of knowledge. Without such a possessive claim, faith can be a trusting self-giving that includes a discrete stepping back, being convinced and seized, but mindful of the controversial character of what is thus being acknowledged. Thus belief cannot serve as a justification for violence. On the contrary, it practices precisely that attitude that overcomes violence: the humility of being ready to learn. In Vatican II language, this is "dialogue."[10]

We have presented a theological understanding of religion that sees faith as humility. It has shown three things at the same time: a suspicion against religions because of their potential for violence is justified; where it comes from; and how, of all things, theology can counteract that potential violence. When faith becomes ideology, it is easily used to justify violent power; but is all power necessarily violent? Is there no good power? Does not religion, if it is political, also have to do with political responsibility? Is it a priori wrong to place public power on a religious basis? Can we not, indeed, must we not, justify power religiously?

Religion, Law, Representation

According to sociologist Max Weber, there are "three *pure* types of legitimate rule."[11] Its justification, its "legitimacy validity," could either have a bureaucratic-rational character, or a traditional-sacred one, or a charismatic-individual character. By these types, he wants to describe the respective "belief." Weber only wants to show on the basis of which grounding patterns a certain society recognizes its ruler. Jürgen Habermas will rightly question such a justification of power, which is after all nothing but "*belief in* legitimacy."[12] On what basis is the respective claim at legitimacy made? The question is thousands of years old. A thinker who has examined justifications of rule in terms of universal history will be presented here.

THESIS

Political systems may have legislative, judicial, and executive power, but they cannot justify that power by themselves.

THE STATE WITHIN WORLD ORDER

Eric Voegelin's approach

In 1958, political scientist Eric Voegelin returned to his native Germany. Born in Cologne, he grew up in Vienna and began his academic career there. After the 1938 *Anschluss* of Austria, he fled to the United States. After the war, he was appointed to the Munich Chair of National Economics, which Max Weber once held. Since 1920, the position had remained vacant. Voegelin was not only Weber's immediate successor, but he was also one of his greatest critics. He made this explicit in a lecture series held at the University of Chicago in 1951, where he presented his political approach, *The New Science of Politics*.[13]

Weber had claimed that his sociology was "value free." For him, values were the unjustified, the unjustifiable, and therefore the "demonic," mere "belief." Voegelin had three objections to that argument. First, he insisted, if Weber had studied pre-Reformation Christianity, he would have been able to see how argumentative a faith can be. Second, he contended that Weber himself in fact did use values. If he was such a convincing teacher that his students fundamentally changed their minds, that was nothing demonic, just a change of values. Third, he feels that if Weber examined assumptions of faith as factors affecting history, then he explicitly recognized values as effective.

However, Voegelin does not simply continue the discussion on values. He wants to reinvent political science as the science of order. His project is not to examine concepts that justify rule, but to expose the preconceptual ideas of order. This is close to what scholars like Charles Taylor will later term the "social imaginary." Voegelin's key analytical concept for this is "representation." First, he examines the symbols of power of the old empires and finds there that rule is understood as an image of the cosmic order.

Voegelin's magnum opus is a five-volume history of how political power has been imagined, *Order in History* (1956–87). In the style of Voegelin (and partly with his ideas), something of a history of political power is attempted here (in all brevity, of course).

Göbekli Tepe: Organized Cult before Organized Polity

The excavations on Göbekli Tepe (southeast Anatolia) reveal, according to the current state of research,[14] something surprising. Pre-Neolithic groups were building a large sanctuary. Nomads without a ruler figure, like a king, and without a permanent dwelling, making their first attempts in the social order and agriculture, erected huge stone pillar circles with what was evidently religious significance. The structures go back to 10,000 BC. What does this mean? Here, the elaborate cult-building did not serve as a subsequent justification for an existing state, but itself became a crystallization point, catalyst, and model for a gradually consolidating society. Religious rites seemed to facilitate political rule.

Egypt: Greeting the Son of the Gods

On pyramid walls, again and again, inscriptions can be found that address the dead Pharaoh. A god calls to him, for example,

This is my son, my firstborn.
This is my beloved, in whom I have been well pleased.[15]

In ancient Egyptian religion, the ruler was son of the gods. What is interesting behind such a title is that it justifies legislative power by birth. What the son of the gods, the Pharaoh does, and decrees, is valid due to an authority that humans cannot produce, and therefore also cannot eliminate.

Babylon: Appointing the Legislator

A ruler of the first Babylonian dynasty issued a collection of 282 law cases, perhaps a model codex for its beauty.[16] In any case, a deep black stele with the text can be admired at the Louvre, larger than the human observer. The legislator was Ḥammurapi, who reigned 1792–1750 BC. The text would, for example, rule these cases:

> Supposing a man has knocked out a tooth of another man who is equal to him, he will have a tooth knocked out.
>
> Supposing that he has knocked out a lower class man's [muškēnu] tooth, he will pay half a silver mine.

But the prologue does not look at earthly Babylon; it looks toward heaven. The Codex Ḥammurapi begins with the words,

> As the exalted Anu, the king of the Anunnaki, and Enlil, the Lord of heaven and the earth, who determines the fate of the land,
>
> ordained to Marduk, the first-born son of Enki, to rule like Enlil over all humanity and elevated him among the Igigi,
>
> when they called Babylon by its exalted name, made it overpowering in the regions of the world, and transmitted to him an eternal kingdom, the foundations of which are fixed like heaven and earth,
>
> at that time, Anu and Enlil called me, Ḥammurapi, the exalted prince, the worshiper of the gods, to let justice govern in the land, to destroy the evil and wicked one, so that the strong would not oppress the weak so that I, like Šamaš, would appear to the black-headed and enlighten the land.

What is said here in detail?

The text is written in Akkadian. But the name of the god *Anu* is Sumerian, meaning "heaven" or "above." Anu is also the god of heaven, ancestor of all gods. The Anunnaki are the gods of the underworld. Enlil is the main god of the Babylonian pantheon. These two *universal* gods, Anu and Enlil, now make a *particular* decision. For Marduk is the city god of Babylon. Enki, his father, is the god of wisdom from which the Euphrates and Tigris spring. Marduk, the city god, should now have universal significance like Enlil, the main god: to rule over all people. For that, he is also elevated over the Igigi, the servant gods.

Once the city god has been appointed, the two greatest gods can also appoint the city itself. Babylon is to *have* a ruler and is to *become* a ruler itself, a secure kingdom. Only after this legitimizing introduction can the king himself have his say; he now has the authority to express himself as "I" and to enact laws.

At the end of the quoted passage we hear of the "black-headed." This was the Sumerians' self-designation. Šamaš is the sun god. The Louvre stela also contains an image. We can see how the king stands before the enthroned sun god and receives from him the insignia of dominion.

Human rule is, then, in ancient Babylon, divine election and gift, and only thus legitimate justification to legislate and adjudicate. Earthly rule represents the entire world order and it can therefore claim legitimacy. Voegelin speaks of cosmological truth in the cosmological empires.[17]

Jerusalem: Enthroning the King

Biblical Israel's relation to the issue of kingship is constant controversy. Indeed, the Bible documents that there were contrary views on monarchy among the people of God. When looking back to its origins, Israel can at any rate find no ruler's election, institution, or justification. God creates nature and the human being. God calls the patriarch from Chaldea and later calls his people from Egypt. There, we hear of a monarchy, but in a mixture of respectful and critical irony: the great empire can, through the foresight of Joseph the Israelite, also feed its hungry neighbors, including Israel. At Egypt's court, however, intrigue prevails. Despite all resistance, we suddenly see, later, a king in Israel, Saul.

With due caution, a type of ceremonial can be reconstructed for the installation of a king in ancient Israel. The enthronement protocol of the Jerusalem royal house probably saw five steps:

1. The new king is anointed (*m-š-ḥ*, the Hebrew root that is behind the "Messiah").

2. He receives words of assurance, such as the adoption formula: "You are my son; today I have begotten you" (Ps 2:7), and throne names such as "Wonderful Counselor, Mighty God, Everlasting Father, Prince of Peace" (Isa 9:6).
3. Now he will be placed on the throne, which is on Zion; palace and temple are close to each other. Israel's God and Israel's king visibly belong together.
4. Now the insignia of dominion are passed on to him, scepter and diadem.
5. The end of the celebration is an acclamation by the people and possibly the handing over of a confirming document.

This is the ritual as can be reconstructed from extant texts and images. It reveals at least two things. For one, Israel has adopted motifs from its environment to present the king as superhuman. The scepter is an extension of his arm, the throne is a seat of the gods, the titles speak of a power that no human can have out of himself. But Israel has not simply copied the entire Middle Eastern repertoire; it also sets contrasting accents. The king is not the son of the gods by birth. His destiny does not originate in a mythical prehistory. Rather, he is divinely adopted one day, in this history's "today," on the day of his enthronement. Another biblical passage, however, shows that the cosmos is also represented in Israel's monarchy.

STUDYING A PSALM: ORDER OF CREATION

Psalm 72
2 O God, give your judgment to the king;
your justice to the king's son;
That he may govern your people with justice,
your oppressed with right judgment,
3 That the mountains may yield their bounty for the people,
and the hills great abundance,
4 That he may defend the oppressed among the people,
save the children of the poor and crush the oppressor.

5 May they fear you with the sun,
and before the moon, through all generations.
6 May he be like rain coming down upon the fields,
like showers watering the earth,

7 That abundance may flourish in his days,
great bounty, till the moon be no more.

8 May he rule from sea to sea,
from the river to the ends of the earth.
9 May his foes kneel before him,
his enemies lick the dust.
10 May the kings of Tarshish and the islands bring tribute,
the kings of Sheba and Seba offer gifts.
11 May all kings bow before him,
all nations serve him.
12 For he rescues the poor when they cry out,
the oppressed who have no one to help.
13 He shows pity to the needy and the poor
and saves the lives of the poor.
14 From extortion and violence he redeems them,
for precious is their blood in his sight.

15 Long may he live, receiving gold from Sheba,
prayed for without cease, blessed day by day.
16 May wheat abound in the land,
flourish even on the mountain heights.
May his fruit be like that of Lebanon,
and flourish in the city like the grasses of the land.
17 May his name be forever;
as long as the sun, may his name endure.
May the tribes of the earth give blessings with his name;
may all the nations regard him as favored.
18 Blessed be the Lord God, the God of Israel,
who alone does wonderful deeds.
19 Blessed be his glorious name forever;
may he fill all the earth with his glory.
Amen and amen. (NABRE)

These verses seem to contain an interesting political theology. Let us study them.

Verse 2 This psalm, like many others, uses parallelisms: a verse's first and second half say the same thing in different words. This is relevant because we see that the "king" and "king's son" are the same person. What does it mean that the king is also called the "king's son"? The monarch is not in power because he is the son of the gods. Justification of rule is dynastic here. And what Israel's king is meant to receive is not simply "righteousness." The word translated into English most often as "justice," *mišpāṭîm*, really means "legal cases," "the judge's business," or "authority." God hands his own power over to the king. In the verse's second half the word is *ṣədaqâ*, a key concept of the Hebrew Bible: "righteousness in government."

Even though God *hands over* authority, it is *God's* people that the king directs, not his own. And justice expressly includes standing up for the poor. They, again, are first of all not the poor of the people, or of the country, but are under divine protection, so that they are God's poor.

Verse 3 Righteous rule does not only affect social life. Nature also plays its part. A good king receives support from the "mountains," too. Here the cosmological dimension of Israel's understanding of monarchy is obvious.

Verse 4 Righteous rule means service to the common good. Righteous rule's antonym is "oppression" (`-š-q`). The fact that the king proves victorious against the oppressors does not permit the people to feel superior to others; rather, a victorious ruler is a guarantor of security.

Verse 5 Why should the king be "feared"? Fear is the attitude to be shown to parents and God: obedient respect (Lev 19:3; Gen 22:12). The wish is that the king should rule until the end of history.

Verse 6 The fruit of good rule is lasting order in unthreatened balance.

Verse 8 And the king's people do not only wish him temporally unlimited rule, but also geographically. World rule ensures peace.

If we compare this psalm with Hammurapi's code, we see a double *rationalization* of kingship here. No legitimizing myth has to preface the rule. The king receives his power from God now ("Give!"). Furthermore, while the rain, which comes down to earth, serves as a metaphor for rule, the sun remains in the sky. It is no longer a point of comparison, let alone a source of the king's rule. The sun is only measuring the extension of royal rule.

In addition to these tendencies toward rationalization, two *idealizations* can also be seen in the psalm. First, the poor are now so prominent that they have become the criterion for righteous rule. Second, the psalm attributes to the king a counterfactual power. The ruler in question, possibly in the seventh century BC, in reality controlled nothing but a tiny territory. Israel's monarch was a tributary to the Assyrians. His rule was highly endangered. At the same time, his people celebrated him as a world dominator. The psalm seems to be more than a petitionary prayer in homage; rather, here Israel at prayer seems to surrender into God's own hands. When they call their ruler to secure dominion until the end of history, they actually entrust themselves to the dominion of God. It is God whom the king represents. The king receives, as the psalm reminds us in its present tense, God's *mišpaṭ*: jurisdiction. "Give your jurisdiction to the king, O God," and God's jurisdiction is, of course, worldwide.

Divine Legitimacy

In the old kingdoms, legitimation of power worked apparently in what we may call the "cosmo-theological" realm. This is in fact a combination of two types of state justification. For one, the local legal order is in harmony with the permanent world structure. On the other hand, there is a particular divine decision for this particular ruler. If this is seen clearly, one also understands that any political order presupposes two claims at legitimacy. On the one hand, why should the legal structures be organized precisely this way; why is that just? On the other, why should precisely this person govern?

Voegelin's thesis has been confirmed in our exploration. Behind the political orders, a variety of representational relationships can be discerned. In "our polity," the cosmos gets its tangible *cosmion*, a corresponding microcosm. The king's power to order represents the entire world order; his territory represents the four "world quarters." Likewise the cult, especially the sacrifice, represents the cosmic liturgy; and the feasts represent the world rhythms.

Now, however, further representational relations come into view. A paradigm shift is announcing itself. It becomes visible in the light of this question: What does the representational structure, as observed by Voegelin, mean in terms of a theology of law?

A state consists of organized rule. In the state, people exercise power over people. How do the rulers justify their power? They can say that the political order is justified because it has to stipulate law and guarantee its validity. This is true, but that is only a justification in terms of purpose. It is not yet a justification that derives power from an origin. A democratic answer would be that rulers are delegates of the sovereign, which is the people. What remains unclear, however, is why something should be right just because a majority of a people voted for it at a certain point in time. From where does a sovereign derive legitimacy? We need an answer to the question of the ruler's justification, an answer that justifies stipulated law as legitimate, an answer that provides a standard that the rulers are not setting up by themselves.

King Ḥammurapi will end his prologue by announcing he will establish justice in the country through his laws, because he has the city god Marduk's mandate. The ancient empires recognized a prestate right that founded them: they claimed to be divinely instituted.[18]

When studying ancient justifications of rule, today's political theorists normally try to enlighten and disenchant any claim that behind royal power is divine decree. They want to expose such strategies as a bluff. The king constructed a world of religious imagination in order to acquire superhuman authority and secure it. But if one wants to see religion only as a ruler's self-legitimization strategy, one must solve two problems. On the one hand, it seems that religion was practiced before the rule of law. That is what we may learn from Göbekli Tepe. There was no earthly ruler to draw up for himself a heavenly background. Rather, religious cult was there first, and then social and political rule became possible. The other problem is this: What makes the law legislated by the legislator legitimate? Where does the right to legislate come from? The mythical notion of the divine justification of law thus hints at a problem that exists at all times. Legitimacy cannot be established by vote. For the first time, this difficulty surfaced in the city-states of Greece in the fifth and fourth centuries BC. Voegelin studies this crisis.

JUSTIFICATION AND LIMITATIONS

Human Consciousness

We do not have many original remnants of Greek thinkers before Plato. Their works are largely lost, but many of their thoughts are preserved in quotations. Heraclitus (around 460 BC) is the first of them to present, in Ephesus, a theory of the human soul. His language borrows heavily from poetry. We encounter thinkers who develop their anthropologies mainly from introspection. Voegelin therefore calls these authors "mystical philosophers." How should they, of all people, bring about a political crisis? They open access to truth that shakes both cosmological empires and their patterns of self-justification. The mystical philosophers discover the individual's interiority: the *psychē*—the "soul." That means everyone can have an experience of transcendence. Everyone can personally relate to the god. Each person, however, also possesses their own standard of judgment. All of a sudden the awareness grows that the laws can be changed. They are mere *nomoi*, "allocations." What was tightly fixed before is now put in question. In the *polis* of the fifth and fourth centuries BC, it is vital to recruit others to your view. What counts now is *peithō*: the art of convincing.

Thus the societies of the Greek city-states came to live in new relations of representation, beyond the theological-cosmological. One can trace this shift in representations all the way into new concepts. Three typical new spaces of representation have been created:

> *Tragōdia*: **the tragedy.** The theatre created a public empathizing for the autonomous human being's unsolvable conflicts in the tension between law and morality.
>
> *Dialogos*: **the dialogue.** The truth is brought from the stage to the marketplace. Here, it is not compassion that is at work, but the persuasive power of argumentative reasons.
>
> *Polis*: **the polity**. The political order is no longer an image only of the cosmos, but also of the cosmion:[19] of the microcosm that every human being forms with his or her own reason.

The question behind the theological-cosmological justification of rule continues here, but it gets a new answer. Which presupposed true order of things is represented by the state? Now it is no longer divine decision and world structure; the political system rather has to represent "us" now: human beings in their rationality and in their society.

Let us put some order into this survey of representative paradigms by the help of two pairs of concepts. In antiquity, there was a transition from a "theological-cosmological" idea of representation to an "anthropological-sociological" one. Since it is human reason (in Greek, *nous*) that is to be represented in the polity, one can, for the sake of accuracy, also speak of a "noo-anthropological" representation. This distinction is appropriate because late antiquity will then see another anthropological form of representation of the political; we might call it, by contrast, the "somato-anthropological" one. The human body in its symmetry finds its correspondence in the geographical—and then also in the ethical—order of the civilized city: this is the description given in Sura 90. And the *ekklēsia*, "the Church, the assembly," understands itself as the body of Christ: it is, in the variety of its members' charisms, representing Christ.

Axial Ages

As noted earlier, Eric Voegelin had fled to the United States. Why did he do that? On March 12, 1938, Austria was annexed to Hitler's Nazi Germany. A few weeks later, Voegelin published a small book in Vienna titled *The Political Religions*. The publication went hardly noticed. But Voegelin fled that same year. Although it was not recognizable at first glance, his work was in fact a fundamental criticism of Nazi ideology. He was not explaining Hitler in the usual way. Hitler was not a return to the Dark Ages, nor a relapse into barbarism. Rather, Nazi racism had grown from a secularized idea of humanity, he argued. It was a substitute religion. The "political religions" in Voegelin's title are those totalitarian constructs that people build autocratically but under religious guise. Pope Francis, for one, would diagnose behind this the false belief that life works by possessing; life is, rather, a process, processing even resistance. To see this means living, as he puts it, with the priority of time before space, which "helps us patiently to endure difficult and adverse situations, or inevitable changes in our plans."[20] The opposite to Voegelin's political religions would be a dialogical approach to world shaping.

In order to liberate the world from Gnostic totalitarianisms, from the "political religions," Eric Voegelin was pleading for a political Christianity. When exploring the history of the political orders, however, he does not see the decisive change in Christ, but before him. Thus he seems to feed on another great idea in history, the "Axial Age." Karl Jaspers (1883–1969) was its propagator. In 1929, Voegelin studied for one term in Heidelberg, where he attended Jaspers's classes.

With his approach to universal history, the philosopher Jaspers was reacting to the Hegelian understanding of history. For Hegel, the one historic hinge, the point around which history revolves, is the knowledge and acknowledgment of God as triune: the recognition of

Trinity. Jaspers, on the other hand, held that there was not only one such transformative moment in history but many. They, he claimed, form a series of points at which the spin changes, an axis. He calls this great change "the Axial Age." Jaspers did not see it in one point, in Christ's coming. He saw it as spread out between 800 and 200 BC, and spread across half the world.[21] During that period, several cultures were transformed; a movement in mentality and spirituality opened up previously closed-in cultures in China (with Confucius and Laotse), India (through the Upanishads and the Buddha), in Iran (with Zarathustra), in Palestine (by prophecy), and Greece (through the poets and philosophers). The Axial Age thus identifies a multifocal and fairly simultaneous revolution of mentality, which in many places in fact led to the founding of empires.

Reflected Sacrality

The attempt to insert an axis into world history may sound artificial; but the key question is not whether a number of intellectual transformations throughout the world fit on a single axis or whether they are even interdependent. What is interesting for us is to study that very change of attitude. Thus, other helpful ways may be uncovered to conceptualize the relationship between religions and politics. What was this transformation, which we were, so far, only vaguely indicating? The sociologist Hans Joas (1948–) describes the Axial shift from seven different angles:

- As insight into the symbolism of symbols;
- As the replacement of the heroic ethos by an ethos of nonviolence.
- As the introduction of second-order thought, that is; reflexivity as a search for proof in mathematics, but also in ethics. Thus,
- As the beginning of a generally critical attitude;
- As the dawning of moral universalism;
- As the emerging idea of transcendence; and (summarizing all that)
- As the disclosure of "reflected sacrality."[22]

Reflected sacrality (one might also speak of "holiness cast back") arises when thinking (reflection) recognizes the human being as mere echo (reflection) of the sacred. What human beings can see in this light is that their power is conditioned, we are not God, but each person's dignity is unconditional. He or she is God's image.

How we can be responsive to reflected sacrality will be discussed later; what we have to study now is how Jesus and the first Christians dealt with power.

Jesus's Authority: Participatory-Liberating

How does Jesus justify worldly rule? We had already seen how far Jesus understood his kingdom as not of this world. In the same scene, the Johannine Christ, a few hours before his execution, reveals to the Roman governor, "You would have no power over me unless it had been given you from above" (John 19:11).

The Gospel of John works simultaneously on different levels. It involves several ways of understanding and misunderstanding in the process of revealing truth. Pilate must have understood Jesus to say, "You are appointed and empowered by the Roman emperor." Anyone who tries to justify a "political theology" with Jesus's words would, by contrast, understand that "God has given you power." In fact, however, when Jesus says "it had been given you," this does not seem to refer to "power" in John's text (because "power," *exousia*, is a feminine noun in Greek, whereas "given" is in the neuter gender). Rather than only to Pilate's authority, the Johannine Jesus is referring to the whole situation the two are presently in; Jesus says something like, "The heavenly Father has guided our paths to cross in such a way that now you too are a station in my passion that leads to the cross. You are part of the history of guilt, but also of salvation."

There is no clear theological justification of state power from Jesus's mouth. Nevertheless, he offers a foundation of earthly power, a new one. For Jesus, rule is a form of representation, but it clearly differs from the representation relationships uncovered so far. The authority that Jesus confers is both the transfer of power *and* the critique of rule in one: the kingdom of God. It can only be unfolded in its full dynamic in the following chapter, which examines the relativization of human power. But already now we can see that Jesus's understanding of power is not "charismatic-individual" (to quote Weber's typology).

A comparison is helpful here; Muḥammad understood himself as having been chosen and sent by God for a particular proclamatory

115

purpose, but not as being entitled to choose and send others in God's name. Muḥammad's understanding of authority was markedly charis-matic-individual. This explains both the disputes about his "succes-sion" (*ḫilāfa*) and Islam's wavering relationship to institutions. Jesus, however, understands and experiences himself as entitled to elect and send others in God's name. For this, the New Testament offers a whole gamut of vocabulary. The best example can be found in the oldest canonical Gospel:

> [Jesus] went up the mountain and called to him those whom he wanted, and they came to him. And he appointed twelve, whom he also named apostles, to be with him, and to be sent out to proclaim the message, and to have authority to cast out demons. (Mark 3:13–15)

Here, "authority" (again, *exousia* in Greek) is manifested as a sharing of power, and this in the service of liberating people from oppressive powers. The sharing occurs through election, appointment, even as name-giving, empowerment, and institution. Therefore, an institutional dynamic is present in the Church from the first months of Jesus's public ministry: institution as the handing over of authority. The transfer of power also includes the authority to pass it on again. The Christian type of rule, then, does contain a "traditional-sacred" element. But in the Church, even after Easter, ministry is based on a personal vocation through Christ. The Christian idea of leadership also has an individual-charismatic element. In view of the apostolic ministry, then, Weber's triple typology of dominion needs an extension. Here, a "participatory-liberating" rule emerges. For Jesus, God's kingdom and the authority to proclaim it is, and must remain, the critical counterpart to political power (Mark 10:43), and, only as such, its possible legitimation.

During the first centuries of Christianity, however, there was a resort again to earlier models of rule, along with their justification, which I will discuss below.

Studying Paul: The Legitimacy of Worldly Governance

How can Christianity's relapse into pre-Christian political theo-ries be explained? The New Testament itself provides an answer, in Paul's first letter. He had just called on Rome's Christian community not to take revenge on their enemies but leave retribution to God (Rom 12:17–20). Previously Paul had talked about "love," a topic to which he would return. He moves on to discuss not community relations, but "the powers that be" (as the King James Version translated Paul's *exousiai ousai*). The instruction has an audibly different character from the rest of the letter. This, however, cannot be explained through a later, non-Pauline insertion. There is no evidence of this. Paul simply touches on another subject, and an extremely delicate one. So his language changes as well. He no longer addresses "you," but demands something from "every soul": each one should submit to the worldly authorities.

> Let every soul be subject unto the higher powers. For there is no power but of God: the powers that be [*ousai*] are ordained of God. Whosoever therefore resisteth the power, resisteth the ordinance of God: and they that resist shall receive to themselves damnation. For rulers are not a terror to good works, but to the evil. Wilt thou then not be afraid of the power? do that which is good, and thou shalt have praise of the same: For he is the minister of God to thee for good. But if thou do that which is evil, be afraid; for he beareth not the sword in vain: for he is the minister of God, a revenger to *execute* wrath upon him that doeth evil. Wherefore *ye* must needs be subject, not only for wrath, but also for conscience sake. For for this cause pay ye tribute also: for they are God's ministers, attending continually upon this very thing. Render therefore to all their dues: tribute to whom tribute *is due*; custom to whom custom; fear to whom fear; honour to whom honour. (Rom 13:1–7, KJV)

Anyone focusing on the transformative power of Jesus's proclamation will probably be disappointed at this Pauline passage. This is political theology in the interest of existing power structures. Apparently, Paul does not wonder whether they are unjust, in need of reshaping, or even of a revolution. He does not seem to ask any question. He rather proceeds pragmatically: The government has power of the sword, therefore, it can execute the death penalty. This puts everyone in fear, which is what was intended. Those who obey, however, have nothing to fear.

Yet, Paul is not ignoring fundamental questions. He does introduce theological considerations. Although state authority comes *from*

God, this does not mean that it is of divine descent. But it does rest on the divine decision to establish it (*hypo Theou tetagmenon*, Rom 13:1). Here, Paul is speaking about the Roman authorities. Hence he implies that Rome's rule is analogous to the king of Israel's! Moreover, Paul teaches, Rome has an eschatological function. It carries out "wrath" (Rom 13:4). In the apostle's language, this means that Rome is a cooperator in God's judgment.

But is Paul's political theology then encouraging servility to the state? It is not, for three reasons. First, Paul is not familiar with any form of participatory government. According to his knowledge, political power can only work by means of subordination. Second, Paul leads the Roman congregation from a heteronomous, fear-driven obedience, to a convinced, understanding acceptance. He speaks to their "conscience" (Rom 13:5). Third, he inserts into his political theory an opening that is only recognizable at second glance. While he felt everyone should pay taxes, he finishes with an ambiguous phrasing: "Render therefore to all their dues: tribute [*phoron*] to whom tribute *is due*; custom [*telos*] to whom custom; fear [*phobos*] to whom fear; honour [*timē*] to whom honour" (Rom 13:7, KJV). Intitially, it seems like he is saying, Fear and honor the emperor with your conduct and your contribution. But here, perhaps, Jesus's word resounds: give the emperor what belongs to him, but give your whole life to God. The conclusion to Peter's first letter is quite similar to Romans: "Fear God. Honor the emperor" (1 Pet 2:17). Paul may be saying here that money is due to the emperor, but save "fear" for God; that is, acknowledge him as your life's end, guidance, and source.

Jesus, through his proclamation of the kingdom of God, made life possible in a new power dynamic, in participatory-liberating rule. How did Paul bring that to bear in his proclamation? In his letters, he emphasizes that no class should occur among Christians (Gal 3:28; Phlm 16). While he did not have the abolition of slavery in mind, his words in the long run contributed precisely to that.[23] Paul introduced the participatory-liberating dynamic into community life. He was not thinking of how states were run. He could not see what today's readers expect him to see, nor could he write what they would expect him to write. Nevertheless, his theology does communicate the world-shaping power of God's kingdom.

Believing in Christ, Serving the Emperor

The Roman historian Tacitus (56–120) describes an *exitiabilis superstitio*: an "ominous movement of enthusiasts," hated by the people, known as "Christians."[24] With growing nervousness, Roman authorities perceived that they rejected sacrifice "to the emperor." At first the law did not require sacrifice *to* the emperor, but *for* him. However, this obligation was suitable to identify belonging, and so distinguish the total subject from the one God's servant. A "test sacrifice" demonstrated who was a Christian. Christians, seeing a challenge in this test, took an unambiguous approach: honor to the emperor, but worship only to the one true God.

Around the year 180, the Platonic philosopher Celsus warned against Christianity in a polemic, placing "true doctrine" against Christ's testimony. He titled his warning *Alēthēs logos* ("the true word"). His text, however, is lost. Christianity, Celsus apparently warned, would destroy the Roman Empire. Origen, the Christian theologian from Alexandria, wrote a response some seventy years later. In his *Contra Celsum*, Origen argues that Christ and the Roman emperor actually worked together. Augustus was the emperor of peace, he writes, the preparation for the reign of Christ. Augustus got the ground ready on which Christianity could spread. For Origen, Christ's birth fulfilled what the royal psalm had predicted:

> For "in his days righteousness arose, and a fullness of peace," which began from his birth. God prepared the nations for his teaching and made them come under the rule of the one Roman emperor. There should not be many kingdoms, otherwise the nations would have remained alien to each other, and Jesus' mission: "Go and teach all nations," which He gave to the apostles, would have been more difficult to implement. It is clear why the birth of Jesus took place under the reign of Augustus, who had so to speak assembled the great majority of the people living on earth by means of a single empire.[25]

In 293, the Emperor Diocletian introduced a reform into an ungovernable Roman Empire. At first, he wanted to entrust its eastern and western regions to one emperor each, but then he decided on a four-part division. To two emperors, each called "Augustus," he assigned a "Caesar" as coemperor. In the West, the senior emperor would reign in Milan/Aquileia, with his Caesar in Trier. In the East, the senior emperor would reside in Nikomedia (now İzmit, Turkey). His Caesar had various residences in the region between Asia Minor and Italy. This four-emperor system also employed a "political theology." It is reflected in the title Iovius for the Augustus and Herculius for the Caesar. Jupiter, the father of the gods, and the demigod Hercules were to have their counterparts in secular authorities.

In this system, which was never fully stable, a Caesar's son (from modern Serbia) came to power: Constantine. He followed his father as a Caesar in the West, but by AD 324 he was able to gain control of the whole empire.

Bishop Eusebius, an early Church historian, considering the new geopolitical situation in 336, offered his own interpretation of imperial rule. In doing so he built on Origen. With a programmatic eulogy he celebrated the thirtieth anniversary of Constantine's reign. As the first Christian emperor, Constantine considered himself the servant (*famulus*) of the highest God, executor of the divine will. Constantine employed New Testament terms to justify his mandate, declaring himself *apostolos autokratōr* ("a ruler sent like an apostle") and *episkopos tōn ektos* ("supervisor of those outside"). He may have meant he was a sort of bishop for nonclerics.

In fact, however, Constantine even reigned *in* the Church. In the year 325, he summoned the first ecumenical council and presided over it as arbiter. What was born here, however, was not yet a state church. (Only in AD 380 did Christianity become the only permitted cult of the empire, hence the official state religion.) But what began in 325 was "Caesaropapism." In order to theologically substantiate this empire, Eusebius, the court bishop, founded a new theory of rule for the emperor's thirtieth anniversary: "one God, one empire, one emperor." After Constantine's death, Eusebius praised "godlike Constantine" not only as the new Moses, but as Christ's vicar on earth.[26] The historian Alexander Demandt (1937–) comments, "The pagan god-emperor has become a Christian emperor by God's grace. However, we now also have a God by the emperor's grace."[27] Under Constantine, theology and church have become subject to earthly power.

Is this the whole truth? Patriarchs and bishops were not court officials, but rather the emperor's counterpart: architecturally, atmospherically, and administratively. Byzantium's imperial-ecclesial *symphōnia* gave Christianity unprecedented possibilities of influence. This included the Byzantine people's right to refuse obedience to an emperor who deviated from the true faith.

Constantine's political theology sounds like a comfortable ideology, an instrumentalization of God's name, a pragmatic acquisition of power by religious means. Was his conversion a shrewd career move? A political religion in Voegelin's sense? Did he feel unable to oppose the rising new religion? Christianity was still too marginal a phenomenon in the empire to challenge the state. Constantine's huge basilicas should not be interpreted as houses of prayer for the Christian masses. Rather, they were a stone display of his splendor.[28] Christianity was a welcome support for the emperor's autocracy, which downplayed the original fourfold imperial division. While the dynamics of the Christian world mission corresponded to his universal rule, previously existing Church institutions helped him administratively. Furthermore, Constantine connected his role to biblical ideas, for example, the apocalyptic image of a long-awaited good ruler bringing heavenly structures of rule to bear on earthly affairs (Dan 7:13), as well as Christ's handing over authority to his elect. Thus Constantine acquired a degree of sanctity that was both new and yet traditional. Even his tomb bespeaks this notion. The emperor was buried in the Church of the Apostles at Constantinople, as the thirteenth of the Twelve, the uninterrupted continuation of early Christianity. Constantine and his theological supporters created nothing less than a new edition of the cosmo-theological representation. They saw Christianity as the earthly image of the heavenly hierarchies. A Christian empire now only had to realize that sacrality in worldly terms.

The Constantinian theology of earthly rule amounted to an ideological abuse of the apostolic doctrine of God's kingdom. The kingdom's proclamation does not lend itself so directly to the justification of earthly power. Nevertheless, the history of this first Christian empire poses a key question in political theology: How can the gospel contribute to shape the political situation; and indeed, how can the gospel justify political power?

From Authority to Justice: Looking Back and Looking Forward

In the Book of Genesis, the image of God is by no means only that of a king. It is "the human being" who is God's image; and God hands rule over to humanity. The *ādām* has the divine mandate to steward creation (Gen 1:26). A similar transferral of power will also characterize Jesus's ministry. He chooses and calls people into his community of life, and subsequently makes them part of his own mission by commissioning them and sending them out to the world. They are now authorized envoys: "apostles." Through this participatory-liberating rule, they participate in the power to free people from the enslaving rule of demons opposing God's reign. This is particularly evident after Easter, as the apostles become the leading figures in the emerging Church. Participative authority as a healing power becomes leadership responsibility.

This (apostolically authorized) self-understanding is also invoked by monarchs professing faith in Christ. But the leaders are under the call to "pursue righteousness" (in Greek, *diōke dikaiosynēn*; 1 Tim 6:11). It echoes God's urgent supplication to Israel's judge: "Justice, and only justice, you shall pursue" (in Hebrew, *șædæq șædæq tirdōf*; Deut 16:20). God thus subordinates the exercise of human power to the "righteous community order," *șædæq*. It is the fundamental condition for the life made possible by God.

If Greek-speaking Jews use *dikaiosynē* for the Hebrew concept of justice, they strike another tone. The Greek word invokes a doctrine of order, in Latin, *suum cuique* ("may all get their due"). It remains unclear, however, what their due is. The dynamics of biblical justice, by contrast, are not reactive, but active, creative. God *bestows* justice: the ability to shape the world according to God's plan. God's justice is the forgiving mercy and creative wisdom that incorporates what has happened into his good plan and thus makes new life possible (Ps 51:14). Reigning according to God's will must be done according to this concept of justice: in integrative and creative righteousness. This justice creates the condition whereby each person's "due" becomes visible. In this context, a person's current situation does not decide what is due to them. God's justice acknowledges what is already there but also transforms the person. For this justice recognizes in every person their dignity and their vocation. They are always present but still scarcely brought to bear: this person's destiny as having been called to live in God's community.

The Byzantine Emperor Justinian seemed to have had such an integrative-creative ideal of just rule in mind. In 537, he dedicated the rebuilt palace church in Constantinople to "holy wisdom," to the Hagia Sophia. In its architecture, God's wisdom (as operative in creation) was to become visible. And God's wisdom is Christ, who gives measure and place to everything created, so that it is assembled into one great whole (Ps 104:24; Col 1:16). This is also how the emperor wants to rule, and how he wants his empire ordered. Like the promised Son of David, he wants to represent divine wisdom in his person and function, in his legislation and jurisdiction (Isa 11:2, 4).

Relationships of representation are to be found in all justifications of power that have been examined here. The more rule is founded, not simply on a divine appointment, but as an image of, and in accordance with divine laws of order, the more an attempt to justify legitimacy also becomes its criterion. The ruler in charge refers not only to a divine measure as elective act, but to a divine measure as a standard. This standard is visible throughout creation. The ruler is verifiable through it. But what precisely are God's criteria in order to verify just rule? No one can present a yardstick that can be used without discussion. No one possesses the tablet of natural law; and in spite of that, rule is justified insofar as it is just. The person entrusted with the responsibility of government must "govern your people with justice" (Ps 72:2, NABRE).

The fundamental question is this: What is righteous rule, what is just government? Part of the answer depends, of course, on how the relevant persons gained power. Was the entire eligible population able to vote freely? Then, again, how do we decide whether those who gained power through a fair majority vote really act justly? A majority vote does not automatically create justice. Justice is a target concept. Whether or not it is being realized ultimately eludes human decision. Again and again, conflicting claims and legal interests must be weighed against each other. No solution will be acknowledged by all as ideal.

Justice would seem to mean this: subjecting all actions, structures, and laws to the standard of whether they recognize human destiny: life's fulfillment. The "Basic Law for the Federal Republic of Germany" of 1949, for example, subordinated all state ruling to the criterion of every human person's inviolable dignity. Concepts such as dignity and justice remain, however, abstract. What do they mean in individual cases? How should they be implemented? That must be negotiated in the social process; but time and again we also must ask, What do these target concepts signify? The various worldviews, traditions, and religious communities must learn to explain this in an understandable but nonreductive language, and thus propose, within the public debates, "social imaginaries."

The most important means of bringing the public order closer to justice is therefore not the power of the ruler; it is rather the education of citizens. Each one should be able to listen attentively to their formed conscience, to be solution oriented with the view to a higher good, but also to examine and justify social claims. While society must reintroduce the concept of justice as criterion again and again, it must also keep explicating it. In that continued educational process the Church's witness is an independent and an important contribution. The Church should not just take part in educational programs that might also be provided elsewhere. Rather, its great contribution is to question political power in terms of representation of the kingdom of God. Earthly rule must represent God's rule. But that must not happen in one of the forms of representation presented so far: no earthly rule simply presents divine order, neither cosmological harmony nor heavenly hierarchy. Rather, Church testimony challenges every human action by asking, To what extent does it contribute to better representing God's kingdom on earth? It is always aware that God's kingdom cannot be produced by earthly means and that each worldly representation is only provisional. The Church's contribution to just rule is, therefore, making God's kingdom present in a new form of representation; it consists in self-distinction from that kingdom. This idea of government is now to be examined: power relativized as anticipation.

RELATIVIZATION

Previewing the Fourth Chapter

We are gradually developing a political theology here, and we are approaching its essence. In the following chapter, we will first show how different religious forms of presence can have a critical role toward human rule. For example, a people may have a holy scripture. Their ruler is not the author. It can thus dictate what true, good rule is and thus be even the ruler's rule.

Then we will turn to the kingdom of God that is breaking into this world in Jesus's ministry and person. Here, we draw heavily on Wolfhart Pannenberg's theology. What is the political significance of the Christ event? The Church is already witnessing to the destiny of humanity. We are called to unlimited communion with God; but the Church insists that this destiny is not yet fulfilled. The religious community that already celebrates the end of history, the Church, *relativizes* all earthly claims to power. These are understood as provisional and imperfect in the face of the coming kingdom of God, but they can submit to this standard of true humanity, and thus prove to be legitimate.

4

Religion as Relativization and Critique of Worldly Power

On July 20, 1944, Claus Schenk Graf von Stauffenberg made an unsuccessful assassination attempt on Adolf Hitler's life. The dictator survived. A few days later, members of the "Kreisau Circle" were arrested for alleged complicity. This was a resistance group thinking beyond ideological and religious divisions, and beyond Hitler's Germany. Members met on Helmuth James Graf von Moltke's farm, which was called Kreisau; among them was a Jesuit, Father Alfred Delp (1907–45).

Delp was placed in a Nazi prison. On January 11, 1945, the most infamous judge in the National Socialist judicial system, Roland Freisler, sentenced him to death. On February 2, 1945, Delp was hung, three months before Germany's surrender. The reason for the execution was not his complicity in the attempt to assassinate Hitler. Following his conviction, Delp wrote two friends how Freisler had justified the verdict:

Things seem to be moving the other way after all. As the Lord wills. To His freedom and kindness all be entrusted and commended.

RELATIVIZATION

Thank you for all goodness and love. That was no legal court, but an orgy of hatred.

They could not uphold the charges of the original accusation.

Now through the trial life has received a good theme worth dying for, and worth living for. The justification of my condemnation stated four reasons—all else is nonsense; important is: no relationship to July 20th!

1. Ideas about a German future after a possible defeat—Freisler by contrast: "With us dies the last German, together with the party, the Reich, the people."
2. Incompatibility of Nazism and Christianity. Since founded in that, my thoughts were declared wrong and dangerous. Freisler also declared what he called Moltke's "idea of re-Christianization" was an "attack against Germany."
3. The Society of Jesus was declared a danger and the Jesuit a scoundrel, we are by principle enemies of Germany.
4. The Catholic doctrine of social justice was declared to be founding a future socialism.

The trial has been recorded. One will perhaps be able to use that at the appropriate moment. If I have to die, at least I know why. Who, among the many who die today, knows that? We will be killed as witnesses for these four truths and realities; and if I may live, I will also know what I will be there for, exclusively, in the future. Greetings to all friends![1]

The Jesuit was facing his execution, but what he wrote here sounds calm and collected. He knows what to live and die for. Now he lives and experiences what he had previously, in the Kreisau Circle, called for as the basis of any new order in Germany, "reconnecting—*religio*—the earthly spheres to the eternal truths and laws." The Latin word does not only mean "religion" but also "reconnecting." Where many let themselves be seduced into criminal collaboration or desperate confusion, Delp does not despair. His *religio* gives him strength and allows him to see another reality. Every totalitarianism fears such an independence among its citizens.[2]

Religions as State Critics

To believe that the ultimate, and therefore definitive, judge of history is God, and not human beings, can free people to courageously resist the rulers presently in power. They can "kill the body," but after that, they have no more to say (see Luke 12:4). Thus the power of the powerful is already relativized. Peter and the other apostles profess before the Sanhedrin: "We must obey God rather than any human authority" (Acts 5:29).

This is what the tradition calls the "Petrine reservation" (in Latin, *clausula Petri*). Such a relativization, however, raises this question: How can people say with certainty that their resistance to a state's command is not even more a case of human will, some private conviction, than is the command itself? Neither the question, nor the relativization, are specifically Christian. Before exploring the typically Christian form of power relativization, two extra-Christian instances of relativization must be examined.

THESIS

Religion can represent divine power over against earthly power structures and thus limit and correct them.

KING UNDER TORAH: DEUTERONOMY

An ancient example of relativized state power is envisioned by the Deuteronomic reform. In its "laws concerning public offices" (Deut 16:18—18:22),[3] the Book of Deuteronomy allows for a king in Israel, provided that the people so desire it, that the king is chosen by God, and that the king's power be immediately restricted. He shall not have too many horses, women, or gold. Yet these explicit power restrictions do not reveal that Deuteronomy actually stipulates much more radical limitations of royal power. The laws concerning public offices, in fact, constitute a legal revolution. This will be examined in detail, but first it is necessary to see what is said here about the king:

> When he has taken the throne of his kingdom, he shall have
> a copy of this law written for him in the presence of the
> levitical priests. It shall remain with him and he shall read

in it all the days of his life, so that he may learn to fear the LORD his God, diligently observing all the words of this law and these statutes, neither exalting himself above other members of the community nor turning aside from the commandment, either to the right or to the left, so that he and his descendants may reign long over his kingdom in Israel. (Deut 17:18–20)

Written, and therefore immutable, legislation has been made public already on ancient Near Eastern stelae. It has thus come to grant rule of law, represents a warning against transgression, and is a demonstration of the king's power. Here the king presents himself as the righteous and lawful ruler. Israel promulgates the law orally and liturgically (Josh 8:30–35; Neh 8). The law calls not only for publication, but also for internalization. A "copy" (Deut 17:18) is to be made; these are the *mišnê ha-Torâ ha-zôt* (in Greek: the *deutero-nomion*). Thus transcribed, the Torah copy penetrates the king's private existence. As a scroll, the Torah also becomes a life companion. There are no more Torah-free areas in life. It is no longer restricted to the legal function of judging in disputes, but now also has the ethical function of navigating any decision. It has become a fundamental life orientation. The Torah realizes its presence as written and transported word, but also as "read," that is, "mumbled contemplatively" (*h-g-h*, Ps 1:2). Here the notion of "individual reading and contemplative listening" find their first expression. Scripture thus established demonstrates that it is not the king who is Israel's lawgiver, but God. The king is not author of the word, but a doer of the word, because he is a hearer of the word (see Jas 1:22). So the ruler is subject to God, and subject to the same criteria as any other Israelite. Hence under the Torah, human power is controlled and relativized.

Deuteronomy had expressly excluded foreigners from becoming king in Israel (Deut 17:15). As we read carefully, we will see here a kingship being sanctioned that is fundamentally different not only from Israel's environment, but also from Israel's early history. In Psalm 72, God was asked to grant to the king the office of judge. Now, by contrast, the people are instructed:

You shall appoint judges and officials throughout your tribes, in all your towns that the LORD your God is giving you, and they shall render just decisions for the people. You must not distort justice; you must not show partiality; and you must not accept bribes, for a bribe blinds the eyes of the wise and subverts the cause of those who are in the right. Justice, and only justice, you shall pursue, so that you may live and occupy the land that the LORD your God is giving you. (Deut 16:18–20)

Even before the king is mentioned, God (as opposed to the text or even the people) establishes a jurisdiction. It is a professional, local jurisdiction, independent of ruler and state, complete with procedural law (Deut 17:2–7). There is also an equally independent central court for cases that cannot be solved by witnesses or through the use of documents (Deut 17:8–13). Priests are involved in the judicial process, but since there are also judges acting in the central court, the Deuteronomic reform does not reestablish a classical temple jurisdiction. The central court is the place where legally valid oaths are taken. People pay priests at sacrifices and harvests (Deut 18:3), but that does not mean financing a state religion because in that way the religious administration is independent of the royal court. So it can speak and act autonomously.

For Deuteronomy's Israel, the reference to God is by no means a covert authorization of the state: it is a guarantor of the people's freedom as regards the ruling house of the land.

SEPARATING POWERS AND CRITICIZING RULERS IN ISLAM

Based on the Qur'an's Medinan Suras, one can construct a political theory in which religion, society, and state are in complete congruence. Does that mean that Muslims, if they wish to take the Qur'an seriously, cannot distinguish between politics and religion? Before answering this question, however, another question needs to be tackled: Why does the Qur'an design such an ideal at all?

Why Politics and Religion Coincide

Making a distinction between the religious sphere and the political realm is not a modern achievement. Early states also made that distinction, as evidenced in the division of labor between different civil servants.

Some were entrusted with government affairs, while others, be they civil servants in the full sense or otherwise, were responsible for religious affairs.

But wasn't everything in antiquity justified through religion, wasn't every war sacred, wasn't the power hierarchy a theological representation? Yes, it was. The premodern ruler united the highest secular power on earth with the spiritual. That is why, for example, the pre-Christian Roman emperor was the supreme priest (in Greek, *Archiereus Megistos*, *Pontifex Maximus* in Latin). Below him, however, separate hierarchies had responsibilities for the two realms. Similarly, the Christian emperor took care of the spiritual concerns, particularly doctrinal uniformity, and was able to utilize certain priestly or episcopal motifs. Still, the Church had its own administrative structure. The Byzantine model sees itself as Church-state harmony: a *symphōnia*, as noted earlier. Now, a model of collocating state and church as body and soul suggests itself. This is not separation, but differentiation. Similar distinctions can be found almost everywhere. Why does classical Islam not know such a distinction? Four factors can be identified.

Ethos of self-determination. Before Islam, the social system of the Arabian peninsula was tribal, largely without state institutions. Contemporary poetry, the richest source for pre-Islamic anthropology, creates an ideal figure in the Bedouin, who is his own master. For him, a state institution would reduce his own sovereignty. So he would reject it. Even if the Bedouin ethos is severely shaken by the Qur'an, the new message still retains a distrust of all kind of mediation and emphasizes personal responsibility (Sura 39:43). Thus, clergy have a questionable status already in the Qur'an (Sura 5:44; 9:42).

Umma **as type of society.** The original context of the Qur'an's was a world where no state yet existed. Criticism of rulers, therefore, is not a prominent theme. The political message of the Qur'an is rather to proclaim a new type of society. People should no longer live partitioned into competing tribes but should see themselves as one community. The common ground is now "belief" (*īmān*). The "believers" (*mu'minūn*) become one transtribal, religiously united people: the *umma*. Within this basic social impulse, the political and religious dynamics already overlap.

Nontransferable authority. The biblical Jesus transmits his healing, reconciling authority to those whom he chooses (Mark 6:7; Matt 18:18; John 20:23). Later, a Christian emperor might understand this

132

as conferral of political power (see Matt 19:28). Christianity, however, was long enough a persecuted minority to understand Christ's apostolic authority as received by an unambiguously spiritual mandate: to unbind, in eschatological perspective (Matt 16:19).

Muhammad too sees himself as God's messenger (in Arabic, *rasūl*; *apostolos* in Greek). He understands his religious experience as a personal commission from God. But it is a mandate (in Arabic *risāla*, literally "mission") without a full handing over of power and authority. He may not pass it on any further. Does not a messenger need helpers? He does, but he is not allowed to appoint them himself. Muhammad does not commission any "helpers" (in Arabic *anṣār*, sg. *nāṣir*). Jesus, according to the Qur'an, does have helpers, but he hasn't chosen or empowered them himself. Rather, when Jesus is wondering who would help him "beside God" (*ilā llāh*), the apostles (*hawārīyūn*) answer him on their own initiative: "We are the helpers of God. We believe in him. Witness that we are devoted [*muslimūn*]" (Sura 3:52).

Accordingly, Muhammad does not appoint any assistants, either for political or religious administration. This may be so for the theological reason that an immediate relation to God for either one is necessary. At play may also be a cultural factor: an Arabic aversion to institutions. Or it may be a tactic to concentrate power on Muhammad. The consequence, in any case, is that after Muhammad's death, there was indeed a political central leadership, even if bloodily challenged from the beginning, but no distinguishable religious administration. The Islamic dynasty in Damascus, the Umayyads (641–744), actually did have top-level scholars on their payrole who were experts precisely in religious questions. So there was actually an early attempt to create a Sunni clergy: theologians who were civil servants.[4] But that line was interrupted when the dynasty (and with it, public order) faded. Now a distinction between the spiritual and the temporal realm was no longer represented in state structure.

Political and religious mission. Only one tribe inhabited Muhammad's hometown. They lived together in relative unity. The Meccan shrine, focal to the whole region, was a point of intersection for different religions, and a point of attraction for profitable pilgrim and trade trips. Muhammad's proclamation, with its criticism of the cults practiced there, was consequently seen as dangerous, destabilizing, even destructive. In Medina, by contrast, the more diverse population, with several Jewish and pagan tribes, lacked unity. Here, Muhammad's charism, which seemed driven by an energy strong enough to found a whole new society, was highly welcome. Therefore, Muḥammad could emigrate with his (at the time, few) followers from Mecca, which provided him with security but offered little resonance, to a city whose population wanted him precisely for his enthusiastic sense of mission. Muḥammad's claim to be divinely commissioned was meant to solve Medina's social conflicts, to overcome the city's religious and political disunity. Hence his mission was spiritual and political. He was now prophet, arbitrator, and commander. (This was a role similar to that of ancient Israel's "judges.") Political decisions were made with a claim to revelation. But Muḥammad's Medina was not a theocracy. Even under his leadership, no institutionalized rule existed. Problems were solved on an ad hoc basis. Solutions came with the claim of divine authorization; but no fully constituted polity emerged and no state was yet formed.

Why Politics and Religion Can Be Divorced

Medinan Suras call in one breath for obedience toward God and toward the prophet (Sura 4:13.136). The explanation is as follows: "In obeying the messenger, one obeys God" (Sura 4:80). After Muḥammad's death, however, it is not clear how this demand is to be met. How should Muslims now make their political and personal decisions? From an early stage, the Qur'an was consulted. Soon a leader was appointed: ḥalīfa, "caliph." But this designation was remarkably unclear. The title can mean "deputy" or "successor." Later it is interpreted to mean "vicar *of God*," whereas at first only "*ḥalīfa* of the *messenger* of God" was meant. The next question is this: Which of Muḥammad's roles would the caliph take? He had no new revelation to deliver, but neither was he merely the faithful's leader of prayer. He was *imām*, "model," in every respect. But he was also a military commander. When Islamic administration was institutionalized, the caliph was designated head of the state. But Islamic state theory would have to process three challenges.

Loss of unity. Though the *umma* was founded as the new, united people, it has been at war from the beginning. Who should lead? While the Sunnis-to-be elected Abū Bakr, others believe it must be Muḥammad's cousin and son-in-law ʿAlī. His supporters are called *šīʿat ʿAlī*, "Ali's party," the Shiites. Ali actually did become caliph, not the first after Muḥammad's death, not the second or third, but he was elected fourth caliph. When that happened (in 656), a rival from the influential Meccan Umayyad clan proclaimed himself a countercaliph. No wonder that Muslims call the inner division of their religious community *fitna* (in Arabic, "temptation"), the eschatological test (in New Testament Greek, *peirasmos*).

Loss of humility. As soon as the caliphate moved from Medina to Damascus, Islam lost its pioneering novelty. The caliphate established itself after the model of ancient rulers. The imam was no longer elected but came to power by dynastic succession. Proto-Sunni Islam had a ruling dynasty for the first time. The imam's rule was authoritarian. He now wore a crown and other insignia of power. Full of contempt, contemporary religious scholars now call the imamate *mulk*. This is a strong criticism, because it considers Islamic leadership to be "kingship." Royalty was a trap the transtribal, unireligious community sought to avoid. *Mulk* has yet another meaning in Arabic, "possession." The criticism points to another painful apostasy from early Islam. The ruler now regards power as his personal possession. But in reality, according to the early religious experts, it belongs to God alone. It is lent to the ruler to use for God's ends. What would be God's cause during, say, the Damascus caliphate (the Umayyad dynasty)? The caliph-imam is responsible for the spreading of the faith; and when the theological reflection speaks of God's cause, they mean those goals that go beyond private interests. "God" had thus come to mean the community itself.[5]

Loss of power. Under the Umayyad dynasty, the Islamic empire expanded west and east at a unique pace. But by the year 756, the caliphate began to lose importance. First, the emirate of Córdoba defected from the empire, and more territory came under other rulers. Although they had political power, they acknowledged the caliph since it made their own rule legitimate in Muslim eyes. Hence the caliphate's status shifted to a simply religious and symbolic power, as opposed to those holding "earthly power" (in Arabic, *sulṭān*). But at the end of the Russo-Turkish War (1768–74), the Ottoman sultan let himself be acknowledged by Russia (and so, internationally) as "sovereign caliph of the Muḥammadan religion." This was at the price of his claims of the Crimea. It was only then, at the end of the eighteenth century, that Ottoman imperial historiography developed the legend that in 1517 the last Abbasid "shadow caliph" transferred the caliphate to the Ottoman sultan. The Muslims, however, now found themselves under a caliphate that had no earthly power. Yet it gained a symbolic worldwide power, a power over the hearts of the Muslim people. The caliph had by now become something like a pope.

Kemal Atatürk abolished that caliphate in 1924. Why did the founder of modern Turkey consider banning a now harmless and powerless office necessary in the first place? By doing so Atatürk admitted that he did see its real influence and so confirmed the political power of religious symbols in general. After all, the caliphate appealed to a history long before the Republic of Turkey, and to a geography far beyond its national territory; the caliph was the reference point for all Sunni Muslims worldwide. A figure so charged with spiritual power could by no means be subordinated to the state apparatus. Every single day, its mere existence would have questioned the total claim of Kemalism. By its abolition, the caliphate proved that religion is the relativization of human power.

Islamic Political Theory: A Modern Example

Modern Muslim state theorists can use this de facto (albeit forced) separation process to justify the notion that a separation of powers, indeed a secular state, is something genuinely Islamic. That is the approach of the Sudanese scholar ʿAbdullāhi Aḥmad an-Naʿīm (1946–).[6] The argument runs in a three-step manner: legal-theologically, legal-historically, and social-theoretically. His legal-theological consideration is that according to Islamic law valid actions, such as the ritual prayer, presuppose the individual's religious intention (nīya). Already the Qur'an sees all people as solely responsible for themselves in the last judgment (Sura 53:38). Consequently, the individual is the focus of Islamic law. Furthermore, an-Naʿīm adduces the legal-historical observation that in classical Islam the state did not understand itself as either the focus or the source of Islamic law. But how can Islamic ideas then have public bearing? This is where his social-theoretical call is employed: convinced Muslims must introduce their views into society as a "civic reason."

Defensive Theory?

Classical Sunni state theory, however, followed a different path. The constant starting point was the question, Who is the valid imam? The question is relevant for salvation, as we will explain below. *Imām* here means more than "leader of the ritual prayer." It refers to the leader of the *umma*, of all the Muslims. And if you find out that you have joined the wrong group, you understand that here, you will never reach your goal. So which is the true *umma* under the true *imām*? The religious scholars play an ambivalent role in answering this question. As preachers they can castigate the Muslim leaders' decadence, and their forgetfulness of God, and call them back on the path of true Islam. A third generation Muslim stands out here, the ascetic (*zāhid*) Ḥasan al-Basrī (642–728). He put in front of the eyes of his contemporaries their situation, the fact that time was running by:

> O Adam's child, you are stuck between two mounts, which, as much as you may resist, do not stop with you night and day, until you come to the hereafter, and then either to paradise or to hellfire. So who would be in greater danger than you?[7]

This is to say that even if you try to fight against it with all your might, you have no chance. The end is drawing near inexorably, hastily; and what opens there isn't your certain elevation. There also lurks the abyss; lurks for all, including the sovereign.

Scholars of a less ascetic-prophetic character, however, prefer to come to terms with their present regime. We encounter Sunni religious scholars who, after each turn of events in a (so far) "un-Islamic" way, bend over backward to explain why the imamate in its current form does in fact comply with Islam in spite of everything. The Arabic word classically used for "polity" was *madīna* (meaning "place for legal decisions" or "city"). But from the nineteenth century on, Arabic uses a different word to refer to the state: *dawla*, which means "stroke of fate" or "change of time." That choice of word provides a deep and telling look into the history of Sunni political experience and theory, which can be summarized here in a few strokes.

The first Sunni political doctrine was *al-afḍal*, the notion that the "best man" is to become the imam. The generation after Muḥammad's death (632) elected their imams, first by acclamation then by vote. But from 661 onward, sovereignty was handed on through a ruling dynasty. By 750, suddenly, the dynasty experienced another change as several simultaneous caliphs were now in place. Was there a complete loss of power? It certainly meant the loss of temporal power, but religious experts now stressed that what really mattered was *spiritual* authority. Each time one could find theologians who would prove that the present form of government was precisely what Islam stipulated.

Why do the classical Sunni state theorists develop such implausible doctrines? One could describe their basic gesture as "cover thinking"—covering in the sense of justifying the status quo. But thus they themselves were also protected, namely from the punishment that a ruler could impose on his critics. There is, however, another reason for this. Legitimate rule is a soteriologically relevant question. The imam guarantees Muslims that they are in the right community, the salvific company. One can be sure one is in the salvific community if one can argue for the imam's legitimacy. To know which of the many pretenders is the true imam is therefore relevant for salvation. This opportunistic cover thinking unwittingly established something like a religious sphere in contrast to the political one. The caliph needs no temporal power, said the religious scholars; and they themselves had started constituting a clergy again.

Radical Criticism of Human Governance: The Kharijites

Now the entire political theory of Islam did not fall into what we have just called "cover thinking." One group was particularly consistent—in other words, particularly radical—the Kharijites (*Ḥawāriǧ*). Their name means, "those who move out (of the camp/into the fight)." The group was formed in 657 during a dispute over the question of who should succeed the third caliph (counting in the Sunni manner). The two main parties wanted to decide the question through an arbitrators' tribunal. It was to be based on Qur'anic instructions. That idea may seem particularly obedient to God; but the Kharijites objected that this was merely human judgment. If the decision is based on the Qur'an, then that means the text must be interpreted. What, if not consulting the text, was then the immediate divine decision? For the Kharijites, that was to fight! Why should the battle, of all things, be God's decision? Because here, they claimed, God decides the outcome. In order to justify their view, however, they also had to refer to a Qur'anic verse (and thus also interpret it)! From the Qur'anic "only God is entitled to decide" (Sura 6:57), referring to the Last Judgment, they inferred the principle *lā ḥukma illā li-llāh*—"God alone is entitled to decide." Thus, religion becomes a relativization of human power, but at the same time also the legitimation of violence.

The State: Hebrew Bible and Qur'an

Israel, by contrast, as seen in the Bible, does have institutions. While the state is a representation of the divine, it is also challenged, in the name of God. How does that compare to Islamic political thought?

Before answering this, we need to ask a fundamental question: What is Islamic? Shahab Ahmed (1966–2015) tackled exactly this question, and proposed, after some four hundred pages, the formula: Islamic is what is meaningful through hermeneutical engagement with the revelation to Muḥammad as pretext, text, and context.[8] One might also respond more succinctly, with a deliberately ambiguous formula: Islamic thinking is "the world understanding of the Qur'an." The world always tries anew to understand the Qur'an; and what is proclaimed and confirmed there as divine revelation allows us to understand the world. In Islamic thought, God, human beings (as individuals and community), and God's creation as a whole are living entities in relation to one another. Institutions, however, were originally foreign to Islamic thought.

From the beginning, the Islamic unfamiliarity with institutionalized power, in its importance and imperfection, has a consequence that can still be felt today. God, the charismatic leader, and the community can all live in fruitful tension with one another. God empowers both the ruler and the community. And God's will is almost synonymous with the common good. But the question of how to create structures that could justly regulate life seems absurd: a breach of trust, so to speak, in the God who cares for his people ever anew. As mentioned, the "state," something supposed to be stable, sounding almost "static" in our languages, is formed, in modern Arabic, from the verb "to change." *Dawla* means, first, "*turn, mutation, change*, or *vicissitude, of time*, or *fortune*,"[9] and only out of that and later "dynasty" and "state." Today, however, institutions can also be founded and justified on the Islamic side. It can be done either from the pragmatic Sunni thinking that one can always provide a fitting Islamic state theory. Or it can be done from the thought that God's will to order grants orders of life that are comprehensible also for critically thinking people. Due to Islam's early history, however, a greater skepticism toward institutions can always be expected.

The Politics of God's Kingdom and Church

Christianity's particular way to relativize earthly rule only becomes apparent when the gospel's own social form comes into view. That social form is not yet expressed appropriately through concepts like institution, movement, or mysticism, although there is truth in each of them (just as in "culture"). But the gospel's real social form is, as we have seen, sacramental, because it is sign and instrument at the same time. In this sense the gospel's social form is "Church." Church is the eschatological community becoming visible. To what extent should, and how can, the Church be critical of politics and critically political? This can only be understood in view of Jesus's proclamation of the kingdom of God.

THESIS

The Church represents the unrealized destiny of humanity: God's community of love. Thus, it unmasks all human-made order and power as provisional.

POLITICAL CHRISTIANITY

Our fundamental question is how religions relate to politics. The Hebrew Bible is critical of rulers, but it is not anarchic. Even Deuteronomy approves of an Israelite monarchy. It only limits royal power by clear legal conditions. There will only be a king if the people so wish, and he will be subordinate to God, the Torah, his "brothers," and to a system of independent public offices.

What is Christianity's specific contribution to the question? How political is Christianity, or, rather, how is Christianity political? At first sight, the Christian answer seems to be this: politics and religion, the less they have to do with each other, the better. But what does a closer look reveal?

The New Testament may occasionally acknowledge the peaceable achievements of the Roman Empire (Acts 24:2). The first Christian writings contain, however, also a harsh condemnation of Rome. Even the apocalyptic ciphers hardly hide what the New Testament seer thinks of Roman rule.

APOCALYPTIC CRITIQUE OF THE EMPEROR

1 And I saw a beast rising out of the sea, having ten horns and seven heads; and on its horns were ten diadems, and on its heads were blasphemous names. **2** And the beast that I saw was like a leopard, its feet were like a bear's, and its mouth was like a lion's mouth. And the dragon gave it his power and his throne and great authority. **3** One of its heads seemed to have received a death-blow, but its mortal wound had been healed. In amazement the whole earth followed the beast. **4** They worshiped the dragon, for he had given his authority to the beast, and they worshiped the beast, saying, "Who is like the beast, and who can fight against it?"

5 The beast was given a mouth uttering haughty and blasphemous words, and it was allowed to exercise authority for forty-two months. **6** It opened its mouth to utter blasphemies against God, blaspheming his name and his dwelling, that is, those who dwell in heaven. **7** Also it was allowed to make war on the saints and to conquer them. It was given authority over every tribe and people and language and nation, **8** and all the inhabitants of the earth will worship it, everyone whose name has not been written from the foundation of the world in the book of life of the Lamb that was slaughtered.

9 Let anyone who has an ear listen:
10 If you are to be taken captive,
   into captivity you go;
if you kill with the sword,
   with the sword you must be killed.
Here is a call for the endurance and faith of the saints.

11 Then I saw another beast that rose out of the earth; it had two horns like a lamb and it spoke like a dragon. **12** It exercises all the authority of the first beast on its behalf, and it makes the earth and its inhabitants worship the first beast, whose mortal wound had been healed. **13** It performs great signs, even making fire come down from heaven to earth in the sight of all; **14** and by the signs that it is allowed to perform on behalf of the beast, it deceives the inhabitants of earth, telling them to make an image for the beast that had been wounded by the sword and yet lived; **15** and it was allowed to give breath to the image of the beast so that the image of the beast could even speak and cause those who would not worship the image of the beast to be killed. **16** Also it causes all, both small and great, both rich and poor, both free and slave, to be marked on the right hand or the forehead, **17** so that no one can buy or sell who does not have the mark, that is, the name of the beast or the number of its name. **18** This calls for wisdom: let anyone with under-standing calculate the number of the beast, for it is the num-ber of a person. Its number is six hundred sixty-six. (Rev 13:1–18)

Another passage that is hard to understand! But this time, it is even expressly intended (see the last verse). The text must not endanger either the sender or the recipients.

The scene takes up elements of Daniel's vision. Daniel 7 had developed a highly critical political theology. Four empires had been shown to the prophet, all inhuman. The only human rule is when people do not rule over people (that was the point of his vision), but when God himself rules. How does the so-called Revelation of John continue this idea?

1 Just like the Old Testament prophet, the New Testament vision-ary sees a monster with ten horns (see Dan 7:7). There, they were inter-preted as ten rulers. And what about the blasphemous names? Rome's emperors used such titles for themselves. The emperor cult included the invocation of the ruler as *kyrios* and *sōtēr* as well as *divi filius*, that is, as "lord," "savior," "son of the god."

2 The dragon, which was already mentioned in Revelation's pre-vious chapter, intervenes and enthrones the monster.

3 Emperor Nero had killed himself; but rumor has it that he returned.

4 The rhetorical questions evoke Jewish forms of worship, and that is exactly what is happening in reality: the emperor is worshiped as the only one worthy of worship.

5 Forty-two months, 1,260 days: that is precisely how long Jerusalem was besieged by Titus until he conquered it in 70 CE.

11 Now that the beast has already received the honor actually due to Christ (Rev 5:9), it also receives a perfidious help, in the pseudomessias, that is, the antichrist. Who can that be? In any case, this must refer to some support institution of the Roman Empire, perhaps to its priesthood.

14 As in Daniel 3, people are now seduced to commit the shameful sin of making a ruler's image.

15 As is often the case in Greek mythology (but also in the magician's trick bag), the ruler's image now supposedly acquires life and voice—and becomes all the more convincing.

16 Instead of God's seal that Christians bear on their foreheads (Rev 7:4), the admirers of the emperor are now to imprint his badge of loyalty onto themselves.

17 Only those who belong to a guild may be economically active; but the guilds also demanded participation in the public cult.

18 Possibly, the solution to the gemantric puzzle is the numerical value of the Hebrew spelling of the words "Caesar Nero"—which is also documented in contemporary sources:[10] *qsr nrwn*.

The vision is a barely hidden fundamental critique of the Roman imperial rule and its ungodliness. Early Christianity was no supporter of the earthly "powers that be" (Rom 13:1, KJV) and their "political theology." The persecuted community rather hoped for a different justice, a different rule, a different Lord and Savior than the Roman emperor: the Lamb and his Father. With their names on their foreheads (Rev 14:1) and their hymns on their lips (Rev 14:3), the members of the Christian congregation have another prospect. After death, they will find rest because they have died in the Lord (Rev 14:13). But what is the reign of the Lamb and his Father like? Can it be realized on earth?

In search of an answer, Christian theologians have proposed various collocations of human power and God's rule. Some of the formulas they have found are of lasting significance. This is especially true of Luther's clarifying contrast of "two regiments." What does it entail? And, first, what were similar theological proposals on the way to Luther's solution?

Two Citizenships

The New Testament is the literature of a persecuted minority. Revelation was, consequently, able to juxtapose the community of the Lamb and the Beast of Rome in stark contrast. In St. Augustine's *City of God* (completed in 426), the circumstances can no longer be so clearly divided into two camps. Whether people belong to God's *civitas* is not decided according to place of residence, nor even according to creed, but according to the criterion of whether they follow Christ in their lives. So there is still a contrast between earthly and heavenly citizens; only now, one cannot divide people by mere eyesight.

Two Swords

A few generations after Augustine, Pope Gelasius I (d. 496) had another contrast to propose. He felt the need to defend himself, living in the "eternal Rome," against the emperor's constant interference, which came from the "new Rome," Constantinople. The new capital, he argued, should stay out of theological questions: such an encroachment into spiritual themes would not bring about unity of the empire, but the division of the Church. Thus in 494 Gelasius made a momentous terminological distinction. The pope, he contended, was not subordinate to the emperor in all questions. He distinguished between two areas of competence—state *potestas* and episcopal *auctoritas*: power over against authority. What is the source of episcopal authority? Jesus gave first to Peter, then to all his disciples, the "authority of the keys," namely to bind and to loosen; that is, to administer the forgiveness of sins in the name of God as relevant for eternal salvation (Matt 16:19; 18:18). Gelasius clearly had the handover of *exousia* in mind, Jesus's participatory liberating type of power, as earlier noted. Gelasius justified his distinction between imperial power and spiritual authority with a New Testament passage. At the Last Supper, when Jesus sees the hour of decision approaching and speaks of the equipment necessary for it, the disciples offer him two swords (Luke 22:38). He ambiguously says, "Enough!" That most likely means, "Stop it! We already have enough violence around us!" However, the answer can be heard as if he was approving of armed struggle: "Those two swords are enough to achieve my goals." The pope took the "two swords" discourse as justification for two areas of rule, each necessary, temporal power and spiritual authority.

During the medieval Church-state conflicts, in 1302 Pope Boniface VIII went so far as to decree that the secular world was subject to the spiritual. According to his famous bull *Unam Sanctam*, the emperor was subordinate to the pope. As surprising as this assumption of power may seem, the underlying concern is understandable. Which Christian would not want the Spirit of Christ to shape the world, life, and politics? The collocation is only misbegotten if it is the bishop of Rome, of all people, who dictates the empire's affairs. Neither priestly ordination nor theological erudition automatically qualify a person to be the better politician.

Two Realms

In this field, a millennium after Pope Gelasius, Martin Luther would achieve a breakthrough in theological and legal conceptualization. Must one subordinate oneself to the prince in all regards, even in matters religious? Is the bishop also entitled to wield the sword? In other words, should the Church have the right to force people against their will? Is the worldly sword subject to the spiritual sword? In other words, are the emperor's state decisions to be under pontifical control? Or, again: Should the spiritual *auctoritas* have political *potestas*?

No, says Luther, following Paul (Rom 13:3). There is only one sword, and it belongs to the worldly authority. Is the Church, then, subordinated to the state? Luther says it is not. Luther acknowledges "two kingdoms," or "two regiments," by means of which God rules.[11] The Reformer uses an image here from the last judgment (Matt 25:31–45). To the right of the universal judge stand the people transformed by the gospel. Here, without any compulsion, the Spirit of Christ rules. Here, the sword has nothing to say, the conscience everything. Luther declares, "For faith is a free work to which no one can be compelled; indeed, it is a divine work in the Spirit: external violence can neither force nor create it."[12] But there is also that other kingdom on the left, the *civitas terrena*, as Augustine called it, "the earthly state," where evil is powerful. Here, the "sword" is needed for physical security. Here, the state is responsible. Luther's two empires do not fall flatly apart. Christians do live in the realm on the right, but they can, indeed should, get involved in the "realm on the left." The two empires cannot be separated, they must be distinguished. Attacks from one side to the other are, however, not rare. A prince-bishop, or Caesaropapism, or a theocracy, contradict the free work of God's Spirit just as much as a religious war.

Spiritual and Secular: The Gospel Distinction

Why did that clear distinction of the religious and worldly spheres grow on the ground of the gospel, of all places? Blatant abuses of power undoubtedly provided an occasion for such ideas, but they did not only exist in the realm of Christianity. The oldest Christian texts, however, exhibit particular dispositions, which flourished after fifteen hundred years in a clear distinction between the state and the religious community. First, there is the opportunistic-egoistic injustice Jesus and his followers experienced on the part of the state, through persecution and execution, without fundamentally rejecting the political order. The first Christians accepted this worldly power, but only with regard to secular issues. No emperor could make decisions on eternal salvation. Second, in Jesus's actions (one may recall blind Bartimaeus or the tax collector Zacchaeus), and in his preaching (the shepherd, for instance, who leaves ninety-nine sheep behind to search for the one lost), a special interest in the individual is noticeable (Mark 10:46–52; Luke 19:1–10; 15:4). Third, the testimony to the Resurrection divides minds from the beginning. Faith, so the early Church recognized, is not an insight that can be produced by arguments, let alone by pressure. To be able to believe the testimony of Christ is a gift that is evidently not given to all. Fourth, the parable of the tares and the wheat instructs the Church to let also those live who do not correspond to the Christian expectations. To pull them out would also mean to eliminate the good (Matt 13:30). So one cannot produce purity of faith by force. This would destroy the entire field of faith. Fifth, for the first time in a religion, early Christian texts speak of the conscience, thus opening up a space of personal freedom for different life decisions (see 1 Cor 8:7).

Martin Luther was able to develop a distinction of lasting relevance. The formula of the two kingdoms can be justified well through New Testament motifs. It can be lived well in a functioning state and can be accepted by many non-Christians. However, Luther's distinction between spiritual and temporal power does not answer the crucial question: How do politics and religion, state and Church, go together? This requires another exploration.

146

THE POLITICS OF GOD'S KINGDOM

"The kingdom of God has come near." With this proclamation, Jesus himself summarizes the reason and relevance for his coming (Mark 1:15). The announcement needs to be heard at six different levels. What begins here with this proclamation are a new proximity, rule and authority, a new community, order and representation.

A New Proximity

On the one hand, Jesus speaks of temporal proximity. He thus follows John the Baptist's apocalyptic proclamation. John had just warned of the coming of judgment with the same words (Matt 3:2). This announcement is a shock, a call to responsibility. As for the Baptist, in Jesus's proclamation, the kingdom is near in the temporal sense: it is coming soon.

On the other hand, for Jesus, the kingdom has also come close in a local sense, and here his call differs from John's preaching. The nearness of the kingdom is not frightening, but joyful and accessible. Those seized by Jesus's proclamation also have the courage to enter the kingdom. The entry step is called "faith." Jesus enables his listeners to transcend themselves and trust that what is testified to here is indeed the kingdom of God, that one can already participate in it by entering into communion with Jesus, and that the new life that begins in this way is the fulfillment of all expectations.

But Jesus does not demand that faith be blind. In his actions, his contemporaries can experience and see the beginning of God's rule. It can be felt physically. Jesus "cast out many demons" (Mark 1:34). What is that? A question that only arises to people in "enlightened" environments. For many cultures, demonic obsession is an everyday phenomenon. One does not do justice to it by reducing it to pathologies that can be diagnosed in a different way, perhaps "scientifically." Possession and Jesus's exorcisms were nothing unique for his contemporaries, and neither were his healings. One had heard of other healers. Still, they were new, a bodily sign of God now overcoming the powers of evil. God's reign begins palpably.

The faith to which the proclamation of Jesus challenges and enables people is, then, risky. On the one hand, because it is a life investment. On the other hand, it is not blind, as if it lacked all evidence. People are free

147

to respond to Jesus's call. Many do not follow him, but rejection does not obstruct the growth of the kingdom. His call can grab people. Those who let themselves be seized, however, do not lose their freedom. They can live in a (previously unknown) authenticity. To enter into the freedom of God's kingdom means to finally be able to live one's own destiny. The kingdom of God is, however, not merely a call to the individual. Biblical talk of the kingdom of God is rather a truly political dynamic. In which sense? We need to consider that kingdom's new proximity from five more angles: the kingdom of God as new rule, new authority and community, new order, and as a new type of representation.

A New Rule

Jesus's proclamation that the kingdom of God is near is at the same time the answer to the question of who rules, and to the question of where God rules. Who rules? Early on, the visionary Balaam cannot help but call out a blessing on God's people:

> He has not beheld misfortune in Jacob;
>   nor has he seen trouble in Israel.
> The LORD their God is with them,
>   acclaimed as a king among them. (Num 23:21)

Many other nations have their human kings; in Israel, only God shall be king. The antimonarchy voices of Israel understand this as a rejection of any state order. In contrast to all other nations, which need powerful institutions, the people of God can find their order of life solely from their divine calling. However, there are also Israelites who support a monarchy for Israel. Like their opponents, they know the prophetic, state-critical "Only God Is King" doctrine. For the promonarchy Israelites, that does not mean a rejection of the state, but its spiritual relativization. Ultimate trust is not placed in institutions, but in God's acting through history.

The kingdom of God is, however, not just a question of whom to ultimately trust. It also has its place. Where is the kingdom of God? Jesus's proclamation gives a concrete answer to that. The answer is local, but it contains its own opening dynamics. When Jesus proclaims the nearness of the kingdom, when he testifies to it in his healing action, when he calls people to follow him: this is not a reference to looking for another place. Jesus says that the kingdom of God is "here"; and though not pointing to himself, his entire proclamation contains, in word and action, the message that the kingdom of God is coming through Jesus himself.

Some particular features of Jesus's actions, however, reveal that the "place" of God's kingdom is evolving. It is the wine that serves as Jesus's sign of recognition. He chooses twelve apostles precisely in order to represent the twelve tribes of Israel. Jesus declares the tax collector Zacchaeus ("also him") to be the son of Abraham (Luke 19:9). The lost, the erring, the forgotten are to be invited to the feast. What is happening here? The kingdom breaks in. Its anticipation becomes celebration, and of course Jesus does not celebrate alone. All Israel is to join in the feast. No one shall be excluded. Therefore, his rules for belonging to the kingdom of God are different from those of the Pharisees as the New Testament portrays them. It is true that the Pharisees are close to Jesus's basic convictions because they live a lay spirituality. That is, every Israelite should practice the priestly holiness of the temple, in everyday life at home. With this holiness profile Israel is to fulfill its vocation of being the witnessing people among the people. Jesus, by contrast, understands holiness as a process of transformation. It is not something that can be produced. Holiness is, then, purity of the heart, in the sense of a perceived dependence on God's mercy. To live holy, as God is holy (Lev 11:44; 19:2), means that Jesus is seized and transformed by the mercy of the heavenly Father. Thus, holiness becomes a vocation. Even the prostitute and the collaborator with the Roman regime should feel in themselves the dignity of belonging to that holy people. The people of God become the place of mercy. The kingdom of God is God's love overflowing in his people. For this reason, it is no specific territory, but the process by which the people are re-created. It is the process of the Spirit. Where is the kingdom of God? In the people from whom no one is excluded any longer. Therefore, the kingdom of God must not be limited, but expected, proclaimed, experienced, acknowledged, accepted, entered, celebrated, and witnessed. The fact that after Easter, even people who cannot ethnically belong are grasped with this new spirit of God's people, and begin to be counted among them, follows the same dynamic.

A New Authority

Right at the beginning of his public ministry, people sense that Jesus has a special authority. He can cast out demons, but even before

149

his first exorcism, people are "astounded" at his way of teaching (Mark 1:22). For it is also palpably with authority (*exousia*) that he teaches. Word and reality obviously come together in him in an unusual manner. What he says is becoming reality. This applies not only to the command against the unclean spirits, but also to his proclamation. When Jesus says that the kingdom of God is near, his listeners can enter into communion with God at the same time. Jesus himself received this authority (Matt 9:8), and he can pass it on to his disciples (10:1). But the authority is not an authorization to exercise power in the style of earthly kings. The royal rule (*basileia*) of God that begins is a healing reshaping of human relationships.

A New Community

From the beginning, the Gospel of Luke has a downright ironic relationship to earthly power. It lets the devil say that all the power (*exousia*) and glory of the kingdoms (*basileiai*) are left to him and that he passes it on to whomever he wishes (Luke 4:6). Luke will then present, during the Last Supper, how the new social order of God's kingdom forms the counterprogram to the power relations familiar to Jesus's disciples.

> A dispute also arose among them as to which one of them was to be regarded as the greatest. But he said to them, "The kings of the Gentiles lord it over them; and those in authority over them are called benefactors. But not so with you; rather the greatest among you must become like the youngest, and the leader like one who serves. For who is greater, the one who is at the table or the one who serves? Is it not the one at the table? But I am among you as one who serves.
>
> You are those who have stood by me in my trials; and I confer on you, just as my Father has conferred on me, a kingdom, so that you may eat and drink at my table in my kingdom, and you will sit on thrones judging the twelve tribes of Israel. (Luke 22:24–30)

In purely physical terms, the person sitting or reclining at the table is lower than those serving, who are on their feet. But, by reflection, one sees that the person serving is a servant, a subordinate. This initially banal remark suggests that the relationship between ruler and servant must be reconsidered continuously. The rulers of the world, as Jesus observes here, bear divine titles (ruling as lord, benefactors: in Greek, *kyrieuein, euergetai*, Luke 22:25). But the real rulers are not those who display dominion. A special place is given not to those who dominate, but to those who have walked the path of nonviolent, listening service with Jesus. And what is that special place? They will sit "at [his] table" and "on thrones judging" in his "kingdom," that is, in the community of God that is already livable now, but will be completely manifest only at the end of history. This can be understood as follows: the fellowship with Jesus celebrated in the meal will not end. And the lifestyle of loving existence for others (as practiced now during the meal) will prove to be the principle and criterion of true life.

A New Order

If the kingdom of God is political, how can its reshaping dynamics be lived in everyday life, which is often unfree? A key passage on the relationship between politics and faith may answer this.

> **13** They sent to him some Pharisees and some Herodians to trap him in what he said. **14** And they came and said to him, "Teacher, we know that you are sincere, and show deference to no one; for you do not regard people with partiality, but teach the way of God in accordance with truth. Is it lawful to pay taxes to the emperor, or not? Should we pay them, or should we not?" **15** But knowing their hypocrisy, he said to them, "Why are you putting me to the test? Bring me a denarius and let me see it." **16** And they brought one. Then he said to them, "Whose head is this, and whose title?" They answered, "The emperor's." **17** Jesus said to them, "Give to the emperor the things that are the emperor's, and to God the things that are God's." And they were utterly amazed at him. (Mark 12:13–17)

It is worthwhile to explore the passage verse by verse.

13 We are looking over the temple square, a few days before the Passover celebrations. One can imagine how charged the atmosphere is, because Israel remembers its peculiarity at this place: right here, in the midst of his elect, the Lord who led them to freedom wants to live; and Israel remembers exactly at this time its liberation. The forthcoming feast represents the exodus from the slave house. Guards patrol the temple walls. The occupiers want to eliminate immediately any sign of turmoil.

The emissaries of the Pharisees and Herodians represent the tension in their own way: the Pharisees stand for the purity of the whole people of Israel. No compromise should be made with the project of a uniform world culture that would, in theatres, temples, and submission to Rome, make God's people forget its particular history and mission. In other words, for the Pharisees, any adaptation to Hellenistic culture is out of the question. The Herodians by contrast stand for prosperous coexistence: better adapting than losing all influence. Thus, the trap opens at Jesus's feet.

14 The introduction to the question reminds us that an opportunistic compromise formula is ruled out, however great the pressure, however dangerous the situation may be. The "way of God" is the challenging ethic to which the Lord himself calls his people; but the "way of God" is also the manner in which God already acts on earth. The question poses a radical dilemma. For whether Jesus answers yes or no, he has always lost. Yes, paying taxes to the occupying regime means betraying the freedom God has given to his people. Not paying means revolution and its foreseeable suppression and thus even more submission than before.

The word for "tax" is Latin in the Greek text. The question mentions the *kēnsos*, the census. The theme is, after all, the Roman administration. But the questioners do not want to know the truth in order to be able to follow it. Rather, they want to let Jesus fall into the trap and thus fall into meaninglessness. Either he gives up the calling of God's people and loses his followers; or he proves to be a rebel and can be arrested and thus stopped. Jesus exposes to the questioners their own dishonesty. It would be honest to take a stand against him: to "profess" him or to "deny" him (see Matt 10:32–33). Thus, however, the actors, the hypocrites remain safely behind their masks. It is not their life they put at risk, but his.

15f. The coin depicted probably the Emperor Tiberius. His coins bore the inscription *Tiberius Caesar divi Augusti filius Augustus*. By asking the emissaries to show him a tax coin, Jesus says that he does not have one himself. By asking them what is on it, he speaks as a rabbi. The rabbis regularly respond to challenges by making the interlocutor give the answer himself. At the same time Jesus shows that it is impossible not to take sides. No one can remain a protected observer behind the actor's mask. Rather, his message is this: unlike myself, you already carry the world of the Roman occupation in your hands; you have proven to be familiar with this world that deifies its rulers.

17 Jesus's answer can be heard in five different ways.

On one level, his response is simply this: pay your taxes.

Second, he says that what they are holding in their hands does not belong to them, and they should keep their hands off worldly things.

Third, Jesus says that money belongs to the emperor, and everything else to God.

Fourth, he asks if they are really ready to give God what belongs to God. And what is God's due? Jesus also seems to suggest that if the emperor's name is on the coin, it belongs to him and should be returned to him. But in reality everything belongs to God. Jesus thus calls them as if saying, serve him, entrust your life to him, expect your liberation from God, and your vocation to cooperate in it. To love God undividedly is the most important thing of all, Jesus will add (Mark 12:30).

Finally, however, he says something else. One might blame him for avoiding a clear answer. Is he a coward? No. He says that every person has to answer the crucial questions for himself or herself. Jesus does not want to win a debate with his answer, and he certainly does not want an uprising. He wants to win the consciences of those who listen to him. But for this, he must speak in such a way that the other can be grasped in freedom. That is what he has done with his complex answer.

A New Representation

Let us summarize our findings on the basis of a paradigm that has already been introduced. To rule is to represent. Eric Voegelin used this idea to describe the patterns in which ordered polities justify themselves. The public order of power may represent cosmic structures, a divine election, social relations, or the individual's rationality. Is the kingdom of God as proclaimed by Jesus also to be understood as such a representation? The concept of representation is actually helpful here. But we discover a new form of representation. Jesus lives from the experience with the one he calls his Heavenly Father. In his own realm, God's rule is, according to Israel's religious imaginary, already realized: an ordered community, the heavenly court (Ps 89). That is the community of loving service. In his public ministry, Jesus now enables people on earth to take part in this heavenly community. Whoever enters Jesus's community enters the kingdom of God. So, from now on, people can live with dual citizenship (Phil 3:20; 1:22). They are already experiencing the joy of God's boundless communion. This is manifested in a detachment that liberates people. They are liberated for service, that is, for participation in the life of God's kingdom. In its dynamic, therefore, representation does not legitimize an existing earthly power system. The heavenly order itself becomes the impetus for the new order on earth. This is what the Lord's Prayer asks for in its line "on earth as it is in heaven" (Matt 6:10). Thus, every earthly relationship can, and indeed should, become an image of heaven, here, in history, including relationships of responsibility and leadership. All earthly construction, however, will until the end of history lag behind the heavenly community thus represented.

Is the idea of the image of God's kingdom on earth not simply the Christian continuation of the old cosmo-theological forms of representation? No; because earthly justice, power, and responsibility do not receive from the community of God, from "heaven," their legitimacy, but their measure and their hope. The kingdom of God on earth is a project for the future. It is not represented by an earthly system of power, but by a person, by Jesus. But he also wants his community to represent, as Christ's body, the future of heaven until his return. Thus, humanity can see its destiny: humanity's destiny, that is to say our vocation, our yet unfulfilled nature, our goal. What is human destiny? It is life in the infinite communion of love in God. This presentation of humanity's future is a source of confidence, orientation, and strength for those who recognize that so far nothing on earth corresponds fully to the kingdom of God. The anticipatory presentation of the kingdom in the Church, however, puts into question and puts into its limits all earthly rule. If the Church is thus relativizing (rather than replacing) human rule, it is a protection against totalitarian claims to power.[13]

THE POLITICS OF THE CHURCH

The kingdom of God, proclaimed by Jesus and presented by anticipation in the Church, is critical of human power over human beings. But it does not want to abolish human power. It wants to transform it. How does Christianity want to achieve this? Primarily, the Christian witness does not resort to the means of the critical word, nor to the means of exemplary action (both are necessary). But the specifically Christian way of the religious community to pursue political transformation is, as we have seen, sacramental. That is, Christianity witnesses, through the visible community, in its constitution and existence, its celebrations and signs—that the future of humanity is reconciled life in God. Only from there flow the words (proclamation, science, dialogue, and criticism) and actions (aid for the suffering, pastoral care, and education). The visible Church is a constant reminder to those in power that rulemaking, decision-making, and acting are never able to produce paradise on earth. Thus, human rule gets its necessary relativization and orientation.

That is how the New Testament's political theology could be summarized. Already such a summary is of course more than the result of a text study. Otherwise, all generations of Christian exegetes would have come to a similar result. The political theology of Christianity in the course of the last two millennia was, however, largely a history of incomprehension and instrumentalization. Our interpretation of the text hopes that we have learned from old mistakes. Some of the most important misinterpretations (and some of their best solutions) are now to be studied.

Political Religions

In his 1951 Chicago lectures, Eric Voegelin again asked how totalitarian ideologies came into being. He now sharpened the descriptive model of his Vienna days, studying the Christian history of ideas, proposing an explicatory model. Can Voegelin's new (now American) approach be reexpressed, reconstructed in an explicitly theological manner? Let us give it a try.

Christ's call is the challenge to believe in the kingdom of God, which is only slowly becoming visible. As such it contains an element of uncertainty. But the presence of the kingdom of God can be celebrated in an anticipating way by the disciples: as Church. Uncertainty or celebration—in this consists the fundamental tension between "still awaiting" and "already activating" the kingdom. On the one hand, the faithful in distress expect God's final conspicuous revelation. On the other hand, the kingdom of God can be sensed already, indeed can be brought to bear in the world by believers. Consequently, two types of Christian life emerge. Those who "await" look out from the present concerns toward God's redeeming coming, which will put an end to history and its suffering. Thus they live in the "not yet." Therefore, they are "not of this world." One such "awaiting" tendency we have just encountered in the Book of Revelation. Constantine, on the other hand, was inclined toward the other type: "activating." An "activating" life recognizes God's coming into the group of the faithful already now. Consequently, the eschaton is now, and the "activating" people feel that they are already perfected. They have everything that is needed to shape the world. They have the knowledge and the strength. For they have the spirit. One can see how far this attitude is still Christian; but at the same time one can already sense its predisposition to radicalization. The faithful of the "activating" type experience the spirit so much as given to them that they believe they possess it. They no longer have to receive it again and again in gratefully surprised humility. Rather, they think they already have knowledge (*gnōsis*).

With this, Voegelin introduces another of his analytical key concepts, that of the "Gnostic." What follows is predictable. Any reference to a supraworldly reality, in front of which one is small, is removed from sight, resulting in a loss of transcendence. Such movements take a "religioid" outlook; they present themselves as something *like* a religion. They claim to know the meaning of history and claim to be able to bring it about. Such a movement is, in this sense, a "political religion."

Where did the breakthrough from a Gnostic loss of transcendence to the ideological pseudoreligion happen? Voegelin locates it at the end of the Middle Ages. The thirteenth-century Italian city-states instilled into society a new sense of security, which had an effect on spiritual life in two ways. Either one longed for the insecurity represented by the gospel, and allowed it to call out oneself. St. Francis of Assisi is the best example of this desired insecurity. On the other hand, one might also take the enthusiasm, which for Francis was a surprising gift, into one's own hands; what will happen thus is, one will, in order to overcome

156

insecurity, ring in the last phase of history, that is, the autonomy of the Spirit. Joachim of Fiore is the epitome of such a theology of history.

Political Church

Voegelin was a political scientist, but it seems that we were able to reconstruct theologically without distortion his dual scheme of how Christians can relate to the end of history. It thus pointed all the more clearly to a trap in Christian eschatology. If one lives the kingdom of God "already now" and the Spirit as "possession," the other dimension of the Christian faith is cancelled. This other dimension is to acknowledge that the end is still to come, and thus also our perfection. Voegelin emphasizes the "not yet." Indeed, in order to avoid all sorts of Gnosticism, he sees human knowledge so strongly restricted that *meaning* cannot be an object of perception for us at all. He writes, "The meaning of history, thus, is an illusion."[14] Here, Voegelin possibly lacks a conceptual tool from theology. The life of the Church, just as much as its theology, must always be characterized by mutually balancing movements. That would mean to stitch together programmatic terms by means of what is called a "Catholic And"[15]: already and not yet, faith and works, scripture and tradition. It is helpful that Voegelin is not satisfied with some vague "both." But the solution is neither in a dogmatic "and" nor in cancelling one side: theology must try to name the dynamics that hold both sides together.

Political Sacrament

Voegelin warns against a claimed possession of the spirit, as practiced by the Gnostics, and rightly so. But should the Church suppress every celebrated presence of salvation? Is every attempt to recognize meaning within history "Gnostic"? The category that helps here was mainly introduced and explained by Wolfhart Pannenberg. It has already been used above to explore God's nearness: the dynamic of *anticipation*. In joyful expectation, the coming kingdom can already be experienced; but it has not yet been fulfilled. Seized by the good news, people can already now take part in the way of life of the future kingdom of God. But they know how much they still lag behind it. In God's great actions, especially in the resurrection of Christ, the meaning of the

157

world as God's history of salvation can already be recognized; but that will remain a controversial recognition.

The conceptual tool of anticipation is relevant also for describing the Church's political role. The Second Vatican Council was able to rediscover the Church as sacrament. Now, this characterization becomes more comprehensible. The Church is, in the world, the anticipatory sign of the coming kingdom of God. It is not the kingdom of God. But it testifies to its coming and thus allows people to experience it in advance and to connect with it. Anticipation therefore contains not only a dynamic of representation, but also of self-distinction: we are not the kingdom.

The dynamic of self-distinction also clarifies the Church's role in relation to human power. Not only by doing something specific, but already because it exists, the Church testifies to the coming of God's kingdom. It thus relativizes all human constructions of power as provisional. It thus criticizes all power infringement as arrogant presumption. It thus orients all human models of societal life toward the lifestyle of God's kingdom, that is, toward respectful, serving love. And it thus directs all human conceptualizations of humanity toward the human destiny as eternal community of all in God.

From God's Kingdom to the Weakness of the Witness: Looking Back and Looking Forward

How do Judaism, Islam, and Christianity fulfill their task of being a critical counterpart to politics? Judaism has developed a particular self-understanding through its multiple exodus experiences, but above all by its diaspora life after the destruction of the Second Temple. Jews can see themselves as the nation among the nations, testifying to God's presence and justice in front of all people.

For centuries and in many places, Islam was the majority religion, and that was taken for granted. A minority situation, by contrast, was often seen as an occasion for worry. Today a Muslim self-interpretation does not have to proceed from the regret that there are still non-Islamic areas. Rather, Muslims can see, in a new way, their own task in God's plan; they can recognize themselves as one voice among many and discover this as an interesting challenge: as a minority in many nontraditionally Islamic countries and as a voice in the global maelstrom of voices. Now, they find themselves in a situation similar to Islam's early years. The Qur'an urges people in the name of God to work for the establishment of God's polity.

A politically significant impulse lurks in the Christian self-designation as "Church." Long before the birth of Christ, the Jewish translators of the Hebrew Bible had reproduced *qāhāl* in Greek by *ekklēsia*: Israel's worshiping "assembly." Here, one can sense a divine vocation that differs from the other nations: *ek-klēsia* is the community "called out." However, for the Greeks, *ekklēsia* at first did not stand for an exodus community. Rather, it referred to the citizens' council. The self-designation of Christianity as *ecclesia* (Church) indicates, then, at the same time life in a special vocation and politically public life. In its name, the Church claims to be more than a particular people. Its name reminds us that despite all its distinctiveness, the community of Christ represents the whole of society.[16]

Christian faith therefore lives with the hope that all may be one, and the Catholic Church sees itself as a sign and instrument for the unity of all humanity.[17] For centuries, however, the Church was a persecuted minority. It was therefore able to produce a self-image based on Israel's vocation: that of the nation among the nations, the people among the peoples. The Church of the peoples recognized itself as accepted into the people of God in order to make visible what the destiny of humanity is, the communion of all, ready to serve, in which the particularities of each individual are not blurred, but come to their fullness.

In late antiquity, the Church adopted a model of Christian presence that resembled anything but a persecuted minority. The Church was declared the religion of the state. The Roman Church officially advocated this as Christianity's ideal realization until the twentieth century. Only with the Vatican II declaration *Dignitatis Humanae* (1965) did Catholicism move away from that aspiration. The claim, however, remains that there should be a Vatican City State, albeit tiny, that does not belong to any other national territory. That claim is different from the idea of a state religion. With a territory that is not subordinate to any other state, the Church can rather dialogue with every nation state.

Caesaropapist theologies feed themselves on this opinion: "We can only shape the world if we are a state religion." Western Christianity was able to free itself from this notion in the wake of the Reformation. The transformation came at a bloody cost and was forced upon the Catholic Church. An emerging bourgeoisie resisted Church paternalism, and intrareligious wars required a legal and theological shift. The focus of the creed was no longer the state but the person. Thus Christians could once again shift back to their original foundation. The texts had always been transmitted, and the rites had always been celebrated. Christians were therefore theoretically able at any given time to know that their beginning was a story of persecution, that the founder did not answer violence with counterviolence but with self-commitment, and that for this reason they had actually always proclaimed the way of humble justice and reconciliation. But they had not always lived it. They had not always sensed the mystery of *infirmitas* (in Latin), of weakness (in Greek, *astheneia*, 2 Cor 12:9). Only when this came to bear again could state, society, and religious community become distinguishable spheres of activity.

From that, however, misunderstanding arose, too: the notion that faith had no public role and religion was a private matter. In fact, by contrast, each of the three spheres (society, state, and religion) must assume important tasks in front of the other two and *for* the other two. For that task, the religious community does not need any physical force. Precisely a Church that affirms its weakness and its poverty gets a new role in society, the role of witness. It applies to itself the claim of justice, gives a voice to poverty and the poor, and can thus, in its weakness, influence society and contribute to the shaping of state structures. How a religious community presents poverty and how it inspires society: those are the themes of the following two chapters.

WEAKNESS

Previewing the Fifth Chapter

The preceding chapter argued that the kingdom of God, as breaking forth in the person of Christ, is indeed political. It neither legitimizes nor delegitimizes human power over people. But it relativizes such power. This now allows us to unfold the political theology of the kingdom of God, to which we can only witness *in poverty*. Poverty again opens a double perspective for the next chapter.

People who sense the need and the hope for a better world will open themselves more easily to God's new life, to God's coming kingdom. Already in this respect, the poor are the criteria for a way of life corresponding to the message of Christ. But the kingdom is not only an attitude, but also active care for the poor. Indeed, the criterion for world shaping, in view of the kingdom of God, must be more than attention to the poor. It must be integrating the disadvantaged as participants in creative action.

One can only witness to the kingdom of God in poverty. That means it cannot be enforced by external power. The way of a serious religious testimony can only be to grasp hearts and convince consciences, with the power of weakness, in humble testimony to acknowledged truth. We will explore this in light of the intriguing Habermasian formula that religion is a consciousness of what is missing.

In those various senses, we can now discuss religion as representation of weakness.

5

Religion as Representation of Weakness

Father Pedro Arrupe (1907–91) was Superior General of the Society of Jesus from 1965 until the summer of 1981, when a cerebral thrombosis disabled him. Only months before that, a fellow Jesuit had encouraged him to relay his spiritual journey. One of the events he shared was this:

A few years ago I was visiting one of the Jesuit provinces in Latin America. I was invited to celebrate Mass in a local neighborhood, in a slum (*favela*) which was the poorest in the region, they tell me. About one hundred thousand people were living there in the mud because this district was located in a low-lying area which flooded every time it rained.

I gladly accepted because I know from experience that we learn much when we visit the poor. We do a great deal of good for the poor, but they, on their part, teach us many things.

The Mass was held in a small open building which was in a very poor state of repair; there was no door, and the dogs and cats came in and went out freely. Mass began with hymns accompanied by a self-taught guitarist, and the result was marvelous. The words of the hymn went: "Loving is giving of oneself, forgetting oneself, while seeking what will make others happy." Progressively as the hymn continued I felt a lump in my throat. I had to make a real effort to continue the Mass. These people seemed to possess nothing and yet they were ready to give of themselves to communicate joy and happiness.

My homily was short. It was more of a dialogue; they told me things that one rarely hears in solemn discourses, very simple things, but at the same time profound and touchingly sublime. A little old woman said, "You are the Superior of the Fathers, aren't you? Well, sir, a thousand thanks, because your Jesuit priests brought us the great treasure we were lacking, what we needed most, Holy Mass."

At the consecration I elevated the Host and perceived in the absolute silence the joy of the Lord which is found among those whom he loves. A bit later, while distributing Communion, I noticed big tears like pearls on many of these faces; faces which were dry, hard, baked by the sun. They recognized Jesus, who was their only consolation. My hands were trembling.

After Mass, a big devil whose hang-dog look made me almost afraid said, "Come to my place. I have something to give you." I was undecided; I didn't know whether to accept or not, but the priest who was with me said, "Accept, Father, they are good people." I went to his place; his house was a hovel nearly on the point of collapsing. He had me sit down on a rickety old chair. From there I could see the sunset. The big man said to me, "Look, sir, how beautiful it is!" We sat in silence for several minutes. The sun disappeared. The man then said, "I didn't know how to thank you for all you have done for us. I have nothing to give you, but I thought you would like to see this sunset. You liked it, didn't you? Good evening." And then he shook my hand.

As I walked away, I thought, "I have seldom met such a kindhearted person." Many indeed are the things I learned thanks to that Mass among the poor. What a contrast with the great gatherings of the powerful of this world.[1]

Option for the Poor

For theologians like the Catalan Jesuit Jon Sobrino (1938–), the poor are a *locus theologicus*, that is to say, a source of theological knowledge.[2] What is meant by that?

THESIS

The writings of Israel, of the Church, and of Islam see a particular closeness between God and the poor, between the faithful and the poor, between faith and poverty.

JUDGING FOR THE POOR

The prophet Isaiah proclaims a terrible punishment for Jerusalem. Even the mighty trees will be cut down. But then his tone changes. He promises a new shoot from the stump of Jesse—that is, a new king from David's dynasty. His kingdom will bring about, the prophet declares, cosmic peace: wolf and lamb will be friends. How will the new ruler bring about such a transformative shaping of the world?

> The spirit of the LORD shall rest on him,
> the spirit of wisdom and understanding,
> the spirit of counsel and might,
> the spirit of knowledge and the fear of the LORD.
> His delight shall be in the fear of the LORD.
>
> He shall not judge by what his eyes see,
> or decide by what his ears hear;
> but with righteousness he shall judge the poor,
> and decide with equity for the meek of the earth;
> he shall strike the earth with the rod of his mouth,
> and with the breath of his lips he shall kill the wicked.
> Righteousness shall be the belt around his waist,
> and faithfulness the belt around his loins. (Isa 11:2–5)

What the new, spiritually gifted king does (as suits a ruler) is "to judge" (*š-p-ṭ*). A king thus equipped, and wise, will not judge by appearance and hearsay; rather, he shall "decide with equity for the meek of the earth" (Isa 11:4). Literally, the verse says in Hebrew, "In uprightness will he decide for the poor of the earth" (*y-k-ḥ* hif., *lǝ-ʿanwêæræṣ*). This passage is the only place where the Bible explicitly uses the plural expression "for the poor."

Since the 1960s, the Catholic Church has insisted on a preferential option for the poor. What does "option" mean here? In the light of Isaiah's prophecy, three dimensions emerge:

- An option consists of responsible decision-making that establishes law and justice. But isn't this alleged justice biased when it says that it decides for a particular group? People tend to favor those from whom they expect favors: the powerful and the rich. That is why there has always been an imbalance. That is why one is not impartial in not taking sides. Rather, fair judgment does not judge the other according to their current rank and reputation. Fair judgment opposes the imbalanced inclination to support the powerful; it promotes those who fall out of their society's usual support structures. Their true face, dignified and valuable for all, may be obscured by their present situation. One therefore needs an eye for human dignity, because people's real dignity is often invisible. Since our greed and lust for power keep pressing, resolute countermeasures are vital. Equal treatment means to advantage the disadvantaged in order to bring them into the realm of justice. That is what makes necessary precise analysis and conscious choice; and that is "option."
- What shines through in this is the "historic Or," of which Johann Baptist Metz was speaking, in contrast to the "nonhistorical And." People have to make choices. An option is a real possibility for action (that is why we sometimes say, "That is not an option"). But an option is not a detailed decision; it is, rather, a whole attitude, a whole path. An option consists of the choice for one or the other world. To call it choice does not mean that either would be good. Moses puts the choice before the people of Israel when they enter the promised land and immediately tells them their choice's consequence. You are faced with the decision for life; the alternative would be death: "Choose life" (Deut 30:19). Consequently Isaiah, too, places "deciding for

166

the poor" in the imaginary, indeed, in the project of a new, reconciled world.

• In the course of St. Ignatius Loyola's *Spiritual Exercises*, the dynamics of such an option manifest themselves. My "election" (choice or option) proves to be that I assent to God electing me.[3] God has a purpose for us and a calling for me. My option is nothing arbitrary; it is, rather, acknowledging my destiny.

The Christian ethos, however, does not only *care for* the poor. Christianity does not yet live up to its vocation if it sees itself alone as the Church *for* the poor. There is a difference between a Church *for* the poor, and a Church *of* the poor. In the first case, the poor are objects of Church action; in the second, the poor are part of such action, hence subjects. In such reflections, a fundamental rethinking is already adumbrated. We have to explore it more exlicitly. The Qur'an, too, contains traits of such rethinking. Let us, therefore begin with a Sura.

STUDYING THE QUR'AN—SURA 93: OVERCOMING MEMORY

The tradition of Muslim exegesis considers Sura 96 the first to be revealed. After all, it begins with the divine command that sounds like an order directly to the preacher: *iqra*'—"Read!" or "Recite!" thus "Let it become public Qur'an!" (similar to Isa 29:12). But it is more probable that the Qur'an was not something so public from the very beginning: the way out of inwardness rather led via comprehensible steps into the outspoken sermon. Rather than Sura 96, it is probably the following text that is Qur'an's oldest passage. It documents the transition from personally experiencing God to publicly proclaiming God.

Sura 93 *aḍ-Ḍuḥā* – Dawn

In the name of God, the merciful Mercifier!
1 By the morning brightness;
2 and by the night when it grows still!
3 your Lord has not despised you, nor does he abhor you,
4 and the future will be better for you than the past;
5 your Lord is sure to give you so much that you will be well satisfied.

6 Did He not find you an orphan and shelter you?
7 Did He not find you lost and guide you?
8 Did He not find you in need and make you self-sufficient?
9 So the orphan: do not be violent with them!
10 The beggar: do not chide them!
11 The blessings of your Lord: tell them!

Let us once again explore a text in depth.[4]

1–2 We find such a series of oaths at the beginning of many Suras, and a similar anticipated confirmation is already known from pre-Islamic soothsayers. Combining times of day and prayer of supplication is also a motif already known from the Psalms. The most conspicuous biblical parallel to Sura 93 is Psalm 22, which begins,

> My God, my God, why have you forsaken me?
>   Why so far from helping me, from the words of my groaning?
> O my God, I cry by day, but you do not answer;
>   and by night, but find no rest. (Ps 22:1–2)

The following Qur'anic verse also seems to take up that psalm:
3 God is said to be neither despising nor abhorring; this recalls,

> For he did not despise or abhor
>   the affliction of the afflicted;
> he did not hide his face from me,
>   but heard when I cried to him. (Ps 22:24)

The Sura shows God's work to the addressee, God's saving action here and now. But who is speaking, and who is the addressee? "Thy Lord" does not despise, but gives abundantly. Is, then, an angel of consolation speaking? It is also possible that Muḥammad reminded himself of God's good deeds. But here, in a unique way, a transition can be observed. One may imagine a small circle of confidants around Muḥammad. Whether he now is speaking to himself, *in front of* the others, *to* the others, whether he is speaking in someone else's name or not, cannot really be discerned. What we witness here is the formative process of the Qur'anic proclamation.

Equally ambiguous is the time of consolation, as we will see in the next verse.

4 Someone listening to the Qur'an later will understand that the hereafter is better than this world; but the words can also simply mean, "That which comes later is better for you than the first": a proverb, generally speaking, or a promise of future consolation and salvation, or a reminder of what the listener has already experienced. It is in this sense, that we now hear the triple question "Has God not...?" Here the Sura's style is "Deuteronomic memory." In the Song of Moses, we were already told of the Lord, who is Israel's rock:

> Is he not your father, who created you,
>> who made you and established you? (Deut 32:6b)

That song will then remind us of God's great deeds and call us to faithfulness. Though without the use of rhetorical questions, Deuteronomy knows such memories, in what is almost a chorus refrain. Three times, the admonition runs, "Remember that you were a slave in the land of Egypt" (Deut 5:15; 15:15; 24:18). Here, the Torah practices a renewing remembrance of grace. One might speak of an "overcoming memory." Let us explain this concept. In fact, it works on six levels: First, it is *humiliating* for the now well-off person to be reminded of what they have overcome: their once low status, miserable, pitiful, at the mercy of others. But then the overcoming memory causes, out of grateful joy, a sense of one's own *dignity*. God has favored me, gifted me by surprise, has advantaged me. From this follows the *confidence* that God's care will carry me reliably. So I will be able to overcome future sufferings. But the overcoming memory also aims at *empathy*: because you have experienced it yourself, you know how the needy person feels. The reminder helps you to overcome your selfish block. The goal each time then is that the person thus addressed should take *care* of those who are in need now, but also that the memory should be *celebrated*. The "overcoming memory" of the Qur'an does the same. The overcoming memory also refers to the overcoming of one's own plight, of fear, of self-centeredness and, from that, of injustice.

6–8 These verses may be a reminder of Muḥammad's own childhood. Tradition has it that his father had died already before the child was born; six years later, he also lost his mother. Nevertheless, he gained prestige, mainly because of his commercial success and a marriage: the rich (twenty-five years older) merchant Ḥadīǧa, for whom he worked, offered to marry him. All this can be remembered in gratitude. What follows is a call to care for the poor.

9–10 Care for the poor is not only a concern of the early Suras. When the Qur'an becomes the founding impulse of the new *civitas* in Medina, the early call to solidarity will turn into an institution: a regulated levy, a tax to be paid. It will keep its original intention, but will also take over other areas of concern. Sura 9:60 will determine that it is meant to subsidize the poor and needy, but it will also cover the tax collectors themselves and the spread of Islam: winning new members through gifts and through battles. The tax's Arabic names are suggestive. The Qur'an calls it either *aṣ-ṣadaqa*, or *az-zakāt*: both words are pre-Islamic, most probably taken from Jewish circles. Do these terms disclose their underlying logic? They give interesting hints. Either, one calls the tax "justice" (*aṣ-ṣadaqa*), because it is just to give to those who cannot afford it themselves; or one calls it "purification" (*az-zakāt*, sg.) thus appealing to a sacrificial logic.

11 Just like the concluding ten verses of Psalm 22, the end of the Sura also shows that the renewing remembrance of grace, the "overcoming memory" is not only aiming at regaining confidence and caring for the poor, but also at confessing the great acts of God:

> Future generations will be told about the Lord,
> and proclaim his deliverance to a people yet unborn,
> saying he has done it. (Ps 22:30–31)

The problem that must be solved is not that there are poor people, but that those who can help do not. Early Suras, therefore, work with a method of motivation already known in Deuteronomy: that renewing remembrance, which at the same time creates joy and empathy; the "overcoming memory," as we called it. The poor are still the object of the action of the faithful here; but a decisive step has been taken when memory is not only a call to action, but also shows that even those who can help today have themselves experienced shame and poverty. Such texts want to create a solidarity that is not duty ridden or bothersome, but self-evident. Indeed, these proclamations want to create even more: Just like in the Bible, institutionalized forms of protection for the poor, legal security, and charitable collections are also emerging in the Qur'an. The option for the poor can be seen as a *decision*; now it has, secondly, been rediscovered as an *experience*, the overcoming memory that creates solidarity; but here, vaguely, a third step is already being suggested.

CHURCH OF THE POOR

Reading the Qur'an together with similar verses in pre-Islamic poetry or the Bible, that is, reading the Qur'an by listening to its "intertexts," can turn into an exercise merely in philological-mechanical perfectionism. But it might also bring out particular characteristics that would otherwise remain unseen: particular emphases either added in the Qur'an or omitted by it. The point of intertextual interpretation is not to accuse a Sura of plagiarism. Rather, some sharp observations that promote the Qur'an's appreciation can only be made intertextually. It can now be said, for example, that the eschatological perspective, which will become a key feature of the Qur'an soon, is still irrelevant to the Torah, the Psalms, and Israel's early prophecy. On the other hand, the Qur'an also omits a Hebrew Bible motif. As we have just seen, Sura 93 probably echoes Psalm 22. But the psalm had set an accent that the Qur'an does not develop.

> The poor shall eat and be satisfied;
>> those who seek him shall praise the LORD.
>> May your hearts live forever! (Ps 22:26)

Who are the poor mentioned here? The poor are not only those to whom food is to be given. Rather, the Psalms are marked by a trace of the poor, who are themselves the people speaking here, the people at prayer. The royal enthronement hymn examined earlier (Ps 72) was praying for the king:

> May he judge your people with righteousness,
>> and your poor with justice. (Ps 72:2)

If the parallelism of Hebrew poetry says the same thing in both half verses (twice, only in different words), then one can conclude that the members of God's people are at the same time "the oppressed, the poor" ('ănāwîm).[5] Those who pray the Psalms, then, not only remember their own former poverty—the Deuteronomic remembrance—but come before God *as* the poor themselves. In the Bible an increasing identification with the poor can be observed. The poor are with you. First, the addressee himself has been poor—then, the person who hears and prays scripture is becoming one of the poor.

Pope St. John XXIII revivified that identification that can be discovered in the spirituality of the Psalms. One month before the opening of the Second Vatican Council, on September 11, 1962, in a radio message, he listed the areas where he hoped the Council would provide clarification. As the last area, he mentioned, "When facing the underdeveloped countries, the Church presents herself as what she is and she wants to be: as Church of all, and particularly, the Church of the Poor."[6] Thus, the preferential option was already making itself felt in 1962. If you want to do justice to all, you must favor the disadvantaged. But more than that: here, a different self-understanding of the Church enters into the papal discourse. The Church's fundamental call is confronting all present social conditions and all present Church conditions. It is the Church of the poor and wants to be so. What exactly does that mean? In order to answer that, we have to engage in dialogue between public objections, Church practice, and New Testament texts.

The majority of the Christians. John XXIII was speaking in the name of the universal Church, the majority of which lives in poverty. On the one hand, most Catholics live in countries experiencing severe economic, social, cultural, and political trouble. On the other hand, in many countries, Catholics are statistically poorer than other parts of the population. The pope recalls that St. Paul had a similar experience some nineteen hundred years earlier. In the early Church, there were few affluent people: "Consider your own call, brothers and sisters: not many of you were wise by human standards, not many were powerful, not many were of noble birth" (1 Cor 1:26). Is the "Church of the poor" merely a description of the Church, the condition that has to be accepted bitterly, rather than the Church's vocation, its definition, its destiny?

In spirit. The Church of the poor is not only a description of an actual, material state that has occurred but might also not have come about. Poverty is, rather, a characteristic of Jesus's proclamation. The most basic evangelic form of speech reveals this: the Beatitudes (Matt 5:3–12). They are promises. That is, they tell people what is happening to them now, as the kingdom is already becoming reality in their lives. Thus, the Beatitudes communicate the proximity of salvation to people in special situations of need. But when the Beatitudes soon speak to

172

"the peacemakers" and "the merciful," it becomes ever more clear that Jesus does not only promise certain consolations to the suffering. He also says how his disciples should live in the anticipated joy about the coming kingdom: without violence, with a pure heart, being as merciful as the Father. Thus, the first Beatitude, which is setting the tone, needs to be heard anew: "Blessed are the poor" is also a call to be poor oneself.

Luke simply transmits the first Beatitude as "Blessed are you who are poor" (Luke 6:20). Matthew, however, has "Blessed are the poor in spirit" (Matt 5:3). Is he watering down Jesus's message? No, because Jesus's first Beatitude is a *call* to a radical form of poverty. It is not only a situation of deficiency from which now a way out is being promised. Rather, only when poverty becomes the attitude of Jesus's disciples, which transforms all areas of their life, namely a trusting openness toward God, in which everything is experienced as a gift of the Father's loving care, only then do people really already live the kingdom of God: "Blessed are the poor in spirit, for theirs is the kingdom of heaven" (Matt 5:3). But then, does the idea of the Church of the poor not sound like a tranquilizer, an "opium of the people"? With this doubt in mind, let us move on to the next aspect.

Advocacy. Pope St. John XXIII has said even more when mentioning "the Church of the poor." The Church is by that making itself the advocate of the poor. Thus it calls for political, economic, social, and environmental decision-making that corresponds more closely to the gospel. The Church does not identify itself with a particular program or party, but takes a critical position for the poor, and in that sense, for justice:

> Learn to do good;
> seek justice,
>> rescue the oppressed,
> defend the orphan,
>> plead for the widow. (Isa 1:17)

So, by giving the Church the task of "advocacy," does the promising title of "Church of the poor" collapse into the banal idea that Christians have to work "for" the poor? Doesn't that actually exclude the poor even more?

The Church representatives. The head of the Catholic Church was, in 1962, not only talking *about* the poor. Rather, John XXIII was speaking here as one of them, as the representative of their concerns, indeed of their life experience. Since he does not only say "pope of the poor," but "Church of the poor," he also instructs other representatives of the Church to be (in their way of life, self-perception, and role) people who are familiar with poverty and who make poverty visible. The 1983 Code of Canon Law, too, stipulates a simple lifestyle for clerics.[7] A person who wants to speak for the poor will either do it paternalistically ("Since they cannot speak for themselves, I do it for them"), or else as one of them. The gospel is not a recipe for self-enrichment. Witnesses of Christ are witnesses to the joyful news, but they also have to proclaim the cross of Christ. When gospel witnesses think they can afford everything, it becomes all the clearer why the apostle must bear witness in simplicity:

> For I think that God has exhibited us apostles as last of all, as though sentenced to death, because we have become a spectacle to the world, to angels and to mortals. We are fools for the sake of Christ, but you are wise in Christ. We are weak, but you are strong. You are held in honor, but we in disrepute. (1 Cor 4:9–10)

But does the Church, if she professes to be the Church of the poor, exclude the rich?

The rich. For those who belong to Christ, any unjust use of wealth is excluded. Christians who rightly bear this name will constantly reexamine themselves as to whether they use their wealth in a way that corresponds to their vocation as gospel witnesses: not only as benefactors, but also in their professional lives, as responsible entrepreneurs, employers, or employees. Within the economic and social conditions of its time, the New Testament already calls for responsibility: "Masters, treat your slaves justly and fairly, for you know that you also have a Master in heaven" (Col 4:1).

Open society. In a real Church of the poor, all people feel accepted: at all levels of society, all ethnic and educational backgrounds, all cultural and financial conditions. A charitable organization easily falls into the trap of handing down alms from the window of its own immaculate image. Then mercy becomes condescension. Then the recipient of help feels even more miserable, if not humiliated. Against that, Pope Francis, when speaking to religious, hinted at a criterion for how the Church can be prophetic: Do those people whose lives are broken feel comfortable with us, a brokenness for which they are perhaps even partly to blame? The Church must not be the community that thinks it is perfect. Rather, it must know about its history of wounding. It is easy to help out of *asistencialismo*—in a paternalistic welfare mentality. However, Francis says, "The problem is not feeding the poor, or clothing the naked or visiting the sick, but rather recognizing that the poor, the naked, the sick, prisoners and the homeless have the dignity to sit at our table, to feel 'at home' among us, to feel as part of a family."[8] That was already Paul's concern. He rebuked a Christian community that gathered around the Lord's table, each member with their own private food. This was insensitive because it was discriminatory. For so, the rich, with their elegant food, embarrass those who cannot bring anything with them. If that is the consequence, one should rather eat at home: "Do you not have homes to eat and drink in? Or do you show contempt for the church of God and humiliate those who have nothing? What should I say to you? Should I commend you? In this matter I do not commend you" (1 Cor 11:22). But does the Church really have to welcome everyone? If it welcomes the racist or the arms manufacturer, does it not bless their fundamental options?

Welcoming and converting. Only an unconditional welcoming of all who want to belong to Christ opens the space for the dynamics of community in Christ. Here, people can sense their need, as well as their ability, to change their way of life. The best example of that is Jesus's encounter with Zacchaeus. It is only when he is very close to Christ that the tax collector realizes how misguided his previous life was. An opportunistic oppressor becomes a generous human being. Why was he able to change? Because Jesus made him feel that he belonged to the holy people. Jesus points out that his visit to Zacchaeus was no act of condescension, but a recognition of his dignity: "Today salvation has come to this house, because he too is a son of Abraham" (Luke 19:9). But what does that mean in the regular, local life of the Church?

The poor showing up. If the Church is really the Church of the poor, if the poor are an active part of the Church, then they are visible in public, especially at Church celebrations. They are not presented but celebrate with others in dignity. They show to observers, such as a television audience, who perhaps live a much safer life, that there are also other situations in life, that people live in need even today. At the conclusion of the extraordinary Holy Year of Mercy, Pope Francis introduced an annual World Day of the Poor for the last Sunday before the Feast of

Christ the King.[9] Here the Church takes seriously its mission to profess itself as the Church of the poor. It thus presents weakness as a human form of life, even in societies where the law of the stronger rules or where one thinks one is safe against all possible disasters: "Let the little children come to me; do not stop them; for it is to such as these that the kingdom of God belongs" (Mark 10:14). But would not a poor Church be a Church that could no longer support the poor?

Rich, in order to help. Poor people who need the Church's help often respond to the question of whether they want a poor Church by saying something like this: "In order for you to support us, you also need to have money." That, however, is not a contradiction to the call of being the Church of the poor. A church relief organization naturally needs material goods for its work. And Christian witness also includes the beauty of the churches and liturgies, the generous hospitality in church centers, and a culture of eating well together. Christians who take their faith seriously will, however, always remind themselves that they cannot rely on earthly solutions in order to have a fulfilled life. They will not "set their hopes on the uncertainty of riches, but rather on God" (1 Tim 6:17). They will also be familiar with the life realities of the disadvantaged. They will not donate with a condescending gesture to the poor, who are otherwise foreign to them, but they will see helping as something natural, because the members of the one body live for each other: "If one member suffers, all suffer together with it; if one member is honored, all rejoice together with it" (1 Cor 12:26). But does the poverty discourse reduce our perspective to material need? Aren't there other, often worse hardships than financial poverty?

Persecuted Church. If Christ's community is the Church of the poor, this self-understanding does not restrict itself to the common consciousness that many of its members lack money. Many lack freedom. Indeed, every day, people are persecuted because of their religion. The Church must not only stand up for the religious freedom of Christians, but for every human being and for all people's rights. The Church also recalls that people were mistreated at all times for professing Christ: "because of me" (Mark 13:9). Christ is scandalous (1 Cor 1:23). To belong to Christ can be seen as an offense, just as Christ himself was perceived as offensive. His gospel is a transformative power that the profiteers of injustice will always find threatening. As Paul writes, "When reviled, we bless; when persecuted, we endure; when slandered, we speak kindly (1 Cor 4:12–13). But speaking of "the poor" and, likewise, of "the rich," sounds simplistic, polarizing, and discrediting. Should a contribution to the public debate better do without such talk?

Scandalous naming. Injustice must be clearly denounced; but it is also necessary to speak precisely and to be personally credible. This includes an exact background knowledge: of the life stories of people as well as socioeconomic contexts. The testimony of Christ is not a demagogic rhetoric claiming that a revolution will eliminate all hardship; the testimony of Christ is, rather, to present to humanity their ruptures. Deuteronomy, although projecting a new society, was admitting that it could not produce an ideal life: "There will never cease to be some need on the earth" (Deut 15:11); and Jesus told his disciples shortly before his arrest, "You always have the poor with you" (Mark 14:7). But can one get involved in a possibly dangerous, sacrificial service for the poor without having the realistic prospect that conditions will actually change?

Shared joy. Is it possible to work, with a palpable renunciation, for the poor without the well-founded impression that one is contributing to changing people's lives, and perhaps even the world? A Christian way of caring for the poor does need quality control, does need to improve itself by wondering what helps more. However, a foreseeable success must neither be motivation nor criterion for successful work. Christian action does not draw its strength from the result (be it expected or attained), but from the Easter joy: it simply wants to communicate itself. A person seized by this joy does not calculate the effect, but lets love pour forth. "Rejoice in the Lord always; again I will say, Rejoice. Let your gentleness be known to everyone. The Lord is near" (Phil 4:4–5); "Do not lag in zeal, be ardent in spirit, serve the Lord....Take thought for what is noble in the sight of all" (Rom 12:11, 17). But the Church is not only poor because there are poor and persecuted Christians; it is after all a faith community and therefore sees today clearly that the use of violence in matters of faith is not only illicit, but also useless. Is nonviolence not also essential to the Church of the poor?

No compulsion. There is faith only when the heart is convinced. One cannot force anyone to believe. Every person must want to believe. Augustine already saw that.[10] However, even this wanting is not the result of an arbitrary decision, but God's gift (Phil 2:13; 3:12). The poverty of the Church is also to recognize: neither by the power of the rational argument, nor seductive presentation, let alone promises of success or even pressure can turn people into disciples of Christ. Paul sees himself as sent "to proclaim the gospel, and not with eloquent wisdom, so that the cross of Christ might not be emptied of its power" (1 Cor 1:17). That is something specifically Christian. How can one proclaim a crucified Messiah? That is a "stumbling block [*skandalon*] to Jews and foolishness to Gentiles" (1 Cor 1:23). However, the poverty of religion, the human impossibility of producing faith, points at something general. Other religions can also be aware of that. On this, a further look into the Qur'an is due!

Faith as Conscious Weakness

THESIS

Where religions are conscious of being phenomena of faith, they can acknowledge freedom: God's freedom and human freedom.

THE POWERFUL GOD AND HIS POWER OVER THE HEARTS (SURA 2:256)

The Qur'an presents God in all his majesty. The highlight of divine sovereignty's linguistic display is undisputedly the "throne verse":

> God: there is no god but Him, the Living, the Independent. Neither slumber nor sleep overtakes Him. All that is in the heavens and in the earth belongs to Him. Who is there that can intercede with Him except by His leave? He knows what is before them and what is behind them, but they do not comprehend any of His knowledge except what He wills. His throne extends over the heavens and the earth; it does not weary Him to preserve them both. He is the Most High, the Tremendous. (Sura 2:255)

The verse uses five double expressions, which all develop biblical wording. Let us look at two of them. "The Living, the Independent" (in Arabic, *al-ḥayy* and *al-qayyūm*) picks up an expression from the Book of Daniel: "the living God, enduring forever" (in Aramaic, *ălāhā ḥayyā wə-qayyām*, 6:26). As in Psalm 121:3, God is not sleeping and slumbering but ever watchful, in a protective or controlling way. He, to whom heaven and earth belong, surpasses everything in greatness and power. But immediately after that, the Qur'an strikes a completely different note:

> There is no coercion in religion: true guidance has been clarified as opposed to error. So whoever rejects false gods and believes in God has grasped the firmest hand-hold, one that will never break. God is hearing and knowing. (Sura 2:256)

Many Muslims take the phrase "no coercion in religion" as a prohibition. One must not force anyone to believe, not even to accept Islam. The same verse reveals in its course that something else is meant. It says something like the following: "The Qur'an does offer a plausible proclamation and a sure guide; and God does notice all decisions of His creatures. Nevertheless, there are people who cannot be convinced, but want to remain idolaters. This is hard to understand and impossible to change." So the verse does not speak about what is not permitted, but about what is not possible: to force people to believe.

Since Muḥammad's emigration to Medina, however, Muslims pursued the spread of Islam in battle. Why are they doing what is declaredly impossible? One should try to persuade others to accept the true religion, by all means, by the expansion of the Islamic territory. Only, one should not be disappointed if not all convert. For people do not always make the right decisions. How do, then, the throne verse and "no coercion" belong together? Some people choose wrong ways: that, too, is so decreed by God's inscrutable, wise will. "He leads astray whom he wills and guides right whom he wills" (Sura 74:31).

The Qur'an warns unmistakably that unbelief will be punished: in this world, and the next (even Sura 2:257 says this). These threats are inserted to motivate people. This shows again how much Qur'anic thinking is aware of human inertia: some simply cannot be moved. God, who was just presented as so powerful, has no power over human freedom. Still, at the end, God will be Lord over everything.

A NEW IDENTIFICATION

We have studied theologies of poverty in the Bible and in the Qur'an. We are now ready to propose a concept to describe the different dynamics observed. In both Bible and Qur'an, we find what we might call, in a multiple sense, "poverty identification." Both start from "overcoming memory." Each is a five-step sequence. In Qur'anic terms, the dynamics of poverty identification develop as follows:

- You yourself were poor.
- You have the poor among you.
- Help them!
- You yourself are poor today, insofar as there are no means to generate faith.
- God will judge in the end, but you cannot understand his ways.

The biblical sequence is not opposed to this; rather, what we saw as the Qur'anic dynamics of poverty identification can also be discovered in the Bible. In the New Testament, however, there is another development of poverty identification, too. It runs as follows:

- You yourselves are poor.
- So was Christ.
- You have the poor among you.
- Christ is to be found in the poor.
- Integrate them!

The royal Son of Man and eschatological judge will, according to Matthew, say, "Just as you did it to one of the least of these who are members of my family, you did to me" (Matt 25:40b). He had just made it clear that he himself was the hungry one, the thirsty, the homeless, the sick, and the prisoner. It would be too little to understand this only as a call to love God and therefore also human beings (see 1 John 4:20). In order to remain within the judgment scene and its motifs: what was clear neither to the helpers nor to the nonhelpers during their earthly lives is now clarified to the hearers of the gospel. It is the fulfillment of all longings, which can only be found in the encounter with God, which takes place in the service of the needy.

Just as God here has transferred his royal-judicial presence to the Son of Man, so the Son of Man transfers his healing-fulfilling presence to the poor. Can one relate to this claim rationally?

In God's name, Christ is exercising the office as eschatological judge. He wants to encounter us especially in the least advantaged person. Obviously, this is another instance of the preferential option for the poor, from God's side. The claim that service for the poor, of all things, is service to God follows an understandable logic of love. Love is all the purer the less it can be justified by foreseeable advantages of our own (even if it is only the attractiveness of the person to whom we show love). The less a service fulfills our own interests and our self-care, the more it can simply follow the impulse to give: the more it can simply be love. That divine option and identification, then, serves to purify our love. And the life God wants to share with all creatures consists in pure loving: it is the kingdom of God (Rom 14:7; 1 Cor 15:28).

The poverty identification from Matthew's eschatological judgment, then, follows the same participatory and liberating dynamic as Jesus's proclamation of the kingdom of God. And again like this, the identification of poverty is a political message, too. It says that if we leave the poor lying untreated, we actually leave God aside. And that means that a Church wanting to withdraw into purely liturgical activity is no longer serving God, either.

Pedro Arrupe told his fellow Jesuit how he succeeded in perceiving Christ in the *favela* people; and Jon Sobrino discovered the poor as a place of theological knowledge. If a theologian consciously pays attention to the poor, even wants to learn faith from them, this line of vision stands in the biblical tradition of poor people's psalmistic piety, the Beatitudes, and the Matthean poverty identification of the Son of Man. When theologians declare the poor to be a theological locus, they go beyond the desk and open themselves to new criteria for theological truth. The question they are thus asking, really, is this: Does my reflection of faith help those who are particularly hurt by this world's structures of sin, and who have to rely, more than everyone else, on God's help? It is becoming more and more apparent how religion needs to make present to its world and to itself the message of weakness.

RELIGION: SHOWING WHAT IS MISSING

Where faith is no longer self-evident, it is no longer "culturally natural," so to speak. Now the roles that religions have assumed in society become more evident. Analyses used to point out functions that are harmful to humanity: faith as a narcotic, faith as blocking the salutary process of enlightenment. Meanwhile, analysts point at positive functions of religion, too, such as transmission of values, consolation, and societal cohesion. The functions, however, that sociologists attribute seldom place religious belief in the place it claims for itself. Faith often does not only want to serve humanity, but first of all wants to show what true humanity is, what the human being is really about. Faith is also something prophetically critical, a dissenting voice. Faith does not only want to satisfy expectations, but to express and transform them, in celebration and in everyday life. A society that claims to be able to choose its own foundations thus wants to clearly define the function of the religious system, as well. Religions should resist that. Thus, they can become a symptom of deficiency, an indicator of what is missing. It is this dynamic that we need to explore now.

Rationality without Scruple

Jürgen Habermas, the theorist of the public sphere, has, in the third millennium, shown a growing interest in religion's social presence. According to him, we live in postsecularity. His observation that human rationality itself is incomplete led him to a key affirmation. Purely rational attempts to justify what is good action do not (or no more) succeed in making people aware of the hardship in which others live:

> Practical reason now misses its own purpose, when it no longer has the strength to awaken—and keep awake—in profane minds an awareness of solidarity (which is being infringed throughout the world!), an awareness of what is missing, of what is crying to heaven.[11]

Habermas suggests that something like religion is necessary in rational societies as "an awareness of what is missing." Is Habermas, with his beautiful formula, not only making yet another attempt of subordinating religion by giving it one particular function in society?

Every such formula, especially if it avoids specifically religious vocabulary, runs the risk of misjudging the liveliness of religion. However, Habermas gladly admits that the formula had flowed into his pen from a theological source, namely when he was reading a book by Johann Baptist Metz.[12] The religions apparently keep awake forms of perception that would be lost within an exclusively rational society. These forms include both linguistic expressions and preconceptual sensibilities. Immanuel Kant (1724–1804) already collocated religious formulations and secular reflection in an intriguing way. In 1790, he observed how Christianity extended the conceptual inventory of the nonreligious ethical discourse:

> That miraculous religion—by its simple discourse—has enriched philosophy with far clearer and purer ethical concepts than philosophy had previously provided; but rationality freely approves of those concepts, now that they exist, and accepts them as concepts, which it could and should have found and introduced by itself.[13]

Kant apparently reminds us that Christianity sometimes so aptly addresses life questions that independently working ethicists have to admit they should have long since come up with such a thinking and wording themselves. At any rate, they now can comprehend and reconstruct with their own instruments what they receive from a religious tradition. Neither Kant nor Habermas say that faith is irreplaceable. But both philosophers see that religious tradition is a useful supplier for rational reflection. For Kant, religion provides themes and concepts; for Habermas it delivers imaginaries and sensibilities. Both at least adumbrate the idea that the religious testimony reveals to human reason its own weakness. Now, does religious witness actually take on the task of showing the supposedly rational world what it is missing and who is missing?

Cain without Brother

Pope Francis drew the attention of an entire continent to the misery of refugees when he visited the island of Lampedusa and made visible to Europe what is missing. What is absent is justice, absent are livable conditions for many. And whole groups of people are absent in the public consciousness. Their suffering, even their existence, is over-

183

looked. Habermas had already spoken of "what is crying to heaven," thus alluding to the biblical scene of the first murder. The pope also hinted at that passage in which the Creator confronts Cain, who has just killed his brother: "'Where is your brother? His blood cries out to me,' says the Lord [Gen 4:9–10]. This is not a question directed to others; it is a question directed to me, to you, to each of us."[14]

Cain will answer in feigned nonchalance that, of course, he is not his brother's keeper: that is, he is not responsible for him. But Cain will now be reminded precisely of his responsibility. He has a responsibility that looks back; he is responsible for his brother's death. And he has a responsibility that looks forward; he is responsible to protect his siblings' lives in the future. But is it not a moralizing instrumentalization of religion when one applies to the present situation a question posed by God according to the Book of Genesis?

Self without Perfection

Religious claims can generate a justified fear or anger; that happens when religion's power to completely seize a person is instrumentalized. What is instrumentalization? If one declares one's own will to be God's will and thus claims obedience from others. Thus the absolute claim of religion can be used for a person's self-absolution. But this pattern also manifests a more general danger, even beyond the religious sphere. Just as dangerous as religious boundary violations (and structurally similar) are attempts to use categories like "humankind" or "reason" to justify absolute demands. Such a use is human and reasonable only if it allows for mechanisms of constantly renewed control and correction. In religion, they should actually be particularly obvious, because its fundamental gesture includes the human person's ever new self-distinction from the divine. Religion is an awareness of what is missing, also in the sense that we all lack perfection, absolute authority. Religion, however, makes us also aware of what is missing in many societies in quite a different sense and context.

Criticism without Addressee

If religions are attacked in public space, the accusations may be justified. A matter-of-fact examination, a self-critical reception, and a humble willingness to dialogue are necessary. Occasionally, however, the criticism of religious representatives has a different dynamic. Sometimes one does not mean at all, or not only, the person and religion concerned. Rather, people sometimes look for someone whom they can blame for a diffuse dissatisfaction. A religious representative or a group can also become a scapegoat. Such mechanisms must, of course, be clarified and tackled. However, religion thus makes visible another deficiency. We are missing authorities, responsible persons, and visible representations that are capable of taking reproach, which one can criticize and even hate without being punished. Such sweeping refusals are often a step on the way to mature conflict competence. Here religion comes into sight as the strong side that reveals a weakness in societies; but is religion not itself also something weak?

The Wound of Faith

Religion can be an indicator of deficiency. Beyond what has been said so far, it indicates that we lack knowledge and certainty. Every believing is also a "not knowing." Of course, religious faith is not the direct opposite of knowledge. And, of course, all areas of life have their uncertainties and require an epistemological modesty. However, the structure and self-understanding of faith show us with particular clarity that we do not approach reality as perfect perceivers. We cannot see everything that is, let alone foresee what will be. Those who believe in a dialogical manner are indeed convinced of the convincingness of some argumentative justification of faith, because faith is no arbitrary decision, but the recognition of reality in its truth. Yet those who believe in a dialogical manner know about other people who, confronted with similar experiences and the same reasons, remain unconvinced. Those who believe consciously, therefore recognize their faith as a gift; and those who believe consciously see their own limitations, see that there is something hypothetical in the reasons for believing: the expectation of a healing future. Therefore, they also have understanding for those who cannot but see differently the world and the end of history. It is sensible of a creed to be called "confession." It thus designates a central aspect of knowing through believing. Faith teaches the believers to see their own limitations, their own guilt and to admit it, that is, to confess it. But what is the point of telling people that they are sinners? Simply putting them in a bad mood?

The Realism of the Sinner

Many forms of religion point out human weakness (see Ps 51:5; John 16:8; Sura 4:28). Even if a theological anthropology stresses that humanity is good by nature, it will still see the basic problem that we want to preserve ourselves and therefore become entangled in ourselves. To see a basic human tendency toward selfishness does not directly lead us to cancel our trust in others. The insight that people become guilty does not prevent us from seeing the beauty of creation and human solidarity. It is true that religions, with their rites of self-abasement and expressions of fear, can influence feelings of inferiority as well as "God-poisoning." But first of all, they help us to see what is all too human, beyond any exaggerated expectation (which leads to the inevitable subsequent disappointment). Religions can have a liberating effect when they present the human being as a sinner in need of healing, who may attain forgiveness and deserves space for a new beginning. Religion then reveals human weakness; a few decades ago it was mainly their preaching on sin that exposed religious representatives to public criticism. Today it is often a different revealing of human weakness that earns critique. That calls for a brief consideration now.

The Weakness of Reconciliation

It seems that a key element of religion is to relegate one's will to what is more sacred. For this reason alone, religious representatives often advocate reconciliation processes—all the more so since many religions contain an explicit message of peace. Therefore, however, the representatives are sometimes criticized by their own people for going too far in their task of mediating between divided parties. Instead of accommodating others, they should take sides for "our own" cause; or so goes the accusation. A peacemaking, solution-oriented dialogue may entail renouncing at self-determination. That can be frightening. Persons working for reconciliation will easily be accused of being starry-eyed romantics: weak, naive, dangerous, even traitorous. In this, religion also testifies to something else, "that is missing": In reconciliation processes, often for years no success can be observed. Enormous patience, ever new imagination is needed, a kind of "hoping against hope" (Rom 4:18). But in this, even a religion conscious of its own weakness might still have an actionistic bias. Therefore, another way of properly living the weakness of religion needs to be discussed.

Adoration without Usefulness

From his prison cell, a few weeks before his execution, Alfred Delp wrote a meditation on Epiphany. The feast celebrates what the Gospel of Matthew recounts. Magi recognize the newborn Jesus as Lord, worship him, and hand over their gifts (Matt 2:11). Because of this movement from worshiping Christ to giving, the feast is also, for many religious congregations, their day of consecration, profession, vows. Taking up this twofold dynamic, worship and self-surrender, Delp writes the astonishing words: "*Adoro* and *Suscipe* are the two fundamental words of human freedom."[15]

"I adore" (*adoro*) and "take!" (*suscipe*). What is so free about worship and self-giving? Religions can motivate people to impressive work, indeed, inspire heroic action. But many religious traditions also know another dimension of service. A generous investment, a well-calculated strategy, a serious effort can fail. People may then find themselves before God's mystery without understanding his ways. In the disappointment, they also encounter the God of surprises. Christians may discover here the "scandal of the cross." The crucified Jesus is supposed to be the Savior. That sounds unconvincing (1 Cor 1:23). To endure God's otherness is adoration. After striving hard in action and supplication, people can experience how all utility orientation vanishes. Their self-affirmation is being transformed into a "not my will but yours" situation (Luke 22:42). In religion, people can understand and acknowledge that they are not the masters of history.

In combining adoration and self-surrender, the Jesuit Alfred Delp binds together two key elements of his tradition. He evokes Thomas Aquinas's eucharistic hymn *Adoro te devote, latens Deitas* (in English, "I adore you, hidden Divinity") and Ignatius of Loyola's prayer of surrender: *Tomad, Señor, y recibid toda mi libertad* (in English, "Take, O Lord, and receive all my freedom").[16] For Delp, to give up one's own power and to surrender to the divine will, entrusting oneself to God's plan is the fundamental act of freedom. Here, still, a heroic courage may resonate, glorifying the uncoerced act. But later, only days before his execution, the Jesuit will be able to sense how autonomy handed over discloses an inner vastness, life in agreement with one's own destiny. This generosity is rightly called "freedom." Delp writes, "One must put the sails in the infinite wind; only then will we feel which drive we are capable of."[17]

From the Poor to Belief: Looking Back and Looking Forward

Religion is a "poor show," in a very good sense. Because the insight that success in life is not programmable is at religion's origin. Happiness is only to be had as a gift. Therefore, it is only given to those who acknowledge that they cannot produce fullness themselves. Fulfilling experiences, in fact, and a fulfilled course of life depend on the other: on favorable conditions, on love freely given by others, and on the joyful gratitude for it. Human life means depending on others. Therefore, a happy life transcends itself, in order to be able to rely on others. Most of the words of the Hebrew Bible for "trust" are formed from the root *āman*, "to fasten." However, the pre-Christian Greek translation of the texts that became the Old Testament, the Septuagint, chooses for this initial dynamic of the Bible, for this "relying on," a Greek word that associates other things, *pistis*. For the Greeks this does not indicate the risky ability to rely on the eternally trustworthy God and thus to find a security that cannot be had otherwise. The word for "believing" in Greek philosophy means, rather, mere opinion, superficial, and therefore wrong judgment. Hence the trust that relies on God's reliability is suddenly in a linguistic environment that declares it to be unreasonable, false. In this way, however, believers are reminded that their religion is not the worldview shared by all, but a matter of trust. There are good reasons for it, but it will still remain controversial. Faith cannot prove its foundation conclusively. Faith can only witness to its reason. Religion, conscious of its own status as belief, thus always carries with it an epistemological modesty. Also in this sense, religion presents itself in poverty. But with that, it enriches societies. For it shows to all that great realms of human life take place beyond conclusive proof and beyond unity in conviction. The different beliefs must interrogate one another; but many of them will remain. In almost no point unity can be achieved; but this does not render human coexistence impossible.

What is to be studied now, is then, how the particular poverty of religions can enrich societies that have no confessional unity.

INSPIRATION

Previewing the Sixth Chapter

Religion can play an important role in a pluralistic society. Its representatives, however, should abandon the notion that one is only efficient when one has the full support of all society. Their testimony will not convince everyone, and even convinced people may not completely identify with their religion. But in such a plurality, religion can renew its task; religion can be inspiration. We shall see that Vatican teaching occasionally expresses this by saying that Christians can *animate* societies.

But does this mean that the task of the Church today is to win over as many people as possible (not to the faith but) to Judeo-Christian values? Values express the priorities in that which is important to people. Religious testimony must not be reduced to the transmission of values. What religions want to communicate would thus be turned into something abstract, banal, static, even sterile. The Church, for one, testifies first and last to the living Christ.

Such tensions need to be confronted when exploring religion as inspiration in a pluralistic society.

6

Religion as Inspiration in a Plural Society

As we have reached a divide, let's first review the way gone so far. Religion had come to the fore as *culture*, as an ambience that must be accepted, hardly changeable. Or it was an *identity foundation* that appeals by promising a radically new beginning. Then we encountered religion as *legitimation*, and as *critique*, of rule and violence. Vis-à-vis power, we subsequently studied religion as presenting the *weakness* element. In the light of weakness as part of basic religious experience, we can now once again ask how religion is presenting itself. Today, religion is often, and in surprising contexts, an *inspiration*.

In the fall of 2008, I moved to Rome. After a few months, I was overwhelmed by the impression that hearts were closed there. I found it was difficult to sense hope in the capital of Catholic Christendom. A Muslim colleague noticed that. He suggested, "Let us take a day off and travel to Rondine!"

Rondine is a tiny village in Tuscany. As beautiful as it looks, the inhabitants gradually abandoned it. Its decay began in the 1970s. A psychology student from the area, Giorgio Vaccari, refused to accept this. He gained friends for his vision, which had yet to be clarified.

In 1993, a Gulag survivor, the literary scholar Dmitry Sergeyevich Lichachev, visited the Rondine group. They took him to La Verna, a nearby Francis of Assisi shrine. There, the Russian guest succeeded in doing what the young Italians were not able to do yet, to identify their vision: "If you invite the peoples at war, here they will make peace."

Today, Rondine is the "Citadel of Peace," an academy of intercultural dialogue. Young people from hostile groups of various countries live together there, in order to learn ways of conflict resolution and in the hope of soon being leaders for a more reconciled world.[1]

During the twentieth century, religions felt challenged and intimidated by an aggressively argumentative, or an aggressively disinterested, atheism. Analyses of the religious situation have, however, shifted in the meantime. One began to speak of secularism and then of postsecularism. Religion today has become anything but meaningless. Although the situation is contradictory, it is not unintelligible. Rather, the current relationship between religion and world can be described quite aptly: with the concept of contradiction itself. If we want to understand how religion can be inspiration today, we must look at this "contradictory" relationship from four different angles.

Faith in a Contradicting Public Sphere

On the one hand, testimonies of faith still encounter contradiction. This is not something that should hurt the believers. It can even be positive for them, when it is a sign of interest on the part of others, and improves the quality of discourse. When, however, the contradiction is limited to slogans, it does not offend religion and believers, but the whole of humanity. An insulting term like "the religiots" (i.e., people who are still religious in spite of all reason, and therefore idiots) obscures the fact that human beings can see beyond themselves.

The situation is also contradictory, in that religion has become "optional."[2] Optional, now, means that one is decidedly for or against it. This is contradictory, on the one hand, because the loud affirmation of one stands against the equally decided rejection of the other. But precisely in relation to religion, there is a further contradiction here.

If one thinks that the foundation of life can be established by decision, one proves that optionality can boil down to arbitrariness. If one's life project is just a question of taste, one is not relying on what lies outside oneself: one puts together one's own world. Religious faith, however, develops in growth processes and in the willingness to understand the old in a new way, in view of the present experience of the world. In this way, people attain the capacity for trust, in which both the emotional and the rational capacities can become convinced. Now, one can commit oneself without fast or exaggerated profit expectations. One does not do justice to a claim to truth if one subjects its validity to subjective approval. Anyone who claims something to be true claims that it is true regardless of one's own acknowledgment; and religions in particular want to place people in front of the undisposable. If one makes the truth of one's religion dependent on one's own decision, one thus already contradicts the fundamental religious gesture.

A similar inner clash is found when a religious option is taken in contrast to a hostile world, in order to escape the ambivalence of the present and to enter the calm waters of unambiguous clarity. What is contradictory here is that religions, with their symbols and metaphors, with their historical-cultural diversity and their senses of humor, do not offer the desired unambiguity. A religion lived in its fullness rather equips people with the capacity to continue within life's ever new ambiguity, with a sense of meaning, serenely and creatively.

In this contemporary society, be it "contradictory" in this or that sense, the question is, in any case, what is the function of religious faith? But the question itself has to be questioned. For neither the vague voice of some "society" nor the defining decision of a state has the right to ascribe the tasks to a religious community. The religious consciousness is a contrast to all conscious and unconscious human constructs (be they institutions or mentalities), as framework of interpretation, as stimulus, orientation, and criticism—indeed, as their origin and justification. Therefore it is more appropriate, instead of asking about religion's "function" in the state, to speak of religion's "role." Religion is not a state's instrument. It has, rather, the right to find, in a quasi-personal manner, its own tasks. The state in turn indeed has the right to protect itself against religious boundary violations that limit its independence. The state has the right to formulate what it expects from religions. But the state should not treat religion as its subordinate; the same applies as regards society in relation to religions (and for that matter also as regards the relationship between state and society). But state and society may always become aware of the fact that they have been influenced by religions. What kind of influence is that? Can it, in the course of history, take on other forms? Where is the boundary between constructive partnership and boundary violation?

THESIS

In Europe, Christianity has entered a third paradigm: religion has become inspiration.

Religious traditions, in their thinking and wording, have described religion's attempted influence differently. Ever new formulae have been offered to say how religions shape the world. Regarding the descriptions so far offered here, one might object that they are not really theological: culture, identity foundation, justification and limitation of power, presentation of weakness. That sounds more like sociology of religion than theology. If, however, we find a clearly theological concept and define the Church in the world as "sacrament," the complaint arises that such technical language is meaningless for the uninitiated. Are there then, at least for some part of history and geography, no concepts that are at the same time understandable and theological?

INSPIRATION: A HISTORY OF THE CHRISTIAN RELATION TO THE WORLD

Looking at the Christianization of Europe, three models can be identified that describe the different roles Christianity played in different eras. The designations are ideal-typical but may help to get an idea of the processes and tasks involved. The three categories can be transposed to some other cultural contexts, but clearly not to all.[3]

Nation: Medieval Faith Societies

The mission strategy of Latin European Christianity was territorial. Not persons were converted but territories were Christianized. When the prince was baptized, the people were considered Christian. Of course, the inhabitants were also baptized; but that was the result, not the condition of a country's being Christian. Faith formation was superficial. There was little instruction about either faith contents (catechesis) or faith life (spirituality). Pastoral care was, above all, the administration of the sacraments. The sacrament of penance, which might be a place of personal faith accompaniment, was rarely a place for consolation and spiritual counsel.

But it is not enough to speak of a territorial principle of faith. For, on the one hand, the baptism of the sovereign and thus of the territory did not oblige the population to a uniform faith practice. There were religious subcultures, unofficial parallel worlds, in which pre-Christian practices continued. Under its surface, the unified religion had various niches. Moreover, faith was not, strictly speaking, territorial. Tribes continued religious practice even when they moved away. Therefore, to describe this first paradigm, it is appropriate to speak of "nation." By this designation we are also reminded of the fact that a person was, in contrast to the early Church initiation through conversion and baptism, Christian because they were born (in Latin, *natus*) into a Christian people.

Confession: The Reformations

In the wake of the Wittenberg Reformation, the principle of "nation" lost its validity. Faith became a question of decision. Now it depended on one's "confession." That meant not just a choice between belief and unbelief, but rather *which* belief. Those who decided against their prince's confessional stance had to leave their homeland. Here again a territorial thinking sounds; but now personal choice is possible, if not expected.

In the age of confessionalization (as it is called), the various denominational groups distinguished themselves against one another. They did so primarily by saying what they were not. Religious identity was now a counterprofile. *Catholic* was suddenly no longer a word going back to the early Church creed, designating the worldwide, multiform Church to which the salvific goods were entrusted in fullness. *Catholic* was now, rather, the Roman response to the Reformation movements allegedly reducing the Christian heritage. Likewise, the designation *evangelic(al)* implied that those who did not follow the Reformation had fallen away from the gospel. And the Geneva and Zurich reformers saw in Lutheranism a personality cult around the Wittenberg Reformer, whose *reformatio* was never carried out to the end as a transformation of life according to the gospel. Therefore, they called themselves the *Reformed*, thus declaring all others to be resisting reform.

Education became a driving force for all denominational parties, and education itself became confessionalized. This did not only mean that a certain confession was taught in schools, but that the population had broad, often compulsory, access to education. However, education was now also explicitly about things of faith; and often not only about what was right, but especially about what was wrong with the others.

Until today, many Christian phenomena are marked by the paradigm of confession. An interest in the other, an understanding for the other, a readiness to be challenged or corrected by the other: all this is often blocked by confessional boundaries. The petty, exclusivist distinctions make confessionalism irrelevant in the public discourse. Such self-referentiality is fatal for a religion, if it actually does not want to represent itself alone.

Inspiration: Resistance and Encouragment

In an environment that can be described as "contradictory," where religion is an option, faith traditions can find new ways of shaping the world. They now have to admit, though, that in their cultures the paradigm of self-evident belonging (the nation model) is over; and equally gone is the idea of confessionalist counterprofiling. Postsecularism is interested in religious questions and in the answers of religions, but their representatives cannot expect sweeping obedience. In pluralistic societies, each religion has to cope with the fact that it is only one of many voices and that its members, too, deal selectively with the lifestyle their religious community presents. If, however, a religious community has digested this, it might also find itself consulted by people, by private persons and persons in public responsibility: consulted, that is, with a high competence assumption. Religious communities are typically assumed to be competent in spiritual accompaniment, personal counseling in ethical dilemmas, in helping to explain problematic human conditions such as radicalization patterns, in the cultic expression of life transitions and traumas, but also as a public voice of "the forgotten." This social trust, however, needs religious communities to train competent interlocutors, to leave space for the creativity of prophetic figures, and to cultivate traditional forms without populism or vanity, especially when it comes to the culture of worship. For the religions, too, the world has become a market. There are competitors, and there may be jealousy. But religions do not have to fulfill all expectations. They need not be out to win customers. They always have a critical role that will therefore be offensive for some. Faith cannot be created by a marketing strategy. Religious communities should not measure success in membership rates. Where the world has become a market, that can hardly be changed. But a religious community can rediscover—precisely in view of the marketing temptations—that its task is not to win, but to serve.

A religious community that has become modest in a world of contradiction because it no longer wishes to return to the model of divisive "confession," and from there to unified "nation," can rediscover its present role: namely, to be "inspiration." That is a New Testament word: "all scripture is inspired" (2 Tim 3:16). It is literally "God-breathed; of divine spiriting" (in Greek, *theopneustos*). A community, too, can inspire. It can discover its responsibility for the "spirit" that rules in society—acknowledging, however, that all it can do is stimulate, propose, contribute (critically and constructively) to its shaping, without being able to determine it. It will not work without contradiction. A religion understanding its role to be inspiration also in the sense of "stimulation" faces new challenges. Then, however, an objection can be heard immediately. If you take religion to be inspiration, are you not suppressing the fundamental drive of many beliefs, namely mission? What is "mission," the concept and the dynamic? And in this context, we also have to explore historically and theologically these three related terms: *evangelize, animate*, and *witness*.

MISSION AND *DAʿWA*

Mission is an early Church concept for its project of shaping the world. Throughout the history of Christianity, mission has been suspected of being a form of violence, and sometimes rightly so. If one gets to the source of the Christian mission concept, however, three basic features emerge that cast a different light on Christian mission.

"I am sending you out like lambs into the midst of wolves" (Luke 10:3). Mission first of all means that people are sent by Christ. They accept not only his message, but his lifestyle—and his style is nonviolence. Of course, the term already suggests that you will not stay at home. The way will lead you into a foreign land. The dangers of the journey and the encounter with the unknown already resonate in the way Christians call their extroversion when they say "mission." In addition, of course, the disciples are not simply sent in one direction or area, but to people in their various living conditions. They have to be responsive to local habits. They will even depend on other people's responsiveness and receptiveness. That, too, can be discovered in the very concept of mission.

What about Islam in this context? One Islamic term for conversion-oriented relationship with people of other faiths is *da'wa*, which means "call." The call goes to other human beings: they are to come to God, to the way of the Lord, and to the good (Suras 41:33; 16:125; 3:104). In the concept of *da'wa*, again, there are three insightful points. The designation "call" as verbal act reflects that the response will not be forced but voluntary. The communication of faith is presented as an appeal. However, in Qur'anic understanding people already know what is necessary for salvation, only that they do not realize it. That aspect is also present in the concept of *da'wa*. It does not seem necessary to tell people the story of salvation. People must only be reminded, by that call, of what they already know. Third, *da'wa* also means "invitation." Thus, it makes a friendly, generous gesture; but it does not contain any mention of a risky departure into foreign lands. That idea is, however, present in a Qur'anic word for "prophet," *rasūl*, meaning "messenger" or "envoy."

Instead of *da'wa*, Muslims also speak of *tablīġ*, "proclamation." It goes back to God's order to the messenger:

> *Balliġ mā unzila ilayka min rabbika*—Proclaim what has come upon you from your Lord! (Sura 5:67)

"Proclaim" refers to both faithful transmission and skillful communication. But since that order is addressed only to the messenger himself, the opinion could arise that only God's messengers had a mission for proclamation. In any case, the concept underlines the verbal aspect and this the listener's liberty.

ANIMATION: BEING A CONTINENT'S SOUL

In the search for a profound understanding of mission, in the Catholic context one may encounter another word for the task of the faithful in the world, besides "inspiration." Christians should "animate" the world. Now, animation is a versatile, but not unproblematic concept. Animation can sound like a holiday in a luxury hotel; the professionally good-humored entertainer encourages the guests to engage in an activity that seems primarily intended to protect them from feeling emptiness. Also, *animation* can reveal the arrogance of a unidirectional communication, mere one-way encounter, as if Christians could not also learn from others.

That suspicion is not confirmed, however, when the word's way into Church language is examined. Basically, it goes back to Vatican II. It can be found for the first time in Italian translations of the Conciliar documents. Of the so-called laity, the council teaches, "They exercise the apostolate in fact by their activity directed to the evangelization and sanctification of human beings and to penetrating and perfecting of the temporal order with the spirit of the Gospel."[4] And again they are "to penetrate the world with a Christian spirit."[5] Instead of "penetrating" (in Latin, *perfundere* and *imbuere*), Italian has *animando* and *animazione*. That word usage of "animating" soon reached other languages in translations of papal writings. Vatican II itself already stressed, immediately after speaking of "animation," that its way of looking into the world is readiness to learn.[6] So animation cannot imply a one-way street approach to Christian life and theology.

"Animating" could subsequently be meaningfully used in another sense. Christians should be the continent's "soul" (in Latin and Italian, *anima*).[7] Pope Francis recalled this in his address to the European Parliament:

> An anonymous second-century author wrote that "Christians are to the world what the soul [*anima*] is to the body" (*Letter to Diognetus*, 6). The function of the soul is to support the body, to be its conscience and its historical memory. A two-thousand-year-old history links Europe and Christianity. It is a history not free of conflicts and errors, and sins, but one constantly driven [*animata*] by the desire to work for the good of all.[8]

This is a call for courageous encounter and world shaping; a beautiful formula, itself an act of animation. However, it could also be the basis for exaggerated expectations and subsequent disappointments. The problem arises if the "soul" of a continent is equated with its culture and mentality. The relationship between Christianity and Europe has fundamentally changed. Neither of them should mourn old times. One should rather ask, What is this inspiration and animation concretely? Here another concept may be helpful—an ambiguous concept, though.

EVANGELIZATION: CONTRIBUTING TO THE SHAPING OF SOCIETY

A much-used term from the semantic field of mission is *evangelizing*. During St. Paul VI's pontificate, the word proved to explore a new dimension contained in *inspiration*. For the tenth anniversary of the conclusion of the Council, the pontiff named the Church's role in history to be an "evangelization of cultures": "Every effort must be made to ensure a full evangelization of culture, or more correctly of cultures."[9]

To what was the pope referring? Was he pleading for abolishing a heritage foreign to the gospel? He was not advocating a replacement of indigenous cultures by a (Roman understanding of) Christian culture, which would be a type of colonialism. Rather, Paul VI called for marking out unjust social patterns, and contributing to their transformation. Vatican II's 1965 decree on the laity, *Apostolicam Actuositatem*, points the way here. It had been able to redefine evangelization. It was not only referring to the people who are to be evangelized, but also the "order of temporal things," as we have just seen. With this classical expression the Council says that the existing relations of politics, economy, and society should be shaped and perfected by the spirit of the gospel.[10]

The expression marks a change in the understanding of mission. Theologians and the magisterium now began to speak of "evangelization" if one understood the task of the gospel as going beyond evangelistic projects in evangelical style. The gospel is not only significant for individual conversion; it can also transform structures and laws, in politics and economics, in societal and social affairs.

POLITICAL CHRISTIANS, CHRISTIAN POLITICIANS

Is the gospel meant to transform the temporal order? That sounds demanding, but also strangely impersonal. Does message influence circumstances? How should that happen? The formulation comes from

Apostolicam Actuositatem. That is significant. The Council fathers saw that while the institutional Church has a political mission, official Church representatives should not assume political offices. That would be clericalism in the original sense. Rather, they are thinking of non-clerics, whose consciences are shaped by the gospel, whose imagination is encouraged by the gospel, whose understanding of the human being develops in dialogue with the gospel. They can contribute with special sensitivity and freedom to the societal process, as vigilant voters and critical citizens, as socially committed voluntary or full-time workers, but also as politicians. They act with a special willingness to find truth and solutions, to reconcile and to stand in for the disadvantaged, if indeed they allow themselves to be challenged anew by their "evangelizing" mission.

Giorgio Vaccari, the initiator of Rondine, says his role model is Giorgio La Pira (1904–77). In 2018, Pope Francis opened the process for La Pira's beatification; and La Pira was of all things a politician!

THE PRESENCE OF TESTIMONY

As we have argued, a Catholic understanding of evangelization and animation is intended to help shape the face of the earth in the spirit of the gospel. Evangelizing is the proclamation of the gospel of God's kingdom; and his kingdom is also a social order. Pope Francis says it this way: "To evangelize is to make the kingdom of God present in our world."[11] In contradictory times, there are many obstacles to this. It may therefore be helpful to include, in this theological exploration of the history of concepts of religious world relationships, one last term, *testimony*, that is, *witnessing*.

*Testimony—*philology, phenomenology, theology. *Witnessing* implies that something has happened that must now be testified to in order to be present. Testimony is given personally. As a legal term, testimony indicates that one is presently in court. At the end, a decision on true or false is to come. Testimony is to be "borne" or "given." That also implies that the witnesses must leave it to their addressees to decide whether they accept the testimony, which is made up of apt expression and understanding.

In the New Testament, it is not only the individual Christian who is witnessing but also God, the Spirit, and the scriptures (Rom 1:9; 8:16; 3:21) as well as, to put it postbiblically, the Church (building on Luke 24:58; Eph 3:10; Rev 12:11). It is not only an individual event that is witnessed, but the history of salvation is witnessed as the grand narrative where each person's individual experience finds its place. A testimony of faith is more than mere words. It is life and action. And it is also given through the existence of the testifying community.

Witness is given with courage, with the openness of *parrhēsia*, with the confidence to say everything, even where it is risky (Acts 4:31). As the word suggests (in Greek, *martyria*), testimony is possibly also martyrdom: themselves being nonviolent, the witnesses can become victims of violence.

Witnesses must ask themselves what they can do to convey their witness successfully, even though they may have courage to go to death for their testimony, and may know that many will not accept their witness. Human means were used from the beginning, despite all the necessary weakness. The New Testament testimonies also strive for clear language, use arguments, and manifest witnesses' commitment in mind and body.

Not only the disciples of the first generation are witnesses. Later generations can also experience the Easter event, and can be credible witnesses. If "witnessing" implies that something has happened that must now be testified to in order to be present, the very idea of religious witnessing already includes the claim that God wants cooperators.

How can one now bear a religious witness in a public place that demands that all claims be made plausible?

Religion and Ethics in Contradiction

THESIS

A public theology need not limit itself to the formulation of consensual values. It can offer its own expressions.

VALUES AND HOW GENERAL THEY ARE

If in a society the dwindling visibility of Christianity is lamented, some contributors to the discussion start appealing to "Judeo-Christian values." Quite often, the resonating assertion is that Islamic values should be left out. To see more clearly, it helps to ask first what Christian values are. Here, Christian anthropology has to be explored, and from there, Catholic social doctrine, and also in this context, the idea of "responsibility." But before that, values are to be examined philosophically. At this point, the philosopher and sociologist Helmuth Plessner (1892–1985) may be helpful. According to Plessner, moral claims are anthropologically general and specifically anthropological: that is, all human beings and only human beings know them. Plessner makes a meaningful distinction between two classes of values, a society's legally regulating values and a community's culturally penetrating values.

What thus becomes visible is that values are "general" in a multiple sense. They are something generally human, they are regulating concepts on which different people want to agree, and they are formulated in such a way that they fit different situations. It is their abstract character, however, that also reveals the problem behind values and the claim that religions must safeguard them.

Value: A Term and Its Problems

Plessner has structured his philosophical anthropology around an impressive term, *eccentric positionality*. To what was he referring?

While stones and stars have only a "position," while plants are in exchange with their environment and therefore already have more world reference, namely a "positionality," while more complex animals have an encapsulating center, a "centric positionality," human beings can transcend themselves. They are purely determined by instinct but have the ability to distance themselves and to relate to facts beyond their own interest. Therefore, the human way of life is "eccentric positionality."[12] In the light of such an anthropology, human grandeur becomes visible. Because of their eccentric positionality, human beings "make demands on themselves." They thus transcend themselves, do not only strive for self-preservation, acknowledge other things and other persons. Human beings' eccentric positionality becomes their "so-called *conscience*, the source of morality and concrete morality."

If people now live as "community," they still live "in the objective community of culture, in mutual penetration by help of acknowledged and internalized values." What, however, if a group of people has become so large and diverse as to be "society," with a "public sphere"? It is still based on a "value-based order of communication." But the values are now working in the background. A society does indeed function with regulating values, "which, however, no longer need to step into the individual's vision."[13] This order is, now no more a "voluntary harmony out of conviction," but "legality." So values that lead one beyond one's own needs are for Plessner an anthropological constant. But a society would be overloaded if expected to have community-type values—a certain group's expressly shared moral characteristics. Through his distinction between community values and social values, Plessner is in fact warning his readers against a totalitarian culturalism. How due his warning was would become apparent in National Socialist Germany only a decade after the text's publication. A sense of togetherness and uniformity was demanded and introduced, which immediately led to racist, and soon murderous, exclusion.

However, Plessner must also be questioned. A liberal constitutional state is based on mutual trust. Anyone who demands that values be professed demands too much. So far, Plessner is right; but anyone who wants to base such a polity solely on a functioning bureaucracy demands too little. A free society needs not only regulatory authorities for its conflicts; a society also needs sources that nourish its capacity to live on the basis of trust. Such sources can, in one and the same society, be different for different people; but its importance should not be underestimated. Only, and here again Plessner is right, are these nourishing sources the much invoked "values"? And what is that supposed to be, a value?

Love: Christian Value?

The Christian core value seems to be charity; but we must be careful. Both the Aramaic and Hebrew languages speak of "love." They use one and the same word for active-neighborly and partner-attracted love. Greek, like Latin and English, distinguishes between *agapē* (Greek) and *caritas* (Latin): charity and *erōs*: love (in Latin, *amor*).

Christian faith, growing from a Hebrew/Aramaic root, does not keep the emotional intuitive dynamics strictly out of charity. Loving seems to be more than looking after your neighbor. If loving means more, however, that makes the use of the value of "charity" more difficult in social discourse. Of course, every interpersonal rule needs an intuition, a preconceptual sensation for its truly human application. That is why Paul rightly presents love as the "fulfilling of the law" (Rom 13:10). Formal legalism does not even do justice to the intention of the law. As lawyers say, *summum ius, summa iniuria*, which means "complete law—complete lawlessness"; in other words, a perfectionist implementation of law automatically flips over into injustice. Both public debate, however, and political attempts at world shaping need a more concrete orientation than only the word *love*.

The Bible itself offers four references for the practice of loving. The commandment runs, "You shall love your neighbor as yourself" (Mark 12:31), so *self-love* is not excluded, but presupposed. The Sermon on the Mount furthermore makes it clear that one's "neighbor" also refers to one's *enemies* (Matt 5:44). The Johannine Christ also instructs the disciples to love one another *as he loved them* (John 13:34). This is marked out as the "new commandment" because thus its content seems overburdening, but at the same time its source is offered: despite their weaknesses, people are enabled to really love the same way because of the liberating love they have received from Christ. Finally, however, it is no coincidence that the Bible's fundamental command prefaces "love your neighbor" with another love. The complete formula is this:

> The first is, "Hear, O Israel: the Lord our God, the Lord is one; you shall love the Lord your God with all your heart, and with all your soul, and with all your mind, and with all your strength." The second is this, "You shall love your neighbor as yourself." There is no other commandment greater than these. (Mark 12:29)

Love of neighbor is thus linked, indeed preceded by, the love of God. A supposed love of God without the love of neighbor is a lie (1 John 4:20); but a person committed to charity without looking at the whole context becomes a romantic do-gooder. It would only mean following one's mood, without reflection on meaning and consequences. Max Weber distinguished between ethics of moral conviction and ethics of responsibility.[14] The call for responsible action is in fact based on Christian language. Martin Luther preached in 1532, "The conscience must be responsible to God in such a way that if you pass there, you pass the Last Judgment."[15]

Max Weber, however, claimed that people acting religiously must automatically behave according to what he derogatorily called moral conviction. Here, his distinction, which is meaningful in itself, becomes polemical. He said that there was "an abysmal contrast between acting according to conviction—religiously speaking: 'The Christian does right and leaves the success to God'—*or* according to responsibility: that one has to pay for the (foreseeable) *consequences* of one's actions." Weber's misunderstanding lies in the fact that people who act in view of the history of salvation feel all the more responsible for the foreseeable consequences of their actions, account for them, and try to act accordingly from the outset. Yet they know that there are factors other than their own actions determining the actual outcome. For religious people, putting success at the mercy of God is not an escape from responsibility, but an expression of gratitude, modesty, and simply, realism.

Responsible action always keeps different interests in mind at the same time. Those interests must control, relativize, and deideologize each other. If called to love of God, as horizon to love of one's neighbor, a human person is not only exposed to the fellow person's claim. Every claim, every action, and every nonaction is thus, rather, seen in context.

In this way, four places of response are called into the scene:

- The immediate challenge of the other;
- The temporal dimension with its view to the future;
- Reason;
- The question of God's plan, God's calling, and God's judgment.

So it is always necessary (and always difficult) to ponder and to take the concrete decision. Responsible action therefore happens within what is classically called "orders," that is, in justifiable structures. Responsible charity also inquires critically about the causes of the hardship one encounters, questions itself, critically, with regard to foreseeable and then actual effects. Responsible charity does not only offer a quick remedy, but plans ahead, creates institutions: the hospital, but also a health system; a pastoral care for the imprisoned, but also a just jurisdiction and access to education for the next generation.

Catholic Values

When people call for values, they call for ethics. And in the context of how religions shape the world, we deal with social ethics. In the wake of the Hebrew Bible, the Church, too, has expressed itself in social ethics from the beginning; and in the wake of prophecy, also in social critique. Catholic social doctrine, as proclaimed by the Roman pontiff, started with Leo XIII's 1891 encyclical *Rerum Novarum*. The Church was now utilizing socially, economically, and therefore politically relevant formulae. The form of life envisioned was a third way between capitalism and communism. The usual expression of Catholic social doctrine is to list certain "principles." But the Church teaches them with the claim that they correspond to Christian anthropology—indeed, that they originate from it. But at the same time the Church says that every human being can discover and acknowledge these principles in their validity, independent of his or her religion. Christian anthropology is based on recognizing the dignity of the human person. The Church also expressly states that these principles require constant revision and extension.

At the beginning of the twenty-first century, the Catholic Church presented a kind of catechism of its social doctrine, the so-called Social Compendium of 2006. It pronounces three principles: the common good with an emphasis on the universal destination of goods; subsidiarity with an emphasis on participation; solidarity with an emphasis on sustainability.[16] These principles are then confronted with "values," and there is mutual correlation between principles and values. Values describe the way in which principles are to be acknowledged. Following John XXIII's 1963 encyclical *Pacem in Terris*, the Catholic Church now names four fundamental values that make living together more dignified: a life "based...on truth, tempered by justice, motivated by mutual love, and holding fast to the practice of freedom."[17]

Value: A Concept and Its Problem

To what does the "values" discourse refer? Values seem to be general ethical concepts, expressing the style and aim of our action. If one tries to spell out values, one already recognizes a number of difficulties.

As long as they are addressed by an overall title, as a package ("our" values, or "democratic," or "human" values), they are easily accepted.

But if we begin to unravel the bundle and name individual values, we suddenly find ourselves debating with people we previously imagined to be standing in our own camp. On top of that, we will immediately see collisions of values. Which hierarchy of values is just? That will remain controversial. If one acts in truth, justice, love, and freedom, does that call for "respect" for those who think differently or "tolerance" toward them or "harmony" with them? Do we also have to show respect to those who show no respect for dissenters? Do we violate that respect ourselves if we demand it as a precondition of living together? Which situations fall under this concept and which do not?

Another problem is this: a value, once formulated, then stands before us as a demand. What remains unclear, however, is why we should follow it. Values do not themselves provide their justifications, neither by convincing us rationally nor by motivating us affectively. A value that is no longer mere intuition, but a word, also loses its stimulating power for new perspectives and ideas. It rather sounds average.

Moreover, what remains unclear is how a value relates to fundamental rights, to law, jurisdiction, and sanction. If "our values" are the basis of the legislative and judicial branches, they have already taken on their legally sanctioned form. They no longer allow for dispute, unless one wants to improve the legal situation or jurisdiction. And those who think that values are not the very basis of our legislation and jurisprudence must rather argue about the legal situation and judicial practice than about value formulations.

What the debate on fundamental values actually reveals, however, is the concern about coexistence in society. Free, and therefore trusting, coexistence depends on something that can neither be regulated by particular laws nor secured against deviation, that cannot be articulated in detail by a constitution's text or any other wording.

People calling for a new clarification of our common foundation often cannot sense that foundation within themselves. Are those who most loudly express concern about the decay of social values furthest away from them? That attitude, which lies below the level of concepts and which makes social life possible, could be called the "basic anthropological intuition." It is worth talking about it. Neither heated arguments nor failing agreements or a refusal by a part of the population to even talk have to be signs of fading consensus. There are many different ways of expression and justification. Whether living together fails or not becomes apparent in living together, not in talking about it.

This does not mean that we should not talk about values. But neither the general concept of values nor listing individual ones (which will again be general, then) solve a social problem. Talking about values, however, does a useful service. It makes people think, makes people speak clearly about things they only saw vaguely, makes people talk to each other. Hopefully it also makes people realize that it is not a definition that brings about good coexistence. Living together succeeds, rather, through ever new patience, willingness to learn, and imagination.

However, patience, willingness to learn, and imagination are values, too. The same applies to them: they are general postulates. But here another function of values is turning up; we can call it "elevation of the soul." This becomes clear when looking into the scriptures.

Ethics in Scriptures: Communicating Belonging

It may be disappointing to see that both the Bible and the Qur'an often content themselves with highly general terms. They say that one should be good. That is of course trivial. Isn't the question rather, what the good thing is, and why I should do it, what motivates me, and why I often fail? Particularly significant for the Qur'an's ethical message is a recurring formula. As a legal principle, it was later called (in a rather cumbersome way) *al-amr bi-l-ma'rūf wa-n-nahy 'ani l-munkar*: "Enjoining good and forbidding wrong" (Sura 3:104).[18] The Qur'an says that a community (*umma*) doing this already exists among the "people of the Book," without specifying who exactly belongs to it (Sura 3:114). Now it is meaningful that the word used here for "good" literally means "known" (*ma'rūf*); because according to the Qur'an, humanity already knows what is good. What is new in the Qur'an (as opposed to its perception of its environment) is only that the community and its leaders also act accordingly, rather than for their own advantage. But why does one need a claim to revelation like the Qur'anic proclamation if one then only hears what everyone knows anyway: that one should be good?

The answer can be found by exploring how the Hebrew Bible proceeds in order to communicate its ethos.

> A false balance is an abomination to the LORD,
> but an accurate weight is his delight.

When pride comes, then comes disgrace;
    but wisdom is with the humble.
The integrity of the upright guides them,
    but the crookedness of the treacherous destroys them.
Riches do not profit in the day of wrath,
    but righteousness delivers from death.
The righteousness of the blameless keeps their ways straight,
    but the wicked fall by their own wickedness.
The righteousness of the upright saves them,
    but the treacherous are taken captive by their schemes.
When the wicked die, their hope perishes,
    and the expectation of the godless comes to nothing.
The righteous are delivered from trouble,
    and the wicked get into it instead. (Prov 11:1–8)

Biblical Wisdom literature offers formulas that are clearly beautiful to listen to, and easy to learn. And that is precisely the point. We are listening to a kind of textbook for young people to memorize. How will the words become ethically fruitful beyond aesthetics? First of all, five motivational strategies can be identified: (1) Being evil does not pay, not even in this world. The Book of Proverbs suggestively recalls this experiential knowledge. (2) Evil displeases God. The text possibly already warns with a view to recompense in the hereafter. (3) The parallel contrasting structures are of a certain beauty and in any case good for memorization. At the same time, however, it seems that the proverbs want to shape not only the pupils' memory, but also their basic attitude. (4) Furthermore, they can pause after each verse to reflect, explicate, and debate. (5) Finally, mentioning the good may cause what we have just called "elevation of the soul." That is to say, one senses how good the good is, and therefore strives for it. "Elevation" is aptly ambiguous, by pointing, at the same time, at a passive and an active movement, both being lifted up and going up.

All this could also be said if Proverbs had been handed down in isolation. Now, however, there is a wider context. Through texts like this one, the Hebrew language is being taught. Not only human life experience is being evaluated, but also the experience of Israel. The message is this: You, the pupil, are part of this people. Here you are taught your ancestors' language, here you are entrusted with our nation's ancient wisdom. Here it is revealed to you that you belong to the people to whom God has done great things; you are part of the elect. What you get by memorizing your people's history and, now also, your people's ethics, is a sense of belonging.

The same can be said of the Qur'an. It communicates what counts, by giving it linguistic weight. It also promises reward. Again, just like the Hebrew Proverbs, it deliberately leaves open whether the reward is in this world or in the next, or both. And the Qur'an creates, comparable to the school situation of Proverbs, belonging and a social context. Here, however, it is even more oriented toward the polity and its constitution: to enjoin good and prohibit evil is not so much individual achievement as the beginning of institutionalization.

The New Testament, too, contains ethical rules and catalogues of virtues. However, there is an originality in the New Testament ethos. The communication of belonging that was already present in the Hebrew Bible is now being centered and radicalized. The testimony of the gospel is a special way of transmitting ethos. In what way? The answer must be given in two steps.

Shaping the Conscience

The specifically Christian way of transmitting values is not naming values and sanctioning them. What is specifically Christian, rather, is that an ethos is conveyed through the formation of conscience. But how does the formation of conscience happen in Christianity? The answer has to clarify on the one hand what conscience is, and on the other hand, what Christianity is. What does conscience mean? It is true, it is the accusatory-reactive inner voice of responsibility-looking-back; but conscience is (in its literal meaning) the accompanying knowledge of oneself: consciousness (in Latin, *conscientia*; *syneidēsis* in Greek). Conscience is in fact also a person's encouraging, creative capacity to recognize in responsibility-looking-forward what one's personal call and destiny is, and thus, what one can and should do.

And what is Christianity now? Only when this has been clarified can we also indicate how one can really educate and form a conscience.

The Church Communicates the Knowledge of Christ

If Christianity is meant to form consciences, that may sound like a moral or an educational institution where people hear what is good and bad. That would be a poor reduction of the movement initiated by Christ. In order to get beyond this, the specific self-understanding of Christianity, and its resulting social form of presence, has to be questioned again. In other words: here again we need to proceed ecclesiologically.

Only in modernity did the designation "Christianity" take a leading role in describing the Church; in doing so, Christians argued that the basic point of the gospel is morality. Meanwhile, we now see more clearly. In the search for a synthesis of culture and religion, we had encountered the understanding of the Church as sacrament. When studying religion as a source of identity, we suggested the category of "liturgical identity." In the light of that, a theologically viable answer can be offered to the question about the typically Christian mode of transmitting values. It must also respond to why the Church should exist in societies in the first place. How can the Church's various tasks be expressed in an appropriate way, without reducing the Church to mere morality, and still describing its ethical relevance? Is the Church's task to justify and transmit general values, or to convert unbelievers? The best answer is probably this: The Church communicates the knowledge of Christ. The formula deliberately uses the ambiguous vocabulary of the Bible.

"Communicating" is sacramental language: sharing (in Latin, *communicatio*), celebratory participation in the communion (*koinōnia* in Greek) with the Lord and in the Lord with others, which is now possible. The basis is the mediation of an experience, the Easter joy. The resurrection of Christ is being witnessed in front of people in order to become their new life perspective. They can be grasped by it (Phil 3:12). If this happens, it causes a change in their fundamental disposition; this frees them from their primal fears. These people have entered into a new sphere and a new form of existence, which they can call, just like St. Paul, "life in Christ," and "knowledge of Christ" (Rom 8:2; Phil 3:8, KJV). But what is this knowledge?

For scripture, "knowledge" is something cognitive: to receive information, to get to know. But biblically, knowledge happens in the heart. There, knowledge can also be acknowledgment, can be affective, and can be sexual. It is love (see Job 19:13; Gen 4:1). The "knowledge of Christ" is, then, not only knowledge about Jesus, but the growing understanding of his "ways" (his way of acting) is to strive for the fulfillment of Christ's project, to begin to "sense" like Christ (in Greek, *phronein*, Phil 2:5), to "have Christ's mind" (in Greek, *noun ekhein*, 1 Cor 2:16).

Christ's spirit can shape people's consciences, that is. Their self-perception can hence be freed for freedom and service (1 Cor 10:29). A person shaped in this manner can make good life decisions, because a "renewed" mind sees with new clarity: "Do not be conformed to this world, but be transformed by the renewing of your minds, so that you may discern [in Greek, *dokimazein*] what is the will of God—what is good and acceptable and perfect" (Rom 12:2). In the knowledge of Christ, people can discern God's will. Ignatius of Loyola is one of the spiritual masters who bring this tradition to life. He knows that life can be difficult when different interests collide. In order to decide then, one cannot deduce the solution from a list of principles. He knows that unforeseen events will always occur. For Ignatius, therefore, the decision-making is subject to the spiritually experienced responsible person's *discreta charidad*, as he calls it in Spanish: the love that is able to discern which of the different possibilities appears in this case to be God's salvific will.[19]

The Church communicates the knowledge of Christ. It does so by witnessing to, celebrating and sharing in, a new grand narrative. Through the witness of a life in communion with Christ, people can be freed to recognize by themselves what the good is that is now required, and to strive for it. But can Christians then communicate values only to Christians? More generally can religious communities participate in public processes of opinion shaping? Can they introduce values there? They can, because such a witness can be an "elevation of hearts," a critical reminder of forgotten points of view or of groups of people, a fertilization of the dialogue by an unusual way of speaking and thinking. To intervene in such a way in a society's discourse is public theology.

THEOLOGY IN THE PUBLIC SPHERE

Theology wants to be "the understanding of the faith."[20] This recalls the new insight made possible by the testimony and act of faith; but "the understanding of the faith" is also recalling a dialogue. Just as the message and attitude of faith wants to stimulate people's understanding of the world, so human rationality wants, in the face of world and self-experience, to examine and possibly accept that to which faith testifies. To enter the debate is in this sense fundamental to theology, because it is the understanding of faith. But how to debate?

A faith group can publicly affirm their view on a particular issue. They can also try to convince, on this point, people who do not belong to the faith group. They can finally try to get a relevant decision through representatives in politics. How do we justify such a view?

For justification, it is not enough to claim that it is thus willed by God, thus revealed, thus enjoined in a holy book. That is insufficient not because every view proposed to the public discourse has to be justified in a purely rational way. A society can live with divergent truth claims, different ways of justifying them, and various concepts of rationality. The justification of claims by mere reference to revelation and the will of God falls short because the will of God is not accessible to anyone in an uncontroversial manner. Nor do holy scriptures create clarity beyond dispute. Scripture must always be interpreted, different exegetes come to different understandings, and different groups respect different texts as authoritative scripture.

In fact, religious communities can place their public justification for a certain view on three levels: on rationality, the future, and belonging. They can, for one, reconstruct religious ideas in a reflective and argumentative manner. Alternatively, believers can try to convince others in looking to the future: such a life makes one happier in this world or in the hereafter; such a life will better realize the human destiny. Finally, however, religious arguments are often appeals to belonging: it is human, it is part of our culture, it corresponds to all faiths, it is fundamental to our faith. Here, however, amazing connections emerge. Out of ignorance or selfishness, believers with a politically relevant view can find themselves in a camp whose ethos does not correspond to their faith. Worldwide, a political shift to the right can be observed. It results from fear of losing self-determination, security, or identity. Now, it is often believing people who opt for authoritarian options and persons. They typically do this with faith arguments like "God is for family values" and let other key aspects of their faith fall by the wayside, like Catholicism's option for the poor.

Those who call for public theology need to see that theology is only one way for a religion to express itself publicly. When presented in the style of some pressure group, a religious community's contribution to the political discourse is merely dry moralizing. Religions have a great variety of forms for their public presence. They are more than a lobbying position. A religion is a whole web of references. A religion is a "culture." It offers a whole context in which to develop, nourish, embed, explain, and justify a politically expressed statement. Let us only point to a few such forms. Among them are the special expressions of religious scriptures (heard both in their strangeness and in transla-tion and transposition). Then there are rhythms (the hourly strike of the clock, the call to prayer, feasts). Furthermore, there are the aesthet-ics (liturgical movements, incense, cantilena.) In art we have buildings, sculptures, paintings, musical instruments, hymns, cantatas. Then there is the grand narrative: creation, this world, and the hereafter. There are signs of presence: the sanctuary light, the headscarf. There are special places: from kindergarten to cemetery. Cultural rudiments include Santa Claus and the *in šā'a llāh* formula with which Muslims throughout the world speak about future plans: "If God so wills." Finally, there is suf-fering, as when people become victims of religious discrimination, per-secution, or violence.

Religious traditions often portray the believers' life on earth as exile. This is what Jacob said as an old man before Pharaoh: "I have lived as a wayfarer" (in Hebrew, *māgûr*, Gen 47:9, NABRE). Like-wise, the Psalmist confesses that he is only a guest on earth (Ps 119:18: *ger ānokî bā-āræṣ*). The New Testament, too, sees how the believers are only guests in this world, pilgrims, strangers (in Greek, *paroikoi*, *parepidēmoi*, *xenoi*: 1 Pet 2:11; Heb 11:13); what they actually are is citizens of heaven (Phil 3:20). This is also how Islamic mysticism calls it: life on earth is life abroad, a stranger's existence: *ġurba* in Arabic.

These strangers, however, are not thus kept in fearful retreat. Their sense of being strangers can become, for the believers, a source of their critical sense, their sense of humor. It can be a healing distance to life, which is, after all, difficult for everyone. Thus, their belief can become to the "stranger in exile on earth" a consolation, "a portable fatherland,"[21] a home that nourishes people's imagination and strength to cooperate with others to shape the world.

It is time to summarize in a final concept the different forms of presence a religion can have in society. First, however, let us reread the tension that underlies an understanding of religion as inspiration.

From Conscience to Person: Looking Back and Looking Forward

State religions justify human power over other humans by acknowledging the sovereign as the image of the heavenly hierarchy or of the cosmic order, as appointed by a god, or as that god's earthly representative. A religion that acknowledges this is run by the state. Should one strive to return to a uniform religious culture, back to the religious "nation"? Such a culture has probably never really existed uniformly; it will also hardly be possible to produce it, and its production by the state would not be desirable at all from a theological point of view. Faith and state power must in fact not appropriate each other. State power should have the monopoly on the use of force. Distinguished from that is the other power of the religious testimony. It can reach human beings so that they can have insight into it as truth; and only so does it convince, "at once quietly and with power."[22] The style of faith communication is, therefore, the testimony. Whether others accept it or not cannot be determined by the witness. So refusal must be expected. Testimonies of faith and divergent claims to truth will remain controversial against each other. This can have a beneficial effect because it challenges ideologically defended stances. Thus, a theology that considers what religious faith is, already points toward a pluralistic society.

But if the religious testimony has political relevance, this question also arises: In a pluralistic society, how can political rule still be justified by religion? The twentieth century saw a magisterial paradigm shift in this, particularly well traceable in the Catholic Church. It was made possible by the Church's worldwide experience, often a minority experience, which stood in constant interaction with theological development. At Vatican II, the universal Church left behind the principle of a Catholic state church, which had so long been held as an ideal. Freedom of religion was recognized as theologically necessary. But now the question arises, How can political power still be justified by religion? The Council itself did this through personalism, more precisely in view of "the interdependence of human person and human society."[23] A constitutional form of society is thus humane, because the human being is person; and the recognition of the personality of the human being by the government can now become a yardstick for the legitimacy of rule.

The concept of the person is promising because it is compatible with philosophical traditions outside of Christianity. But Christians will feed, as "inspiration," their specific understanding of the person into the polyphonic dialogues. It arises in view of what Sacred Scripture testifies to, above all in view of Christ and his proclamation of God's kingdom.

Religion as Inspiration in a Plural Society

The Bible has made a decisive contribution to the history of the self. Here, for the first time the human being says, "I" in confession and responsibility (Ps 51). The human being has, qua human being, the capacity for ethical knowledge, and thus for responsibility and confession (Rom 2:15); in this respect the human being is autonomous: a "law to themselves" (Rom 2:14). The human being thus also has a conscience, and a sense for the otherness of the other's conscience and necessity to respect it (1 Cor 10:29). Nevertheless, the human task is not autonomy as individual independence. The human being is called into the life of God in which she or he already participates when living in communion with Christ (Luke 12:8). In this way, the human being can experience and fulfill the law as the law of love, which is God himself. Since they are called to eternal communion with God, human beings have infinite dignity. From a Christian point of view, this is their human status as a "person." All persons are to be fully recognized at every moment in this dignity, without being able to prove at any moment of their lives that they are fully worthy of this recognition. This is what we have to examine finally, the dynamics of recognition, acknowledgment, will prove to serve also as a synopsis of everything we have been able to develop in the past six chapters.

ACKNOWLEDGMENT

Previewing the Seventh Chapter

We have taken up the *political-theological challenge* of the question of how religions can shape the world. In responding, we have seen how susceptible religion is to abuse. Finally, I shall face a *conceptual challenge*. Can religion be defined in such a way that its definition already shows how violence runs counter to its essence?

To conclude, such a formula is offered here: religion is, in the full sense, the acknowledgment of the Other. This is developed under ten considerations:

- Acknowledgment of the human being by God
- Acknowledgment of God by the human being
- Acknowledgment of the environment
- Acknowledgment of the fellow human being
- Acknowledgment of oneself
- Acknowledgment of the undesirable
- Acknowledgment of what needs to be changed
- Acknowledgment of a tradition
- Acknowledgment of a community order
- Acknowledgment of other points of view

So, all the roads we have taken so far seem to lead us to an understanding of religion as acknowledgment of the Other.

7

Religion as Acknowledgment of the Other

In 2011, Pope Benedict XVI invited the representatives of different world religions to Assisi, Italy, to celebrate an anniversary. Twenty-five years earlier, in 1986, Pope St. John Paul II had convened the first-ever World Day of Prayer for Peace in the hometown of St. Francis, a courageous move, a brave step. But Benedict had one particular worry. Their coming together to pray, he felt, might look like relativism and syncretism.[1] Benedict was the first to invite not only representatives of religions, but also agnostics. It was their presence he must have had in mind when preparing his speech, because he discussed objections to "religion":

> The post-Enlightenment critique of religion has repeatedly maintained that religion is a cause of violence and in this way it has fueled hostility towards religions. The fact that, in the case we are considering here, religion really does motivate violence should be profoundly disturbing to us as religious persons. In a way that is more subtle but no less cruel, we also see religion as the cause of violence when force is used by the defenders of one religion against others. The religious

221

ACKNOWLEDGMENT

delegates who were assembled in Assisi in 1986 wanted to say, and we now repeat it emphatically and firmly: this is not the true nature of religion. It is the antithesis of religion and contributes to its destruction. In response, an objection is raised: how do you know what the true nature of religion is? Does your assertion not derive from the fact that your religion has become a spent force? Others in their turn will object: is there such a thing as a common nature of religion that finds expression in all religions and is therefore applicable to them all? We must ask ourselves these questions, if we wish to argue realistically and credibly against religiously motivated violence. Herein lies a fundamental task for interreligious dialogue—an exercise which is to receive renewed emphasis through this meeting.[2]

One often hears that peace is the essential concern of religions.[3] Benedict, the pope-theologian, however, raises the question how to justify that. In search of such a justification, he was looking for a general concept of religion. In other words, he asked, what is the peace-promoting nature of religion? He did not answer his question, but he did give the word to interreligious dialogue. Let us accept the challenge.

It is difficult to find a definition of *religion* that fits everything that is commonly so called. We have already seen Eric Voegelin's important (but perhaps unconscious) hint when he explained that he understood by religion "such phenomena as Christianity."[4] He hints at the fact that in the concept of religion there is a good piece of projection from one's own faith onto others. This applied also when the modern age said *religio*[5] and when the Qur'an says *dīn*, religion. So the other must have something similar to our faith. Are Hinduism, in its variety of cults, writings, and teachings, and Buddhism in its renouncing completely to speak of God, really "religions"? That depends on the subconscious connotation, or on the explicit definition one has.

At the beginning of this study, we made a suggestion: religion can be defined as the "realization of the sacred." The proposal has a number of advantages. Religion can thus be seen as being both perception/experience ("then, I realized her presence"), and implementation ("she realizes the proposal creatively"). And what about teachings which do not understand the divine to be a personal reality? That is why we employed the term *the sacred* instead of *god*. Finally, "realization

222

of the sacred" also can mean (besides, "people perceive the sacred," and "people make it present in the world") "the sacred realizes itself/himself." Religion is the realization of the sacred; we thus have a relatively open and at the same time accurate concept of religion. What does not, however, follow from it is the rejection of "holy" war. If war can be called holy, then religious people see themselves as obliged to wage it.

Can we conceive of religion in such a way that the rejection of violence already follows from its concept? The six roles we have proposed so far in this book do not fulfill that expectation; they are sociopolitical descriptions rather than stating the nature of religion in a normative way: culture, creation of identity, legitimization of rule, relativization of power, presentation of weakness, and social inspiration. But religion can also be determined in a philosophical-theological manner; thus, and with a consciously suggestive program formula, one might say, "Religion is the acknowledgment of the other in the full sense."

What is acknowledgment? To acknowledge is to avoid both possessive appropriation and unconnected abandoning. Acknowledgment means to perceive but not as one perceives an object. Acknowledging means getting involved in a history of encounters, whose outcome one cannot determine alone. Acknowledging means entering into a dialogue.

Is religion aptly understood as acknowledgment of the other? Three objections to this can be raised immediately: First, *"Acknowledgment of the other" is too general a definition to clarify what religion is. Even the most areligious person recognizes others.* This is true; but the concept of religion proposed here employs the full breadth of the concept of the "other": the other thing, the other person, the transcendent Other. Thus the explanation of the phrase in question contains the question whether persons who, for instance, only acknowledge other human beings, do not have to go further in their movement of acknowledging, if they really want to acknowledge "the other"; and conversely, whether persons who say they acknowledge God would not also have to welcome other points of view with greater interest, because that openness is part of the concept of religion.

A second objection: *But is this broad understanding of the "other" not a trick with which one tries to reconcile what in reality does not belong together at all?* In naming "the Other," authors in the tradition of French phenomenology, for example, want to name the vis-à-vis: that alterity that can both be the familiar fellow human being, or some strikingly strange object; that alterity that can be God or *Oneself as Another.*[6] If a concept that can refer to God and to the other human being is more than a play on words, it must be seen in light of existing modes of expression. There are two relevant examples here. The word for "service" used in many languages under Islamic influence, *'ibāda*, means "worship." And the Qur'an emphasizes that no one but God deserves such acknowledgment. But since God directs people to care for their fellow human beings, service of the poor, for example, is also part of the Qur'anic "worship" (see Sura 90:13–16). Second, the New Testament so closely unites love for God, neighbor, and self (see Mark 12:30) that it can formulate the following: without love for fellow human beings there is no love for God (see 1 John 4:20). The openness of the expression of the "other" obviously reflects this biblically testified solidarity of the various interlocutors and drives us to pursue this trace.

A final objection can say, *The concept of acknowledgment may be justifiable philosophically, but is alien to religious traditions and their linguistic heritage.* In fact, however, the objection is erroneous. The New Testament, for one, certainly knows expressions from the semantic field of acknowledgment. They even shed new light on what has been seen so far. "Acknowledged" is *dektós* in New Testament Greek (Luke 4:24, etc.). The adjective is reminiscent of two different processes. It calls to mind *dekhesthai*, "to accept" or "to welcome," but also the *dokein*, "to have an opinion of someone." From *dokein* is formed the word with which John's Gospel speaks of the relationship between Jesus and his heavenly Father. When Jesus acknowledges his Father and is acknowledged by the Father (and by the Spirit), this is *doxazein*, meaning "to glorify." Also the New Testament expression we have already encountered under the heading of "knowledge" designates in fact an act of acknowledgment: the loving, humble openness toward the other person or thing that allows them to come into their true reality (1 Cor 8; 13).[7]

From ten different points of view, religion can be described as "acknowledgment of the other." Only this before we start: we will be speaking of "the human being" or "the human person." Does that generic "human person" exist at all? Philosophical anthropology presupposes that one can speak of the human being (in Greek, *anthropos*). With that expression, various sciences continue the choice of words with which more than two thousand years ago the basic anthropological theme was voiced in Hebrew: *"mā-änôš—What are human beings?,"* the Psalmist asks God (Ps 8:4). The problem of generalization is to be kept in mind in theological anthropology; but then the various relations of acknowledgment can be named both generically and accurately.

Relations of Acknowledgment

GOD ACKNOWLEDGING THE HUMAN PERSON

The biblical grand narrative can be described as God's history with the human being under the challenge of mutual acknowledgment. God creates the world and the human being. Afterward, Genesis says, in an acknowledging manner: "God saw everything that he had made, and indeed, it was very good" (Gen 1:31). But God's acknowledgment of his creation is not a unique event. Even when the human stops being faithful, God does not let the human being fall into death. He apparently risks appearing inconsistent rather than declaring the history of humankind discontinued. He opens up a new possibility of life. Thus God's acknowledgment is merciful. What does that mean? In the Bible, mercy is historical. It is the love that responds to its rejection creatively. But to what extent is that still acknowledgment? It is obviously not simply "acknowledging receipt" of the creature's rejection. Rather, merciful acknowledgment also takes into consideration that which is not yet apparent at the moment, but which, precisely through this mercy, is made possible and becomes real: the human being who will actually be God's loving and creative covenantal partner. Mercy is acknowledgment in that it already sees the good not yet achieved but made possible by that anticipatory acknowledgment.

THE HUMAN PERSON ACKNOWLEDGING GOD

In religions, people acknowledge a personal God as the sacred and determining reality, or as something more diffuse, something less definable, a force. How does this acknowledgment of God by human beings manifest itself in the holy scriptures of Judaism, Christianity, and Islam? Its first form is fear.

225

ACKNOWLEDGMENT

Fear is generally not a desirable sensation. There is, however, a fear that scripture presents as salutary, namely the fear of God. It is the "beginning of wisdom" (Ps 111:10). How should something as blocking as fear lead to wisdom? The fear of God is nothing that robs human beings of their imaginative and creative powers. With the fear as mood and with the fear of innerworldly objects, the fear of God only has in common that it indicates an encounter with something nondisposable: I am at the other's mercy. Fear of God is not an inhibition, but a life-forming sense of being seized by God, being in his hand. That liberates human beings from fearing the world's dangers. To acknowledge God's great works, to keep God's power in mind, means to understand that no one here can determine the world, nor oneself. Now, this also corresponds more to reality than human fantasies of omnipotence. The right knowledge of the world and of human nature comes from the modesty of that acknowledgment.

Satan asks snappishly in the Book of Job, "Does Job fear God for nothing?" (Job 1:9). The seducer alludes merely to the fact that Job was richly gifted by God and is therefore not only wealthy and happy, but also full of careful fidelity to God's law. This is the other side of the fear of God: it does not acknowledge God's actions in general, but specifically, as happening "for us" and "for me." Fear of God and thanking God are two sides of the same coin. Acknowledgment is also gratitude; in French both are *reconnaissance*.

Thanksgiving is the glad acknowledgment that one could not have done it oneself. Out of gratitude, the human being comes to faith; and faith then happens in faithfulness, that is, without looking at the reward and without making the right action dependent on ever new gifts from God. Faith and faithfulness are related words in Hebrew, too (*âmûnâ, æmæt*, see Ps 86:10). Gratitude has become faithfulness. That both are one and the same movement is indicated by the biblical notion of "blessing" (the Hebrew root is *b-r-k*). It speaks at the same time of God's gift, of the creatures praising God, and the active witness to God when people give blessings to others.

Another biblical word impressively traces the dynamics of acknowledging, to "confess" (in Hebrew, *y-d-h*). Confessing God's great deeds "for us" (Isa 26:12; Ps 126:3) is acknowledging that we are already acknowledged by him. Being acknowledged is what makes possible self-awareness and autonomy. Confession also leads me to the knowledge that I am acknowledged by God through and through, and thus to the confession that in my pettiness I do not correspond to God's mercy. Professing or confessing God becomes confession of guilt; and thus once again an acknowledgment of God as merciful and just (Ps 51:1.3). A third dynamic of faith is also called "confession" in the New Testament (Heb 4:14). The acknowledging consent to the Christ event becomes entry into the divine life itself. This act of entry takes place in the baptismal confession, publicly.

If human beings acknowledge God as their "Thou," each one of them becomes an "I." What however does the claim mean that God is personal? It says that God has a will, his own plan. Therefore, contact with God is encounter. Meeting him is being torn out of one's self-centeredness. God challenges every person to set out. So one form of trusting acknowledgment is obedience. Sura *al-Fātiḥa* voices that in an illuminating way.

Sura 1 – *al-Fātiḥa*: The Opening
1 In the name of God, the merciful Mercifier!
2 Praise be to God, the Lord of all worlds,
3 The merciful Mercifier!
4 Who rules on the Day of Judgment.
5 It is You we worship ['-b-d], it is You we ask for help.
6 Guide us in the straight path.
7 the path of those You have blessed, those who incur no anger
and who have not gone astray.

"Guide us in the straight path" (Sura 1:6)—the prayer leaves open whether the "guidance" is God indicating the way or God taking us to the goal. In fact, this openness makes sense. Both our deliberate collaboration and God's complete activity are always intertwined in the experience of believers. To pray is to acknowledge that one's life is in God's hands. God knows what he wants. He will lead the course of events according to his will. That is why this request (by the way, the only request in this key prayer of Islam) was preceded by an acknowledgment of God as *rabb al-ʿālamīn*, as "Lord of the inhabitants of the world times." God is acknowledged as the Lord of history. On the Christian side, the main request to God, again in the key prayer, is "Your will be done" (Matt 6:10). Those who pray this today, pray with Jesus in Gethsemane (Matt 26:42). Immediately before his arrest he had begged that the cup should pass by him, so that he would not have to go the way of suffering. But then the transformation took place that is part of real prayer. After one has expressed one's own longing and opened oneself to God, one can be freed to assent: not my will, but yours, Lord!

Christians may know from the history of Jesus that God does not impose his will at the expense of humanity, but that he is the Father who wants life in abundance for his creatures (John 10:10). Acknowledging God as the Lord of history has two consequences. The encounter with Christ shapes people's hearts so that their obedience becomes the two-fold faithfulness "to the law and to the spirit."[8] The attitude of prayer is then the acceptance of the otherness of God and his will, confident that the world is in the hands of the loving Father. Even that which seems to come in his way does not really hinder his good plan.

Now we must consider another way in which God is acknowledged as the Lord of history. God wants to make himself dependent on the cooperation of creatures. Thus prayer is already an expression of one's own consent to creative participation.

THE HUMAN PERSON ACKNOWLEDGES THE COMMON HOUSE: CREATION

Religions can have a magical tendency and attribute guaranteed healing powers to an object of nature—a tree or rock, for example. They can also have a degrading tendency and push aside everything natural. Or they can have a subjugating tendency toward exploiting nature and can even claim that their basic writings entitle them to do so. This is how the biblical command was understood: "Subdue [the earth]" (k-b-$š$, Gen 1:28). But why would God command this? In the time of the passage's origin, nature is still threatening the human. It is felt as a danger. Therefore it is necessary to "have dominion over" it (r-d-h, v. 28). For the human person, however, dominion means acting as God's image on earth, as Genesis says immediately before (v. 27); and God's reign is not exploitation. Rather, he lets life "spring forth, sprout" (d-$š$-', v. 11). As soon as nature is no longer a danger but becomes a "garden," God entrusts it to the human being again. Now he is to "work, serve" in it ('-b-d), indeed, he is to "protect, preserve" the garden ($š$-m-r, Gen 2:15). Ruthless exploitation of nature must not be justified biblically. This protective stewardship also corresponds to the general concept of religion explained here. If religions are acknowledgment of the other, they can also convey a special sensitivity for the whole of nature.

To see creation as our common house[9] and to feel oneself as part of the divine order of creation is an attitude that is also present in Qur'anic Suras, as we have seen. Indeed, people can rediscover themselves as part of the process of creation, so much so that they sense all creatures to be one great community of responsibility.

St. Francis of Assisi (1182–1226) sings God's praise in a peculiar way. He lives in a culture of transition, including linguistic development: the vernacular of his homeland (the Umbrian language) and Latin interpenetrate. In his famous hymn of praise, he calls seven times, "*Laudato si', mi' Signore, per…*—Be praised, Lord, for…." People can praise God "for" something; that is familiar from the Bible: "Praise him for his mighty deeds!" (Ps 150:2). What we translate by "for," however, is more open in Hebrew: *bə-*. The Vulgates and Luther still translate: praise God "in." Only the King James Version of 1611 and afterward all modern translations understand, "Praise him *for* his mighty acts." But the other creatures are not only a message to humanity. They are also our companions in the praise of God. Let him be praised *cum tucte le tue creature*, sings Francis: "with all your creatures." So then, his *per*, too, cannot mean only praising "for"; it can also be the Latin word for "through," just as here: "*Laudato si', mi' Signore, per frate focu, / per lo quale ennallumini la nocte*—Be praised, my Lord, for brother fire, *through* whom you enlighten the night."

That Franciscan *per* of praise thus has two directions. It is in a double sense praise of creation: praise for creatures—and praise from the mouth of creatures, as in the Psalm: "Praise him, sun and moon; praise him, all you shining stars" (Ps 148:3). St. Francis already suggests here what can be understood in the meantime not only anthropologically but also ecologically: the creatures are dependent on each other. Human beings must not subdue creation to their desires; they must, rather, administer it responsibly.

THE HUMAN PERSON ACKNOWLEDGING HER FELLOW HUMAN PERSON

According to the Book of Genesis, God commissioned the human being in the Garden of Eden to *'ābədāh* and *šāmərāh*: "to till it and keep it" (Gen 2:15); but already the next generation will show what the creature not acknowledging its borders is capable of. When Cain is caught red-handed in fratricide, he pretends coolness: "Am I my brother's keeper [*šōmēr*]?" (Gen 4:9). That, however, is exactly what the human being is: the one to care for brother and sister. The biblical Cain stands for the hypocritical misunderstanding that the divine mandate "to keep" (*š-m-r*, Gen 2:15) applies only to the garden, not to the brother. But acknowledgment of creation cannot be responsibility for the common house without taking care of its inhabitants.

The Qur'an will tell the story in such a way that Abel, shortly before his brother kills him, says, "If you reach out your hand to kill me, I will not reach out my hand to kill you. I fear [*aḥāfu*] God, the Lord of the worlds" (Sura 5:28). Fear of God is the acknowledgment, in awe, of the Lord of all. Acknowledging him already entails acknowledging and preserving others as his creatures and as one's brothers and sisters. Preserving does not mean that I can protect the other human being from life's hardship, but that I contribute to making their life truly human. But one is also entrusted to oneself.

THE HUMAN BEING ACKNOWLEDGING HIMSELF/HERSELF

Love as "acknowledging the other" thus contains a recognition of one's own neediness; I am dependent on my environment, on my fellow human beings, and on God. However, the biblical commandment to love explicitly presupposes self-love (Lev 19:18; Mark 12:31). Can that also be understood as a relationship of acknowledgment? Monsignor Romano Guardini (1885–1968) writes,

> We are to criticize ourselves, but in loyalty to what God has founded in us. The respect of the human person for herself must be rediscovered. It is rooted in the widely forgotten truth that God himself respects us. There is no cold knowledge of the human being—no knowledge in violence—only in that generosity and freedom which is called love. But love begins in God; begins in that he loves me, and I am able to love him; and in that I am grateful to him for his first gift to me, which is called: I-myself.[10]

To recognize oneself as being wanted and loved is a way of acknowledgment, one that makes possible life in love. Self-love is no vain complacency. Like fellow human beings, one acknowledges oneself as a person who is now only beginning to be what one day one's whole self is supposed to have become. I know that I have not yet reached the fulfillment of my destiny, but I can already see it appearing. It is the self that is to be and that I am therefore called to love and to strive for, in spite of all neediness. The sense of who I am destined to be is my conscience.[11]

ACKNOWLEDGING THE UNDESIRABLE

The faith testified to in the Bible consists in the acknowledgment of a personal God, the Lord, who not only has a will and a mission, but is good. Whoever accepts this recognizes meaning in history. However, the course of history does not always appear to be meaningful, joyful. This can be met with stoic indifference or a generous sense of humor. But believers can also call out their disappointment precisely because they wanted to acknowledge God as a good Lord. God acts "differently," painfully differently: "It is my grief that the right hand of the Most High has [now translated literally] changed" (Ps 77:10). Hence the believer reproaches God by saying, "Why have you forsaken me?" (Ps 22:1). The question verbalizes the greatest need, possibly despair, but the question "why" could also open oneself to a surprise. The Egyptian Joseph, whom his brothers, out of envy, sold into slavery, may have asked desperately for years, why? But his bad fate turned out to be a blessing, for himself, for those entrusted to him, and then even for those who had once sold him. Before them, before his brothers, he can now see an answer to the question why. History has unexpectedly proved to be truly cunning and meaningful. He can console the brothers with impressive generosity, because now he can see meaning: "And now do not be distressed, or angry with yourselves, because you sold me here; for God sent me before you to preserve life" (Gen 45:5). Also in this sense, religion is acknowledging the other. Acknowledgment of the adverse, however, obviously means that human beings themselves must cooperate.

ACKNOWLEDGING CHANGES TO BE NECESSARY AND POSSIBLE

The acknowledgment of the other, which belongs to the essence of religion, entails that religious people have a critical relationship to present conditions. The world situation in fact never corresponds with the message of faith. Many religions draw up a picture of what true justice, good society, is. Thus, they criticize reality and offer a contrasting foil, possibly even the energy to begin change projects. The leitmotif of Pope Francis's programmatic *Evangelii Gaudium* is *apertura*. What does that mean? The Word points at an "openness" for God's mission and for God's action in history, and thus at the will to engage in change and to let oneself be involved in it.[12] The "other" that is acknowledged by religion is also what is not yet there. However, besides that which comes from the future, religion also includes that which comes from the past.

ACKNOWLEDGING A TRADITION

General talk on "religion" is in danger of interpreting other people's understandings of life according to one's own pattern. Wilfred Cantwell Smith (1916–2000) questions the concept of religion. For him, it is a modern Western projection. In premodern times, *religio* referred to personal "piety." Since the seventeenth century, within the context of Christian confessionalization, it was understood as a systematic "doctrinal edifice." Only since the twentieth century is "religion" what sociologists and historians study as a community's "beliefs, practices, values."[13] Because of the danger of projection in the concept of religion, and its multifaceted semantic outreach, today the term *faith tradition* is often preferred. This is problematic in view of "religions" such as Buddhism and Judaism, where the concept of faith can be inappropriate or marginal. On the other hand, the notion of tradition is appropriate insofar as a religion typically represents a past history. Religions are traditions especially under three aspects:

- They transmit rules—ethical, cultic, and intuitive.
- They transmit a heritage of texts—for reading, prayer, chanting.
- They keep alive a grand narrative.

All these can seem exotic, even odd to contemporaries. However, the believers' relationship to something they have not invented frees them from the doubt that they may have been circling around themselves. It challenges them to come out of their self-referential ways. This is especially true when there is a guaranteeing community, a personal instruction, or a written tradition. Where it is offensive even to the believer, it also becomes an impulse for further growth. Where it appears scandalous to others, "the duty of identity" can nourish "the courage of otherness."[14] By contrast, when mere emotion, perhaps in rejection of tradition, is coming to expression, what may be lacking is the depth and variety of a historical legacy and the support it may grant. Remember how liberating it can be to entrust oneself to a traditional form of worship, even abandon oneself in it.

A religion's tradition can contain a message that confronts the faithful by being something they cannot communicate to themselves: an encouragement, a promise, an opening of access from history. The transmitted heritage confronting a person now can also be a guide of high authority: commandments for meditation and cultic practice, but also for the shaping of everyday life and of society. And since tradition forms an environment, a culture, it also shapes the world, is political, and can create community, possibly even a polity.

ACKNOWLEDGING A COMMUNITY ORDER

Caring for the neighbor belongs, as we said, to the dynamics of acknowledging the other; but one can only truly do justice to the others (and is thus only really acknowledging them) if one respects the space in which those people can unfold who cannot or do not want to receive our care. Acknowledgment of the other is therefore also to recognize a social and political order with its style, laws, institutions, and representatives. The authors of the New Testament, too, can feel this way: "Honor everyone. Love the family of believers. Fear God. Honor the emperor" (1 Pet 2:17). Such acknowledgment is not blind obedience. It rather means to acknowledge principles of power administration, power relations, and bearers of power as enabling human development and fulfillment in freedom and solidarity. Thus, a critical standard has already been introduced into this type of acknowledgment.

ACKNOWLEDGING OTHER VIEWS AND LIFESTYLES

Religions can also, if misused or misunderstood, turn human beings into fanatics. Fanatics hardly understand the views and lifestyles

ACKNOWLEDGMENT

of others. But if we try to understand religion as something like "acknowledgment of the other," then religions should precisely be experts in understanding different opinions. Such an understanding cannot, of course, be deduced from a newly proposed concept. However, it allows the question to be asked whether in general one can discern traits in religions, specifically religious traits, which at the same time help people to accept deviations from their own worldview.

People within faith traditions can at the same time be convinced of their belief's plausibility and yet have an awareness that not everyone will be won over. It is true, where there are religions, dispute will not be far: "And never argue with the people of the Book other than in the best possible way," orders the Qu'ran (Sura 29:46a). Not all will be convinced. Why not, when the right faith can be explained so clearly that everyone can see it? The Qur'an repeatedly provides the theological solution that God "leads some people astray" (Sura 35:9, etc.). Thus, proclaimers no longer have to reproach themselves for their failure; and so the persistent unbelief is no proof of God's weakness. Unbelief, is then, in God's hands. Christians are also aware from the beginning that not everyone accepts the Easter witness. Being able to believe is a gift. Seeing this, one can already create an understanding for other points of view; but it has also led to the assumption that God must now be helped in his conversion project, by force of arms. So how can believers become more dialogical? Is there theological justification for that?

For one, there is the argument that when eradicating what seems wrong, one might also destroy what is good. This has been a rather pragmatic but efficient justification of tolerance in Church history, based on Jesus's parable of the weeds that ends in the advice to "let both of them grow together until the harvest" (Matt 13:30).

A theologically more profound argument is this: although the Hebrew Bible has no explicit word for "history," it sees the "deeds" of God (Ps 143:5) and therefore sees a meaningful whole happening. Thus the Bible can be seen as the source of the understanding of all events as one "history." Many religions do similar things. Looking at history can give believers special confidence: God will change everything for the better and will also include the defeats, the experiences of suffering, and the violence suffered. Those who acknowledge this also see the peace potential of religions and a readiness for dialogue, to which "acknowledgment of the other" points. If all events belong to the history of God's salvation, the encounter between believers of other

234

faiths can also become, for both "purification and enrichment."[15] Such an expectation leads not only to tolerance toward others, but to a real interest in them as well.

Also, the profession that "our religion is rational" or even "is the rational religion" sounds dialogical. But is reason at someone's disposal in such a way? Even when it comes to religion, reference to rationality should not be reduced to the simple claim of having the better arguments. It must actually be proven again and again throughout history who the person is with the better arguments. Reason should here rather mean not simply to assume what is believed to be true, but to distinguish truth (as the target concept) from one's own understanding (up to now). Rational is the readiness to see every concept, and everything so far conceived as provisional. If religion is acknowledgment of the other, it modestly admits that what is true is what is to be acknowledged rather than what is at our disposal; and that rational faith therefore means being open for the development of knowledge. So people who want to represent their convictions also by means of reason will not automatically be the winners. Rather, they carry out in it a further acknowledgment of the other, namely of the truth, which cannot be produced, which can even be in opposition to their previous views.

God is not only an experience in one's own heart. He also *confronts* both the community and the individual. God can speak sharp words against his own people. Even the king is forbidden to take advantages and selfish partisanship (2 Sam 12; Isa 1:23). A God whom I acknowledge as "my God" is actually leading me out of my self-made cell—if he really is God and thus greater than my self-centeredness. He will not always fulfill my private interests and requests. Also, all earthly formulas and forms of expression concerning him are relativized before his own reality, for he is ever greater.[16]

Such formulas can, however, contain a "transcendence trick." Then God, defined as the one who eludes all definition, is nothing more than a thought: in the dynamics of the "ever different," but no longer a challenging counterpart. At the same time, however, the biblical testimony presents God as the one who binds himself most concretely: to a certain people, to a certain person in Galilee, to a certain sacramental celebration. Here, too, acknowledgment of the other is called for: namely, acknowledging the scandal of particularity. However, even where God binds himself to earthly things, he cannot be appropriated, his truth cannot be possessed, his presence cannot be restricted. If people believe in the free God, who created heaven and earth and who chooses by himself where he wants to manifest his presence and future, faith in him frees them both from a rationalistic dogmatism and from a tribal party formation.

Thus it can actually be justified how, from the concept of religion or from the "true essence" of religion, there follows not war but reconciliation. Because religion means, in the full sense, acknowledging the other.

Conclusion

We have made seven attempts here. Six times we were following the same course. We wanted to understand how religions can shape the world. For this purpose, we identified different types of religious ways of shaping the world: culture, foundation of identity, legitimization of power, relativization of power, presence of powerlessness, and inspiration of society. However, we have not restricted ourselves to description. Rather, to that sociological framework, we aligned corresponding religious notions, mostly from the Bible and the Qur'an, especially where they are critical of past and present circumstances. Only with the seventh concept of religion did we proceed differently. Now we were no longer limiting ourselves to the various forms of religious world shaping. Rather, we were searching for a formula that is open enough to name the whole range of relationships that are meaningfully described as religious, but which at the same time contains a standard to identify pseudoreligion. A useful formula proved to be, in great breadth of meaning, religion is the acknowledgment of the other. The formula could be unfolded into ten different relations of acknowledgment. All of them thus came into view as religious dimensions. What can the dynamics of acknowledgment of the other now contribute to a better understanding of the various types of religious world shaping?

The six types of social power of religion could be grouped into three groups, in each of which two opposing religious dynamics are at work. Let's sketch this out.

Religion can be like an existing culture, or it can present itself as an attempted new identity. The two belong together because in them two conditions of acknowledgment come into play: the acknowledgment of a continuing tradition and the acknowledgment that the conditions can, indeed must, change. Where religion is only lived like a culture, the world-critical potential of religion remains bound. Where it behaves as a radically new foundation, it avoids consideration for continuities; it then becomes something human made and is thus no longer religion in the strict sense.

Religions can legitimize violence and any human rule—but religions can also relativize them. These two forms of the social presence of religion also belong together. For both are explicitly related to human power. Again, the two can also criticize each other meaningfully, namely from the concept of religion itself. If religion serves only for the legitimation of human power, it suppresses the fact that it also includes the acknowledgment of the other, other human beings, in their claim to shape the world. Where religion shows human power within its limits, it has an important task, but must not now be abused to prevent any earthly order. For acknowledgment of the community order is itself part of the religious relationship of acknowledgment in its breadth.

In another way, the last two social forms of religion examined here belong together: religion as a realization of human weakness and as inspiration. In them, all ten relations of acknowledgment are at work; but each time, the relationship is shaped by the fact that we have to consciously acknowledge it. The fellow human being and nature, the social order and our tradition would be misunderstood, even abused, if one thought they could prevail by imposing themselves. They are dependent on the other who respects them in their dignity, gives them space, that is, acknowledges them. This is also true of God. He does not want to be Lord at the expense of his creatures, but through their participation. So there are theological, conceptual reasons—beyond the boundaries of one particular religion—for why religion is only faithful to itself when it brings to bear its power to shape the world, not by using its power violently, but in acknowledgment of the other.

Notes

I. Religion as Culture

1. Eric Voegelin, "The Political Religions," in *The Collected Works of Eric Voegelin*, vol. 5, *Modernity without Restraint* (Columbia: The University of Missouri Press, 1999), 27.

2. Johann Baptist Metz, *Theology of the World* (New York: Seabury Press, 1973). The book's main theological piece is his "World as History" (originally written just before the closure of Vatican II, for the second edition of the German *Encyclopedia of Theology and Church*, which was edited by his teacher Karl Rahner, SJ).

3. See Hans Maier, "Kritik der politischen Theologie (1970)," in Hans Maier, *Politische Religionen* (Munich: C.H. Beck, 2007), 32.

4. See volume 2 of Karl Rahner and Alfons Darlap, eds., *Sacramentum Mundi: An Encyclopedia of Theology*, 6 vols. (German edition: Freiburg: Herder, 1963–1970).

5. John W. Padberg, ed., *The Constitutions of the Society of Jesus and Their Complementary Norms* (St. Louis: The Institute of Jesuit Sources, 1996), 125.

6. Karl Rahner, "Über den Dialog in der pluralistischen Gesellschaft," *Stimmen der Zeit* 176 (1965): 321–30.

7. Franz Xaver Arnold and Karl Rahner, eds., *Handbuch der Pastoraltheologie*, 6 vols. (Freiburg: Herder, 1964–1972), vol. 2, part 1, 35.

8. Martin Heidegger, *Sein und Zeit* (*Being and Time*) (Tübingen: Max Niemeyer Verlag, 1927), 63: no. 14.

9. This has been explored by Jürgen Habermas ever since his postdoctoral thesis on the structural transformation of the public sphere: *Strukturwandel der Öffentlichkeit* (Frankfurt am Main: Suhrkamp, 1962). In spite of Habermas's attempt to distinguish between *Öffentlichkeit* ("publicness") and *öffentliche Sphäre*, the standard rendering of *Öffentlichkeit* is now "public sphere."

10. "Everything": *ha-kol*, Jer 10:16, etc.; "earth, land": *æræṣ*, *teḅel*; "duration": *ḥælæd* and especially *'ôlām*.

11. Gerhard von Rad, *Theologie des Alten Testaments* (*Theology of the Old Testament*), 6th ed. (Munich: Chr. Kaiser Verlag, 1969), 1:165.

12. This observation—and many more Qur'an interpretations in the following—are based on the research by Angelika Neuwirth, especially in her book *The Qur'an and Late Antiquity: A Shared Heritage* (New York: Oxford University Press, 2019).

13. See Wolfhart Pannenberg, *Systematic Theology*, 3 vols. (Grand Rapids: Wm. B. Eerdmans, 2013), vol. 2, chapter 7, I, 3; chapter 8, 3a.

14. Wolfhart Pannenberg, *Anthropology in Theological Perspective* (Edinburgh: T & T Clark, 1985), 69 (chapter 2, III).

15. Charles Taylor, *A Secular Age* (Cambridge, MA: Harvard University Press, 2007).

16. Jean Calvin, *Institutes of the Christian Religion*, I, 11, 10, accessed April 24, 2019, http://www.ccel.org/ccel/calvin/institutes.iii.xii.html.

17. Calvin, *Institutes*, I, 11, 12,

18. *Gaudium et spes* 4, accessed March 22, 2019, http://www.vatican.va/archive/hist_councils/ii_vatican_council/documents/vat-ii_const_19651207_gaudium-et-spes_en.html.

19. Thomas Bauer, *Die Kultur der Ambiguität. Eine andere Geschichte des Islams* (Berlin: Verlag der Weltreligionen, 2011); Josef van Ess, *Der Eine und das Andere. Beobachtungen an islamischen häresiographischen Texten* (Berlin: de Gruyter, 2011).

20. Henry Chadwick, *The Early Church* (London: Penguin, 1993), 46.

21. The sociologist Georg Simmel (1858–1918) has coined the adjective "religioid" from *religio* and the Greek suffix -ειδής /-*eidēs* ("-shaped") to describe quasi-religious phenomena: *Die Religion* (Frankfurt am Main: Rütten and Loening, 1906), 114.

22. I am here drawing on Rolf Schieder's research. See his *Civil Religion. Die religiöse Dimension politischer Kultur* (Gütersloh: Mohn, 1987).

23. Georg Wilhelm Friedrich Hegel, *Vorlesungen über die Philosophie der Religion*, part 3, *Die vollendete Religion*, ed. Walter Jaeschke (Hamburg: Felix Meiner, 1984), 254, lines 80–81. It should be noted that, for the Lutheran Hegel, "community" can mean something like "church," because Luther regularly rendered the New Testament word ἐκκλησία/*ekklēsia* as "*Gemein(d)e*—community"; at the same time, however, Hegel is referring to "society, people."

24. Hegel, *Die vollendete Religion*, 262, lines 305–6.

25. Hegel, *Die vollendete Religion*, 264, line 383.

26. Martin Luther, *Eyn brieff an die Fürsten zu Sachsen von dem auffrurischem geyst* (Weimar Edition) (Weimar: Hermann Böhlau, 1899), 15:219.

2. Religion as Foundation of a New Identity

1. Umm Khalid al-Finlandiyyah (literally, "Finnish woman whose eldest son is Ḫālid"), "How I Came to Islam," *Dabiq* 15 (July 2016): 36; see https://clarionproject.org/islamic-state-isis-isil -propaganda-magazine-dabiq-50/ (accessed June 5, 2019).

2. Thomas Meyer, *Identitätswahn* (Berlin: Aufbau Taschenbuch Verlag, 1997).

3. See Mark Juergensmeyer, *Global Rebellion: Religious Challenges to the Secular State, from Christian Militias to al Qaeda* (Berkeley: University of California Press, 2008.)

4. Metin M. Coşgel, Thomas J. Miceli, and Jared Rubin, "The Political Economy of Mass Printing: Legitimacy and Technological Change in the Ottoman Empire," *Journal of Comparative Economics* 40 (2012): 357–71.

5. "Strive for God's sake," 22:78, *ğāhidū fī llāh*. "Fight for God's sake," 2:190, *qātilū fī sabīli llāh*. "Kill the polytheists," 9:5, *fa-qtulū l-mušrikīna*, cf., 9:29. An example from the life of Muḥammad is the massacre of all male members of the Jewish tribe of the Banū Qurayẓa in 627. See also, the section in this book on "Holy War in Islam," p. 94.

6. See Josef van Ess, *Der Eine und das Andere. Beobachtungen an islamischen häresiographischen Texten* (Berlin: de Gruyter, 2011).

7. Gottfried Küenzlen, "Moderner Antimodernismus. Kultursoziologische Überlegungen," *Theologia Practica* 1 (1994): 43–56.

8. Pope Francis, *Laudato Si'*, On Care for Our Common Home, 106–14, accessed March 22, 2019, http://w2.vatican.va/content/francesco/en/encyclicals/documents/papa-francesco_20150524_enciclica-laudato-si.html.

9. Ibn al-Ḥaǧǧāǧ, *Ṣaḥīḥ, Kitāb al-Fitan wa-ašrāṭ as-sāʿa* (= 41/44/54), number 6924.

10. Angelika Neuwirth, *The Qur'an and Late Antiquity: A Shared Heritage* (New York: Oxford University Press, 2019), chapter 12, 3. See also www.corpuscoranicum.de.

11. Jan Christian Gertz, "Volk Gottes," in *Religion in Geschichte und Gegenwart*, vol. 8 (Tübingen: Mohr Siebeck, 2005), cols. 1152–53.

12. Joachim Ritter and Karlfried Grunder, eds., *Historisches Wörterbuch der Philosophie*, vol. 6 (Basel: Schwabe, 1984), col. 408.

13. Martin Luther criticized the restriction of the Christian vocation to monastic life: all Christians have a priestly mission, he argued, and any role they take in the society can be a divine vocation. "Vocation" is, then, a mission to get involved in the world: "How could you possibly not have a vocation?": *Wie ists muglich, das du nit beruffen seyest?*; Martin Luther, *Weihnachtspostille 1522* (Weimar Edition), vol. 10/1/1 (Weimar: Hermann Böhlaus Nachfolger, 1910), 308.

14. H. Wheeler Robinson's *The Hebrew Conception of Corporate Personality* of 1936 and his 1937 "The Group and the Individual in Israel" were posthumously published together as *Corporate Personality in Ancient Israel*, rev. ed. (Edinburgh: T & T Clark, 1981).

15. For the entire document see http://w2.vatican.va/content/francesco/en/speeches/2014/november/documents/papa-francesco_20141125_strasburgo-parlamento-europeo.html (accessed May 31, 2019).

16. Wolfhart Pannenberg, *Anthropology in Theological Perspective* (London: T & T Clark, 2004), 200–223.

17. Homer, *Odyssey*, α 4f, accessed June 18, 2019, http://classics.mit.edu/Homer/odyssey.html.

18. *Le métarécit*, as Jean-François Lyotard called it in 1979. See Lyotard, *La Condition Postmoderne* (Paris: Minuit, 1979), 7.

19. Johann Wolfgang von Goethe, Letter to Friedrich Schiller,

July 9, 1796, quoted in Stephen Leach and James Tartaglia, "The Original Meaning of Life," *Philosophy Now* 126 (June/July 2018), accessed June 18, 2019, https://philosophynow.org/issues/126/The_Original_Meaning_of_Life.

20. Muhammad Hamidullah was a Muslim scholar from India; he received part of his academic formation in Bonn, Germany, and in Paris. He taught in Istanbul and Erzurum, Turkey.

21. See, e.g., the Greek *koinōnia*; e.g., 1 Cor 10:16.

22. Martin Luther, *Assertio 1520* (Weimar Edition) (Weimar: Herman Böhlaus Nachfolger, 1897), vol. 7, 98, 40–99, 2: *solam scripturam | regnare nec eam meo spiritu aut ullorum hominum interpretari sed per seipsam | et suo spiritu intelligi volo.*

23. Jean-François Gilmont, "Réformes protestantes et lecture," in *Histoire de la lecture dans le monde occidental*, ed. Guglielmo Cavallo and Roger Chartier (Paris: Éditions du Seuil, 1997), 249–78.

24. Jürgen Habermas, "Bewußtmachende oder rettende Kritik—die Aktualität Walter Benjamins," in *Zur Aktualität Walter Benjamins, aus Anlaß des 80. Geburtstags von Walter Benjamin*, ed. Siegfried Unseld (Frankfurt: Suhrkamp, 1972), 195.

25. *Lumen Gentium*, 1, accessed June 13, 2019, http://www.vatican.va/archive/hist_councils/ii_vatican_council/documents/vat-ii_const_19641121_lumen-gentium_en.html.

3. Religion as Legitimation of Rule and Violence

1. Michael von Faulhaber, "Das Schwert auf der Wage des Evangeliums," in *Waffen des Lichts. Gesammelte Kriegsreden* (Freiburg: Herder, 1915), 131–53, 132, 140, 148.

2. *Gaudium et Spes* 40, 43, accessed May 5, 2019, http://www.vatican.va/archive/hist_councils/ii_vatican_council/documents/vat-ii_const_19651207_gaudium-et-spes_en.html.

3. *Traditio Apostolica*, 16, accessed June 14, 2019, http://www.bombaxo.com/patristic-stuff/church-orders/hippolytus-the-apostolic-tradition/.

4. *Civitas Dei* I, 26, accessed June 12, 2019, http://www.thelatinlibrary.com/augustine/civ2.shtml.

5. Thomas Aquinas, *Summa Theologiæ* II-II, 40, 1, accessed April 12, 2019, http://www.documentacatholicaomnia.eu/03d/1225 -1274,_Thomas_Aquinas,_Summa_Theologiae_%5B1%5D,_EN.pdf.

6. "How Born-Again George Became a Man on a Mission," *The Guardian*, October 7, 2005, accessed June 14, 2019, https://www .theguardian.com/world/2005/oct/07/usa.georgebush.

7. Josef van Ess, *Dschihad gestern und heute* (Berlin: de Gruyter, 2012), 41. See also page 34.

8. Jan Assmann, *Of God and Gods: Egypt, Israel, and the Rise of Monotheism* (Madison: University of Wisconsin Press, 2008). (German original, *Die mosaische Unterscheidung, oder der Preis des Monotheismus* [Munich: Carl Hanser Verlag, 2003]).

9. Jan Assmann, *The Invention of Religion: Faith and Covenant in the Book of Exodus* (Princeton, NJ: Princeton University Press, 2018).

10. *Gaudium et Spes* 40, 43.

11. Max Weber, *Wirtschaft und Gesellschaft (Economy and Society)* (Tübingen: Mohr, 1922), 124 (emphasis in the original).

12. Jürgen Habermas, *Legitimationsprobleme im Spätkapitalismus* (Frankfurt: Suhrkamp, 1973), 134 (italics mine). See the discussion in Wolfhart Pannenberg, *Anthropologie in theologischer Perspektive* (Göttingen: Vandenhoeck & Ruprecht, 1983), 449 (chapter 8.4, c).

13. Eric Voegelin, "The New Science of Politics: An Introduction," in *The Collected Works of Eric Voegelin*, vol. 5, *Modernity without Restraint* (Columbia: The University of Missouri Press, 1999), 75–241.

14. Klaus Schmidt, *Sie bauten die ersten Tempel. Das rätselhafte Heiligtum der Steinzeitjäger. Die archäologische Entdeckung am Göbekli Tepe* (Munich: C. H. Beck, 2007).

15. Eric Voegelin, *Order and History*, in *The Collected Works of Eric Voegelin*, 34 vols. (Columbia: University of Missouri Press, 2001), 1:354.

16. Dietz-Otto Edzard, *Geschichte Mesopotamiens. Von den Sumerern bis zu Alexander dem Großen* (Munich: C.H. Beck, 2004), 123.

17. Voegelin, "The New Science of Politics," 149, 137.

18. "All human laws derive after all from the one divine (law)," Heraclitus (fragment 114) formulated over a millennium after Ḥammurapi; cf., on the whole subject, Pannenberg, *Anthropologie*, 452.

19. Voegelin, "The New Science of Politics," 136.

20. *Evangelii Gaudium* 223.

21. Karl Jaspers, *Vom Ursprung und Ziel der Geschichte* (Zurich: Artemis-Verlag, 1949).

22. Hans Joas, *Die Macht des Heiligen. Eine Alternative zur Geschichte von der Entzauberung* (Berlin: Suhrkamp, 2017), 349.

23. Egon Flaig, *Weltgeschichte der Sklaverei* (Munich: C.H. Beck, 2009), chapter 8.

24. Publius Cornelius Tacitus, *Annales*, 15:44, accessed June 1, 2019, http://www.perseus.tufts.edu/hopper/text?doc=Perseus%3Atext %3A1999.02.0078%3Abook%3D15%3Achapter%3D44.

25. Origen, *Contra Celsum*, book II, 30, accessed June 14, 2019, http://www.newadvent.org/fathers/04162.htm.

26. For Eusebius's *Vita Constantini*, see Alexander Demandt, *Die Spätantike: Römische Geschichte von Diocletian bis Justinian, 284– 565 n.Chr.* (München: Beck, 2007).

27. Demandt, *Die Spätantike*, 93.

28. Jörg Lauster, *Die Verzauberung der Welt. Eine Kulturge- schichte des Christentums* (Munich: C.H. Beck, 2014), 95.

4. Religion as Relativization and Critique of Worldly Power

1. Alfred Delp, *Gesammelte Schriften*, vol. 4, *Aus dem Gefäng- nis*, ed. Roman Bleistein (Frankfurt: Knecht, 1984), 101, 136. See also Felix Körner, "Ekklesiologie im Widerstand. Wieso Religion für Alfred Delp etwas Politisches ist," in *Shifting Locations and Reshaping Meth- ods*, ed. Ulrich Winkler, Religion zwischen Mystik und Politik (Münster: Aschendorff, 2020), 257–76.

2. Delp, *Aus dem Gefängnis*, 389.

3. Norbert Lohfink, "Distribution of the Functions of Power: The Laws Concerning Public Offices in Deuteronomy 16:18—18:22," in *A Song of Power and the Power of Song: Essays on the Book of Deuteronomy*, ed. Duane L. Christensen (Winona Lake, IN: Eisenbrauns, 1993), 336–55. See also Eckart Otto, *Deuteronomium 12,1—23,15*, Herders Theologischer Kommentar zum Alten Testament, vol. 5.3 (Freiburg: Herder, 2016).

4. Josef van Ess, *Theologie und Gesellschaft im 2. Und 3. Jahr- hundert Hidschra. Eine Geschichte des religiösen Denkens im frühen Islam* (Berlin: de Gruyter, 1991), 1:41.

5. Patricia Crone, *Medieval Islamic Political Thought* (Edinburgh: Edinburgh University Press, 2004), 45.

6. ʿAbdullahi Ahmed An-Naʿim, *Islam and the Secular State: Negotiating the Future of Shariʿa* (Cambridge, MA: Harvard University Press, 2008).

7. Hellmut Ritter, "Studien zur Geschichte der islamischen Frömmigkeit. I. Ḥasan al-Baṣrī," *Der Islam* 21 (1933): 20.

8. Shahab Ahmed, *What Is Islam? The Importance of Being Islamic* (Princeton, NJ: Princeton University Press, 2015), 405, 409.

9. Edward William Lane, *An Arabic-English Lexicon*, 8 vols. (London: Williams and Norgate, 1897), 1:934.

10. David E. Aune, *Revelation 6—16*, Word Biblical Commentary, vol. 52b (Nashville: Thomas Nelson, 1998), *in loc.*

11. Martin Luther, *Von welltlicher Uberkeytt wie weytt man yhr gehorsam schuldig sey* (1523) (Weimar Edition) (Weimar: Hermann Böhlau Nachfolger, 1900), 11:229–81.

12. "Denn es ist eyn frey werck umb den glawben, datzu man niemandt kan zwingen. Ya es ist eyn gottlich werck ym geyst, schweyg denn das es eußerliche gewallt sollt erzwingen und schaffen," in Luther, *Von welltlicher Uberkeytt*, 264, lines 19–22.

13. Wolfhart Pannenberg, *Systematische Theologie*, 3 vols. (Göttingen: Vandenhoeck & Ruprecht, 1993), 3:69.

14. Eric Voegelin, "The New Science of Politics: An Introduction," in *The Collected Works of Eric Voegelin*, vol. 5, *Modernity without Restraint* (Columbia: The University of Missouri Press, 1999), 185.

15. See Karl Barth's polemics against a "Theology of the 'and'" in *Kirchliche Dogmatik*, 4 vols. (London: T & T Clark, 1969), vol. 1, part 1, 252.

16. Walter Kasper, *Katholische Kirche. Wesen, Wirklichkeit, Sendung* (Freiburg: Herder, 2011), 142.

17. *Lumen Gentium* 1.

5. Religion as Representation of Weakness

1. Pedro Aruppe, *One Jesuit's Spiritual Journey: Autobiographical Conversations with Jean-Claude Dietsch, S.J.*, trans. Ruth Bradley

(St. Louis: Institute of Jesuit Sources, 1986), 34–36, slightly abbreviated and rearranged; and corrected in two places: "one hundred thousand" (rather than "five thousand," original, *cent mille*) and "those whom he loves" (rather than "those who love him," original, *ceux qu'il aime*).

2. Jon Sobrino, *Resurrección de la verdadera Iglesia. Los pobres, lugar teológico de la eclesiología* (Santander: Sal Terrae Editorial, 1984).

3. Ignatius of Loyola, *Spiritual Exercises*, nos. 98, 146, 147, 168, accessed April 5, 2019, http://spex.ignatianspirituality.com/Spiritual Exercises/Puhl.

4. And once again, my own interpretation is heavily indebted to Angelika Neuwirth's findings.

5. Norbert Lohfink, "Von der 'Anawim-Partei' zur 'Kirche der Armen.' Die bibelwissenschaftliche Ahnentafel eines Hauptbegriffs der 'Theologie der Befreiung,'" *Biblica* 67 (1986): 153–76.

6. "In faccia ai paesi sottosviluppati la Chiesa si presenta quale è, e vuol essere, come la Chiesa di tutti, e particolarmente la Chiesa dei poveri"; see Carlos Maria Galli, "From John XXIII to Francis," accessed May 16, 2019, http://www.raoulwallenberg.net/roncalli/articles-11/from-john-xxiii-to-francis/.

7. Canon 282 (in Latin, *vitæ simplicitas*), accessed April 24, 2019, http://www.jgray.org/codes/cic83eng.html.

8. "Meeting with Priests, Consecrated Men and Women and Seminarians, Address of His Holiness Pope Francis, Santiago Cathedral, January 16, 2018," accessed May 29, 2019, https://w2.vatican .va/content/francesco/en/speeches/2018/january/documents/papa -francesco_20180116_cile-santiago-religiosi.html.

9. Pope Francis, Apostolic Letter *Misericordia et Misera*, November 20, 2016, accessed March 26, 2019, http://w2.vatican.va/content/francesco/en/apost_letters/documents/papa-francesco-lettera -ap_20161120_misericordia-et-misera.html.

10. Augustine, *In Ioannem* 26:2, accessed April 12, 2019, http://www.newadvent.org/fathers/1701026.htm. Augustine writes, "*Credere non potest nisi volens*"—"to believe is possible only if one wants to believe."

11. Michael Reder and Josef Schmidt, eds., *Ein Bewußtsein von dem, was fehlt. Eine Diskussion mit Jürgen Habermas* (Berlin: Suhrkamp, 2008), 30.

12. Reder and Schmidt, *Ein Bewußtsein von dem, was fehlt*, 94. See also Johann-Baptist Metz, *Memoria Passionis. Ein provozierendes Gedächtnis in pluralistischer Gesellschaft* (Freiburg: Herder, 2006).

13. Immanuel Kant, *Kant's Critique of Judgement*, trans. with intro. J. H. Bernard, 2nd rev. ed. (London: Macmillan, 1914), appendix, § 91, n41, https://oll.libertyfund.org/titles/kant-the-critique-of-judgement/simple#lf0318_label_363.

14. Pope Francis, homily at Lampedusa, July 8, 2013, accessed April 13, 2019, http://w2.vatican.va/content/francesco/en/homilies/2013/documents/papa-francesco_20130708_omelia-lampedusa.html.

15. Alfred Delp, *Gesammelte Schriften*, vol. 4, *Aus dem Gefängnis*, ed. Roman Bleistein (Frankfurt: Knecht, 1984), 218.

16. Ignatius of Loyola, *Spiritual Exercises*, 234.

17. Delp, *Aus dem Gefängnis*, 218.

6. Religion as Inspiration in a Plural Society

1. See www.rondine.org.

2. Charles Taylor, *A Secular Age* (Cambridge, MA: Harvard University Press, 2007), 3.

3. Cf. Christoph Stiegemann, Martin Kroker, and Wolfgang Walter, eds., *Credo. Christianisierung Europas im Mittelalter*, 3 vols. (Petersberg: Michael Imhof Verlag, 2013–17).

4. *Apostolicam actuositatem* 2: "esercitano l'apostolato evangelizzando e santificando gli uomini, e animando e perfezionando con lo spirito evangelico l'ordine temporale." See the document at http://www.vatican.va/archive/hist_councils/ii_vatican_council/documents/vat-ii_decree_19651118_apostolicam-actuositatem_en.html (accessed June 25, 2019).

5. *Gaudium et Spes* 43: "l'animazione del mondo con lo spirito cristiano."

6. *Gaudium et Spes* 44.

7. John Paul II, *Ecclesia in Europa*, 116.

8. Pope Francis, Strasbourg, November 25, 2014: "Un anonimo autore del II secolo scrisse che «i cristiani rappresentano nel mondo ciò che l'anima è nel corpo». Il compito dell'anima è quello di sostenere il

corpo, di esserne la coscienza e la memoria storica. E una storia bimillenaria lega l'Europa e il cristianesimo. Una storia non priva di conflitti e di errori, anche di peccati, ma sempre animata dal desiderio di costruire per il bene." See the document at http://w2.vatican.va/content/francesco/en/speeches/2014/november/documents/papa-francesco_20141125_strasburgo-consiglio-europa.html (accessed June 25, 2019).

9. Paul VI, *Evangelii Nuntiandi* 20: "occorre evangelizzare—non in maniera decorativa, a somiglianza di vernice superficiale, ma in modo vitale, in profondità e fino alle radici—la cultura e le culture dell'uomo." See the entire document at http://w2.vatican.va/content/paul-vi/en/apost_exhortations/documents/hf_p-vi_exh_19751208_evangelii-nuntiandi.html (accessed June 25, 2019).

10. *Apostolicam Actuositatem* 2, "rerum temporalium ordinem spiritu evangelico perfundendum ac perficiendum."

11. Pope Francis, *Evangelii Gaudium* 176.

12. Helmuth Plessner, *Die Stufen des Organischen und der Mensch. Einleitung in die philosophische Anthropologie* (1928), *Gesammelte Schriften*, vol. 4 (Frankfurt: Suhrkamp, 1981), 360, 393. The following two quotes are both on 392.

13. Helmuth Plessner, *Grenzen der Gemeinschaft. Eine Kritik des sozialen Radikalismus* (1924), *Gesammelte Schriften*, vol. 5 (Frankfurt: Suhrkamp, 1980), 95. The following quote is on 96.

14. Max Weber, "Politik als Beruf" (1919, "Politics as Vocation"), in *Gesammelte Politische Schriften* (Tübingen: Mohr Siebeck, 1988), 505–60, 551–52. The quotation after the passage from Luther is on 552.

15. Martin Luther, Weimar Edition, vol. 36 (Weimar 1909), 444, lines 19–20.

16. *Compendium of the Social Doctrine of the Church*, 160–96, 466–71, accessed June 25, 2019, http://www.vatican.va/roman_curia/pontifical_councils/justpeace/documents/rc_pc_justpeace_doc_20060526_compendio-dott-soc_en.html.

17. Pope St. John XXIII, *Pacem in Terris* 149, accessed June 17, 2019, http://w2.vatican.va/content/john-xxiii/en/encyclicals/documents/hf_j-xxiii_enc_11041963_pacem.html.

18. See Thomas Aquinas, *Summa Theologiae*, I-II q. 94 a. 2 corpus: *quod bonum est faciendum et prosequendum, et malum vitandum*—"good is to be done and pursued, and evil is to be avoided."

19. Ignatius of Loyola, *Constitutions*, 237, 2; *Spiritual Exercises*, 104, 233.

20. Augustine, *Sermo* 139:1: *intellectus fidei*. See https://w2.vatican.va/content/john-paul-ii/en/speeches/1999/november/documents/hf_jp-ii_spe_16111999_pul.pdf (accessed March 25, 2019).

21. Heinrich Heine saw the Bible as the Jews' portable fatherland: *Confessions*, chapter 7 (*Sämtliche Werke* [Munich: Winkler, 1969, first publication, 1854]).

22. *Dignitatis Humanae* 1, accessed April 1, 2019, http://www.vatican.va/archive/hist_councils/ii_vatican_council/documents/vat-ii_decl_19651207_dignitatis-humanae_en.html.

23. *Gaudium et Spes* 25.

7. Religion as Acknowledgment of the Other

1. Benedict XVI wrote in a 2011 letter to the Protestant missiologist and former Tübingen colleague Peter Bayerhaus, "I very well understand your worry in view of my participation in the Assisi anniversary. But this commemoration had to be celebrated in any case; and after all consideration, it seemed to me best to go there myself and try to determine the direction of the whole event. In any case, I will do everything I can to make a syncretistic or relativistic interpretation of the process impossible and to make it clear that I continue to believe and confess what I recalled to the Church in the declaration *Dominus Jesus*"; quoted in Sandro Magister, "The Truth about Assisi: Never-Before-Seen Words from Benedict XVI," October 26, 2011, accessed April 14, 2019, http://chiesa.espresso.repubblica.it/articolo/1349995bdc4.html?eng=y.

2. "Address of His Holiness Benedict XVI at the Meeting for Peace in Assisi," October 27, 2011, accessed April 26, 2019, https://w2.vatican.va/content/benedict-xvi/en/speeches/2011/october/documents/hf_ben-xvi_spe_20111027_assisi.html.

3. At the end of the First World Prayer Meeting (1986), John Paul II summarized the mood as follows: "More perhaps than ever before in history, the intrinsic link between an authentic religious attitude and the great good of peace has become evident to all." See "Address of John Paul II to the Representatives of the Christian Churches and Ecclesial Communities Gathered in Assisi for the World Day of Prayer, October

Notes

27, 1986," accessed June 4, 2019, https://w2.vatican.va/content/john
-paul-ii/en/speeches/1986/october/documents/hf_jp-ii_spe_19861027
_prayer-peace-assisi.html. In 2002, in the name also of the other reli-
gious communities, John Paul II affirmed that "whoever uses religion to
foment violence contradicts religion's deepest and truest inspiration";
see "Address of His Holiness John Paul II to the Representatives of the
World Religions," January 24, 2002, accessed June 3, 2019, http://w2
.vatican.va/content/john-paul-ii/en/speeches/2002/january/documents/
hf_jp-ii_spe_20020124_discorso-assisi.html. In September 2016, Pope
Francis declared, "Let us not tire of repeating that the name of God
can never justify violence. Peace alone is holy. Only peace is holy, not
war"; in "Visit of His Holiness Pope Francis to Assisi for the World
Day of Prayer for Peace," September 20, 2016, accessed April 3, 2019,
http://w2.vatican.va/content/francesco/en/speeches/2016/september/
documents/papa-francesco_20160920_assisi-preghiera-pace.html.

4. Eric Voegelin, "The Political Religions," in *The Collected
Works of Eric Voegelin*, vol. 5, *Modernity without Restraint* (Columbia: The University of Missouri Press, 1999), 27; but he already added
there, "and the other great redemptive religions."

5. Matteo Ricci, *Della entrata della Compagnia di Giesù e
Christianità nella Cina*, ed. Maddalena Del Gatto (Macerata: Quodli-
bet, 2006), 90.

6. Paul Ricœur, *Soi-même comme un autre* (Paris: Éditions du
Seuil, 1990); see also Ricoeur, *Parcours de la reconnaissance* (Paris:
Gallimard, 2013).

7. See Wolfgang Schrage, *Der erste Brief an die Korinther*, 4
vols. (Zurich: Benziger, 1995), 2:231–35.

8. Quoted in Devin Watkins, "Pope Celebrates Mass on World
Day of Consecrated Life," February 2, 2019, accessed March 1, 2019,
https://www.vaticannews.va/en/pope/news/2019-02/pope-francis-mass
-consecrated-religious.html.

9. Pope Francis, *Laudato Si'*, On Care for Our Common Home,
accessed March 22, 2019, http://w2.vatican.va/content/francesco/en/
encyclicals/documents/papa-francesco_20150524_enciclica-laudato-si
.html.

10. Romano Guardini, "Die Annahme seiner selbst," in *Gläu-
biges Dasein* (Mainz: Matthias-Grünewald-Verlag, 1993), 21, 22, 27.

11. Wolfhart Pannenberg, *Anthropologie in theologischer Perspektive* (Göttingen: Vandenhoeck & Ruprecht, 1983), 300 (chapter 6.4).

12. Felix Körner, "Apertura nella verità e nell'amore. *Evangelii Gaudium* e il dialogo cattolico-musulmano," *Gregorianum* 96 (2015): 123–43.

13. Wilfred Cantwell Smith, *The Meaning and End of Religion* (Minneapolis: Fortress Press, 1962), 48.

14. "Address of His Holiness Pope Francis to the Participants in the International Peace Conference," accessed February 3, 2020, http://www.vatican.va/content/francesco/en/speeches/2017/april/documents/papa-francesco_20170428_egitto-conferenza-pace.html. The official version, "the duty to respect one's own identity and that of others, the courage to accept differences," does not do full justice to the highly suggestive original "il dovere dell'identità, il coraggio dell'alterità."

15. "Address of John Paul II to the Members of the Secretariat for Promoting Christian Unity," November 16, 1984, accessed March 12, 2019, https://w2.vatican.va/content/john-paul-ii/en/speeches/1984/november/documents/hf_jp-ii_spe_19841116_unione-cristiani.html; "Address of His Holiness Benedict XVI on the Occasion of Christmas Greetings to the Roman Curia," December 21, 2012, accessed March 12, 2019, http://w2.vatican.va/content/benedict-xvi/en/speeches/2012/december/documents/hf_ben-xvi_spe_20121221_auguri-curia.html; Pope Francis, Apostolic Exhortation *Evangelii Gaudium* 250.

16. See St. Augustine, *Expositions on the Psalms* (Digital Psalms, 2007), 62:15, accessed June 11, 2019, https://faculty.gordon.edu/hu/bi/ted_hildebrandt/otesources/19-psalms/text/books/augustine-psalms/augustine-psalms.pdf.

Index

Index

Index

representation, 104;
Voegelin, 104
Preferential option for the
poor, 166
Proclamation, 198
Proverbs, Book of, 210–11
Psalms, 107–10, 171

Qaṣīda, 12–13
Qur'an: and the Bible, 66–67;
clarity, 25; coercion, 179;
ethics, 209, 211; God, 16,
167, 169, 178–79; identity,
63; intertexts, 171; and
Muḥammad, 11; overcoming
memory, 167–70; the
poor, 170, 171; poverty
identification, 180; Suras,
11; and violence, 94–96; and
world, 11–16, 24–25; world
understanding, 139. *See also
specific Suras*, e.g., Al-Balad

Rahner, Karl, 1, 6–9
Reality, 101–2
Reflected sacrality, 114–15
Reformations, 22–23, 195–96
Religion: absolute claim, 184;
acknowledgment of the other,
223–28, 238; belief, 188; and
Bible, 66–67; Christianity, 4;
church, 34–35; civil, 1, 33–36;
clarity, 23, 24; coercion, 179;
and community identity, 67;
contradiction, 192–94, 196–
97, 202–15; criticism, 184–
85; and culture, 1, 4, 18–42,
214–15, 237–38; definition,
222–23; and fanaticism, 233–

34; formula, 237; freedom,
32; and identity, 43; and
ideology, 102; inspiration,
191, 194–97; *Institutio*, 22;
instrumentalization, 25–26;
justification, 214; light of the
world, 23; and modernity,
31–33; objections to,
221–22; optional, 192–93;
and peace, 222; phenomenon,
4; and politics, ix, 131–40;
and power, 87, 102, 104–5,
215–16, 238; puritanism,
23–24; rational, 235;
rationalization, 26, 27;
realization of the sacred,
4, 222–23; reconciliation,
186; reform, 21–24, 28;
and society, 182–88; state,
34–35, 193–94, 215–16;
symbolizations, 34; and
tradition, 20–21, 26–27,
232–33; and violence, 92,
223, 238; and world, 4, 7–10,
23, 40, 192; world-shaping, x
Representation, 104, 112–13,
123, 153–54
Rerum Novarum, 207
Responsibility, 206–7
Rich, the, 174, 176
Robert the Monk, 98–99
Robinson, H. Wheeler, 69–70
Rome, 115, 119–20, 141
Rondine, 191–92
Rule: and Christ, 61–62,
115–16, 122, 148–49,
153–54; Christianity, 116–17;
and God, 61–62, 123, 154;
representation, 153–54

Index

Weber, Max, xiii, 103–4, 205–6
Wisdom literature, 210
Witnessing, 201–2
World: and Church, 5–7, 8, 17, 97–98; double-edged, 16–17; and God, 16–17; Hebrew Bible, 10–11; history, 17; light of, 18, 23; New Testament, 11; Qur'an, 11–16, 24–25; and religion, 4, 7–10, 40, 192; temporality, 10–11; theological phrases for, 10; worldliness of, 6, 8–9
World War I, 91–92, 99–100